WITHDRAWN

F826   Wise
W68   Massacre at Mountain Meadows

Keep 2018

DATE DUE		
MAY 1 8 1977		
APR 1 2 1977		
OCT 1 0 1979		
OCT 2 7 1979		
NOV 0 5 1979		
MAR 1 7 1982		
MAR 2 1982		
NOV 2 4 1982		
NOV 1 6 1982		
MAR 2 5 1983		
OCT 1 9 1983		
DEC 1 1983		

MASSACRE AT
MOUNTAIN MEADOWS

MASSACRE AT
MOUNTAIN MEADOWS

*An American Legend
And a Monumental Crime*

by William Wise

THOMAS Y. CROWELL COMPANY
Established 1834   New York

Maps by Donald T. Pitcher

Designed by Ingrid Beckman

Manufactured in the United States of America

Library of Congress Cataloging in Publication Data

Wise, William.
    Massacre at Mountain Meadows.
    Bibliography p.   Includes index.
    1. Mountain Meadows Massacre, 1857. 2. Lee, John
Doyle, 1812–1877. I. Title.
F826.W68   979.2′47   76–16014
ISBN 0–690–01174–1

10 9 8 7 6 5 4 3 2 1

To Claire and Cynthia—
For listening so patiently,
and for waiting so long.

ACKNOWLEDGMENTS

FOR THEIR SEEMINGLY ENDLESS HELP, I would like to thank the staffs of the New York Historical Society, the New York Society Library and the New York Public Library, as well as the staffs of the Yale University Library, the Library of Congress, the Henry E. Huntington Library and the Princeton University Library.

Several individuals were especially generous of their time and assistance: among them I wish to thank Miss Sue Adele Gillies of the New York Historical Society, for her frequent and most useful advice; Kim Matland, for his Washington investigations; Mrs. Ida Cianci and Mrs. Beverly Greenhow of the Argosy Bookshop, for the research material they helped me obtain; and Richard Russell, for the professional facilities that he so freely placed at my disposal. Finally, my thanks to Joseph McQuade, for helping assemble the official documents essential to any understanding of the events in Utah, which reached their climax in the Massacre at Mountain Meadows.

AUTHOR'S NOTE

AT THE CONCLUSION of the text are the names of the men, women and children who most probably belonged to the ill-fated Fancher Train. Because so many obstacles were placed in the way of early investigators only an incomplete list of the train members was published at the time, and even today it is not possible to identify all of the victims and survivors.

" . . . it was a considerable time before more than vague rumors of the crime reached the Eastern States. No inquest or other investigation was held . . . no person participating in the slaughter was arrested . . . and, when officers of the federal government first reached the scene . . . all that remained to tell the tale were human skulls and other bones lying where the wolves and coyotes had left them, with scraps of clothing caught here and there, upon the vines and bushes."

The Story of the Mormons
WILLIAM A. LINN

MASSACRE AT
MOUNTAIN MEADOWS

Chapter 1

IT WAS NO TRIFLING MATTER to travel across the western half of North America in the days of the Fancher Train. Food for several months had to be stockpiled before a party of emigrants could consider itself ready to set out for Oregon or California. Wagons had to be acquired, along with the oxen or mules to haul them; at the same time clothing had to be sewn and tools and harnesses put into working order. And if the men of the party knew what they were about, they made sure of one thing more—an ample supply of bullets, with firearms that were in good repair.

For in 1857, thirst, hunger and disease were not the only dangers encountered by travelers along the unmarked fifteen-hundred-mile trail. On the plains, from Iowa and Kansas to the Rockies, lived a number of restless, wandering Indian tribes. During times of formal peace they usually were harmless enough; yet even then some of the more aggressive bands were not above launching a sudden attack, hopeful of surprising a careless party and running off its livestock.

In addition, there were rumors of more predatory bands, particularly in the remote and desolate sections of the mountains, that made a practice of robbing and murdering small, unwary parties of travelers. Some of these "Indians" were said to possess fair skin, an extensive knowledge of English and eyes the most astonishing shade of blue.

The Fancher Train, however, was neither a small nor an unwary party of travelers. Although many facts remain obscure about its members, it is certain that the train's leaders planned the expedition with care and proceeded at each step with reasonable caution.

1

For the most part the Fancher Train was made up of prosperous rural families from the state of Arkansas. Their homes were mainly in Carroll, Marion or Johnson counties, in the northwest corner of the state. Members of several of the families were related by birth or marriage; others who decided to go West were simply old friends or neighbors.

There were three Fancher brothers. By 1856, the year when the emigrants began to mature their plans to move West, John Fancher already had pulled up stakes and had settled in Visalia, California, a little more than a hundred miles from the Pacific, at a point about equidistant from Los Angeles and San Francisco. It was excellent farming country, and no doubt he had urged his relatives to join him. Certainly John Fancher knew of the emigrants' preparations, the time they proposed to leave and the route they intended to follow.

Hampton, the oldest of the brothers, declined to become one of the party. He was now the middle-aged father of five grown children, a man for whom pioneering had lost its allure. Two of his sons, though, James and Robert, did become members of the train.

The third of the brothers was Captain Alexander Fancher, the leader of the train. He had been born nearly a half-century before in north-central Tennessee and, like many other early nineteenth-century American pioneers, had spent most of his adult life moving from one quarter of the frontier to another. He began by farming in Illinois; there he met Eliza Ingram, whom he married in 1838. Five years later he owned a farm in Missouri, and five years after that he had taken his growing family to Carroll County, Arkansas. Soon this home was sold and a new one purchased in Benton County.

But Alexander Fancher belonged to a restless breed, and before long Arkansas in its turn began to seem less appealing. Either alone or with his brother John, he set out for California, probably herding cattle at least part of the way in order to make the venture profitable. He might have gained the title of captain on this journey, or perhaps he'd earned it a few years earlier for service in the militia.

Once beyond the Rockies, Alexander Fancher discovered for himself some of the advantages of the new state; there was excellent pasturage, a mild climate and high prices paid for cattle and other livestock. It was the best and last frontier, still largely unsettled, offering almost unlimited opportunities to those with the vision and courage to secure them. And so he returned home, some fifteen hundred miles to Arkansas, there to discuss plans with relatives and neighbors and begin making preparations to move his family a final time.

Captain Fancher must have made a convincing impression on many of his listeners as he spoke of the golden land beyond the Rockies and the advantages of emigrating to California. His appearance was reassuring; he was forty-five, a tall, angular man with a dark, weather-beaten complexion and a steady gaze, the sort of leader who instills confidence in others by his calm manner and his measured, unhurried speech.

There was something reassuring, too, in the captain's willingness to risk so much of his own. Compared with a Philadelphia banker or a New York City merchant he was not, of course, a rich man. But by the more modest standards of the frontier he could be considered well-to-do, and now he was prepared to hazard his hard-earned capital, the product of thirty years' toil, and to do so without a qualm.

Also significant was the captain's readiness to take his considerable family on the long, unchartered journey. He and Eliza had eight living children, four boys and four girls. In age they ranged from nineteen-year-old Hampton, named for his uncle, to five-year-old Christopher "Kit" Carson, named for the famous western scout and explorer. Surely the captain would not have considered including the girls and young Kit in the party unless he was confident of a safe passage and a prosperous future.

In all likelihood, too, his listeners needed little enough persuasion before declaring themselves ready to sell their homes and emigrate again. Like the captain, many of them were restless men, with families who were prepared to follow them without a murmur. If Arkansas was becoming overcrowded, what better place to try next than fabled California?

Among the original members of the train were the Bakers, about twenty or twenty-five of them, a large, closely knit family group from Carroll County. Captain John T. Baker, known to everyone as "Uncle Jack," was the clan's amiable fifty-two-year-old patriarch. He and his wife, Mary, were the parents of seven children, and their contemporaries, Abel and Elizabeth, had an equal number. George and Minerva Baker, a couple in their twenties, had one child and perhaps more. Whether or not all the various Baker children left Arkansas in early 1857 is uncertain, but three who did leave were Martha Elizabeth, called "Betsy," William and Sarah Jane. Of the numerous children in the party these three were among the youngest, and one September afternoon, at a distant place called Mountain Meadows, their extreme youth would prove to be their good fortune.

One member of the Baker family played a singular role in the story of the Fancher Train. He was John H. Baker, Uncle Jack's oldest son. Like Hampton and James Fancher—the latter a nephew of the captain—and several other young men in the party, John H. Baker was accustomed to the outdoors. An excellent rider, he eventually found himself called upon to demonstrate his horsemanship against odds that from the beginning were much too long.

Rivaling the Baker clan in numbers were the Dunlaps from Marion County. Jesse Dunlap and his wife, Mary, had six children, and Lorenzo and Nancy Dunlap had five. Both families, including all eleven children, went West in the train.

And even before the Fancher Train departed, at least one man from out of state decided to join the original company. He was William Eaton, born in Indiana and, since the beginning of the 1850's, a farmer in Illinois. Toward the end of 1856 he met some congenial visitors from Arkansas who were planning to settle permanently in the Far West. One day the conversation turned to prospects in California, and it wasn't long before Eaton had caught the western fever. After accepting their invitation to be one of the party, he sold his farm, took his wife and young daughter back home to stay with relatives in Indiana and then hurried south to Arkansas to buy an outfit for the trip.

The Fancher Train was better organized than most emigrant parties that set out to cross the plains in the 1850's; yet from beginning to end there was a good deal of informality about many of the proceedings—an informality characteristic of the way most people planned their journey, and then behaved, once they were on the trail. Before their departure, a typical party of emigrants would select a leader and establish a set of rules for the road, with the further understanding that both leader and rules would be subject to change if they proved unpopular. En route, some of the emigrants might leave their own train and join another, perhaps because there had been a quarrel or they wished to travel more quickly. And if there were Indians in the neighborhood, or other signs of danger, single wagons and smaller parties would merge with a larger group until the danger was past and it was safe once more to express one's independence by traveling alone.

As part of the general informality, few records were kept except by the military trains and by the Mormon authorities who operated their own emigration parties. Certainly in most cases there was no log or official passenger list of the journey. At the same time, a group as large as the Fancher Train would almost inevitably have had among its members at least one or two enthusiastic observers who sensed the novelty and importance of their pioneering venture and recorded in a diary or journal the names of their companions, the curious places they passed and whatever striking events occurred.

Unhappily, all the private papers in the Fancher Train, including any such diaries or journals, were destroyed deliberately. As a result, many things that ordinarily would have been known about the journey remained a mystery. Honest witnesses—and there were a few—spoke of the Fanchers, the Bakers and the Dunlaps, yet never mentioned others who also were in the train—the Joneses, the Rushes, members of the Wood family, and William Mitchell's three sons. At the same time, they spoke of the Stevensons, the Smiths and the Mortons, families whose names never appeared in a single public document. Did these other families really join the train or had the witnesses, after a lapse of time, become confused?

There were any number of other unanswered questions. How many horsemen, for instance, were in the party? Some witnesses said one dozen, some said two. And who were they? Surely they included most of the younger men, like John H. Baker, James and Hampton Fancher, twenty-seven-year-old Richard Wilson and the two Prewitt brothers, John and William.

In the party there was a sheriff named William Wood from Marion County, but the Methodist minister, who rode in one of the wagons and held services each morning and evening on the trail, remained unidentified. There also were the unnamed owners of two or three elegant carriages, which mingled in the train with the heavier wagons and carried a number of the ladies in comparative comfort toward California.

One man in the company had a curious physical abnormality—an extra tooth, or "supernumerary," in his jaw—but whether he was a Baker, a Dunlap or somebody else, no observer ever specified.

Finally—and without question—there were three other families in the train worth noticing, but not one of them ever was mentioned by even a single investigator; nor were its members cited anywhere in a matter of record. Somehow Joseph Miller, his wife and children, William Cameron and his sizable family, and the family of Henry Dalton Scott were overlooked.

Yet as more than one lawbreaker has discovered to his sorrow, the destruction of evidence can sometimes be a slippery business, and so it proved to be in the case of the Fancher Train. For Henry Dalton Scott had a wife named Malinda, and though nothing could have seemed more improbable at the time, ultimately she became the most important member of the party, and the one thing all criminals dread—the unexpected witness who can testify to their crimes.

Chapter 2

In the autumn of 1856, while she and her husband were beginning to prepare for the approaching journey, Malinda Cameron Scott became pregnant with her fourth child. The timing could hardly have been worse. It meant that she would have to endure the most taxing part of the trip while she was least fit to do so, and that weeks before their arrival in California she would have to stop and give birth in the middle of a wilderness. But as she discovered later, her predicament was not unique; there proved to be a number of other pregnant women in the party, as well as several mothers still nursing their infant children.

Long before the train's departure, Malinda Scott's personal life had become less than ideal. Henry Scott, her husband, was a quarrelsome man, and from time to time there must have been disputes with Malinda's father, William Cameron, and with those even closer to him, like his own brother, Richard.

Twenty-eight-year-old Malinda suffered from a disability common among frontier women: she could neither read nor write. So whenever the newspaper arrived at their home in Clarksville from Fort Smith or Little Rock, someone had to read it aloud to her, and on the few occasions when she was obliged to attest to some legal document, she had to mark the papers with her ungainly, lopsided "X."

Being unlettered, though, did not interfere with her usual household chores or with the additional preparations that were necessary before the train's departure. Food for the journey had to be selected, and sometimes preserved, prior to its being set aside for last-minute loading in the wagons. Flour was one of the basic food items; it was milled and stored in sacks and then placed alongside bags of rice and tins of hard bread and biscuits. Ham and bacon were the meat staples, and on the trail they often could be supplemented by wild birds, rabbits and other small game. If the hunters of the party were skilled enough, an occasional deer, pronghorn or buffalo might be added to the emigrants' diet. In addition, fish sometimes could be taken from the creeks and rivers, and for those who cared for it, there even was such an exotic dish as frogs' legs, pan-fried over an evening fire.

Space in the wagons was reserved for a few gallons of vinegar and molasses and for large amounts of beans and dried fruit, especially apples and peaches. Other foods included dried, or what often was called "desiccated" vegetables, small quantities of precious tea and sugar, an abundant supply of Brazilian or "Rio" coffee and a few pounds of the more expensive and esteemed Jamaican variety. Also stockpiled were such nonfood items as soap and sperm candles to provide extra light in the evenings when someone had to leave the circle of the campfire.

Because each of the departing families owned at least several excellent cows, sufficient nourishment for the forty or fifty children in the train did not appear to pose much of a problem, or at any rate, not for the initial weeks of the journey. Later on, of course, unforseen delays might occur, resulting in a shortage for everyone. Yet even if this should happen, there would be a good chance to acquire what was needed, simply by trading with a better-provisioned party of emigrants. Also, there always would be an emergency supply of food close at hand, and if conditions became extreme, a small part of it—a few of the draft animals, or the cows, or even some of the horses—could be slaughtered and eaten.

And there was an additional margin of safety, a very important one, on which the travelers counted heavily. It was true that for the first thousand miles of travel there would be no towns or villages where food could be obtained, but after two-thirds of the journey they would come to Salt Lake City, capital of the vast Utah Territory that the Mormons controlled, and here they could purchase food for themselves, and hay and other feed for their animals.

Although some travelers went to great lengths to avoid the Mormon settlements, most emigrant parties realized that it would be prudent to augment their supplies while crossing the Utah Territory. Therefore they traveled directly to Salt Lake

City, which lay on the main routes to northern and southern California. When they arrived in the Territory, they almost invariably found the Mormons willing and even eager to sell whatever extra stocks of food they had on hand. Most emigrants never doubted that they would receive an openhanded welcome from the Mormons—if not for charitable reasons, then at least out of self-interest—and in this respect, the leaders of the Fancher Train were no exceptions.

Besides selecting various kinds of food for the journey, a woman like Malinda Scott had to decide which of her few precious household possessions could be taken and which were so cumbersome that they would have to be left behind. Sometimes a heavy table, a cabinet or a chest of drawers was put into the wagons, but often, they failed to reach their destination. For when things went wrong and a wagon had to be lightened, it was these cherished pieces, often the sole momentos of a former home, that were among the first objects to be discarded along the trail.

In addition to furniture, a variety of other items began to be added to the growing inventory: kitchen utensils, including a brass kettle or two, powder, caps and lead, for the muzzle-loading "Texas" rifles that the men kept close at hand, and a few pounds of tobacco and some stone or clay pipes, to be smoked by the campfire at night, or to be offered in trade, with silver coins, beads, and brass or zinc mirrors, to any friendly Indians met on the journey.

As the date of departure drew nearer, the packing continued at a brisker pace. Into Henry Scott's wagon went bedding for himself and Malinda, and for Joel, Martha and George, their three young children. Clothing was selected and placed strategically in the limited space so that each article would be readily available when needed. Included were black woolen caps and caps made of brown fur; light shirts and pants, "hickory" or coarse work shirts, boots, overcoats, socks and handkerchiefs, as well as calico and muslin dresses, a variety of shawls, and several straw bonnets to protect Malinda and her daughter from the sun.

While these preparations were being made in Clarksville, some fifty or sixty miles east of Fort Smith, all but one of Malinda Scott's immediate relatives also were preparing to depart in the Fancher Train. The exception was her sister Nancy Cameron Littleton, who with her husband had decided from the beginning to remain behind in Arkansas. Despite all efforts at persuasion, the Littletons kept to their decision.

Malinda's other married sister was Mathilda Cameron Miller, the wife of Joseph Miller and the mother of four young children: William, Alfred, Eliza and Joseph Jr. The Millers had their own wagons and cattle; they planned to meet the Scotts and the Camerons, Mathilda and Malinda's relatives, and join with them, to form a small private company within the larger train.

By now Malinda's father and mother, William and Martha Cameron, had sold their farm, situated some ten or fifteen miles from Clarksville. Their outfit consisted of two large covered "emigrant" wagons, in which they and the rest of their party would ride, and a smaller wagon that would hold their food and most of their other supplies. They had thirty or thirty-five good milk cows, three horses, a number of mules and twelve yoke of oxen to haul the wagons.

Planning to travel with William and Martha Cameron were their five sons: Tilghman, Ison, Henry, James and Larkin, and an unmarried daughter, also named Martha. And riding in one of the two canvas-covered emigrant wagons would be Malinda Scott's cousin, eleven-year-old Nancy Cameron, a child whose fate was to prove far stranger than that of any other member of the Fancher Train.

Unlike most of the other men in the emigrant party, one of Malinda Scott's brothers, Tilghman Cameron, was a businessman rather than a farmer. He had lived in Fort Smith during recent years and evidently had done well for himself. His assets consisted of a part interest in the Cameron mules, some cash and a racing mare named "One-eyed Blaze," an animal well known in several parts of the state. Tilghman had entered her successfully in a number of races, and as a result of her triumphs she was valued at a minimum of $2,000. In some people's estimation she was worth as much as $5,000 or $6,000.

At first glance nothing belonging to the Cameron family seemed to be of great value with the exception of One-eyed Blaze. Yet measured against the standards of the time, their outfit actually represented an enviable amount of wealth. This was true in part because the farther west a traveler went, the more valuable his livestock became, providing the animals did not suffer injury or other harm during the journey. In 1857, for example, a good milk cow might bring only $20 or $30 at Little Rock, while the same animal would bring $50, $75 or even $100 at Salt Lake City.

After traveling a thousand miles on the trail, William Cameron's thirty or thirty-five cows promised to be worth as much as $3,000, and his twenty-four oxen would have a value of $1,500 to $1,800; another $1,500 could be added for the two large wagons and the personal and household effects they carried, and for the small wagon and its supplies; five hundred more for the three horses, excluding, of course, the mare, and a few hundred for the mules; in all, the outfit and animals would command roughly $6,000 to $7,000 in Salt Lake City, a sum not to be taken lightly during an age when money itself was scarce, an American dollar had immeasurably more value than it does today and the salaries of important public officials were correspondingly lower—the President of the United States, James Buchanan, then receiving an annual salary of $25,000, Vice President John Breckinridge $5,000, and the governor of the Utah Territory, Brigham Young, a mere $1,800.

But livestock, wagons and household goods did not comprise all of William Cameron's wealth. He had, in addition, enough American dollars in silver and bills to pay for repairs, extra food and other emergency expenses. And then, concealed inside one of the two large covered wagons, was $3,000 in gold, a sum no doubt realized from the sale of his Arkansas holdings and which he intended to use to purchase necessities in California.

In all likelihood the hoard consisted almost entirely of twenty-dollar pieces, a denomination first minted in 1850. The dull-yellow one-ounce coins, called "yaller boys" on the frontier, when placed within a few soft leather bags, or "pokes," or piled in stacks inside three or four small, empty cigar tins, would have required only a tiny amount of space in a hollowed-out portion of the wagon hounds—the horizontal wooden braces used to reinforce the wagon's running gear—to be hidden away. A single hollow, six or seven inches long, four or five inches wide, and an inch or two deep, would have been large enough to conceal them; and once emplaced in the hounds and sealed over, it would have been difficult to find them unless one had sufficient time to search.

How many other wagons in the train might have carried a similar cache of gold is not at all certain; perhaps William Cameron was the exception, the only one of thirty or forty frontiersmen who failed to convert all his wealth into milk cows, oxen, horses and mules. Yet even so, it was an indisputable fact that the Fancher Train was one of the richest parties ever to set off across the prairies. Some six to nine hundred of the finest cows, an abundance of oxen to haul forty, fifty or sixty light and heavy wagons, twenty or thirty horses, a number of them extremely valuable, and considerable sums of ready cash in silver and bills—a train worth $75,000 or $100,000 according to some witnesses, and twice as much according to others. A prize to tempt unscrupulous men, even without the added lure of hidden gold.

And so the Fancher Train, approximately fifty men, forty women and fifty children, began to assemble from a dozen or more scattered locations in the state. Just before leaving, William Eaton, the out-of-state farmer from Illinois, wrote a cheerful letter to his wife, saying that all was well and that the train would soon be underway. He assured her that he was in good health and spirits and promised to write from California if not before.

Friends and relatives of the emigrants came to see them off, either at their homes or at some rendezvous point for several families, usually at the county seat. Nancy Littleton said good-bye to her sister Malinda Scott, now five months pregnant and already beginning to move with less agility, to her other sisters and brothers and to her parents, William and Martha Cameron. Hampton Fancher took leave of his two sons; his brother, the captain; his eight nieces and nephews, including Hampton, his namesake, and young Kit Carson; and his grandchild, Triphena Fancher. William Mitchell, who had three grown sons in the train, as well as his only grandchild, a boy of four or five, saw them off and then consoled himself with the thought that in nine or ten months he would hear of their safe arrival in California.

It was now early spring, the twenty-ninth of March, 1857, and after months of labor and planning, the wagon wheels finally began to turn and creak, the cattle began to amble along the trail, and the horsemen fixed their eyes on the horizon. An exodus repeated countless times, year after year, in pioneer communities throughout the South and West, but never, either before or after, with such appalling results as in the case of the wealthy party of travelers from northwest Arkansas.

The Fancher Train's leaders had every reason to suppose that their plans were sound and that by leaving so early in the season they had greatly reduced any chance of subsequent misfortune. During April and May they would travel north and west, through hundreds of miles of unmapped Indian country, sometimes called the Cherokee Nation by nineteenth-century travelers. If all went well, mid-June would find them on the north branch of the Platte, making their way along the Oregon Trail, and by the end of July or early August they would be across the Great Divide and safely at Salt Lake City. After resting themselves and their numerous animals, they would then proceed north around the Great Salt Lake and then west again to the Humboldt River, following the much-traveled route to northern California. An early snowfall in the mountains was one of the most serious hazards facing an emigrant party, but long before any snow could fall that year both the Rockies and the Sierra Nevadas would be behind them.

They also were well prepared for other hazards. They were heavily armed and had several dozen marksmen in their ranks, more than enough to repel any attack except one made by a full war-party of Indians. They had sufficient supplies of money, draft animals and wagons—indeed if anything, an eye-catching over-abundance of them—they had experienced leaders, and for the most part, were themselves a sober, hard-working and reasonably congenial party of friends and relatives.

And so there was no sense of haste or urgency in their departure, nor would there have been the slightest need for any in normal circumstances. But the year 1857 was hardly a normal one in the American West. The huge Utah Territory, governed by an extraordinary theocracy, long had been wracked by internal disorder, and its rulers were now on the point of openly defying the Federal Government; meanwhile in Washington, more than two thousand miles to the east, the new President, James Buchanan, not yet a month in office, was drawing up plans to dispatch an army to Utah, in order to reassert the national authority over the territory's remote and seemingly rebellious citizens. Unaware of these events, the travelers from Arkansas were about to advance into what could soon become a war zone, defended by hostile white inhabitants and their Indian allies. Counting on ordinary standards of hospitality and on a liberal amount of fresh food and pasturage, they already had made a serious miscalculation.

The leaders of the Fancher Train were handicapped in judgment by a lack of information. In 1857, most news traveled slowly, when it traveled at all. Few small-town papers printed items from the Far West and many metropolitan dailies offered little more. In early 1857 the New York *Herald* and the *Times* did not have a single official correspondent inside the Utah

Territory, so that they had to depend on whatever information could be smuggled out by anonymous and often terrified local residents. Under these conditions it was not easy for even the most knowledgeable city dweller to form a clear idea of events in Utah, and it was almost impossible for ordinary rural citizens to do so.

In another, even more critical respect, the leaders of the Fancher Train were poorly informed. Like most Americans, they probably had heard a considerable amount of gossip about the people who controlled the distant territory through which they intended to pass; no doubt they were familiar, in a general way, with the controversial reputation of the Church of Jesus Christ of Latter-Day Saints and knew something of its turbulent beginnings in Missouri and Illinois. Yet they could have known but little of the Church's most recently evolved policies, the character and intentions of current Mormon leaders and the political acts then being contemplated in Salt Lake City. Lacking any substantial knowledge about their future hosts, the leaders of the Fancher Train set out for California, unaware of the exceptional risks they were running or even the real nature of their danger.

Chapter 3

SOMETIMES THE ROOTS of a criminal act lie buried deep in the past, and this certainly was true in the case of the brutal and premeditated crime that afterward came to be called the Mountain Meadows Massacre. To fully understand all the complex motives that lay behind it, and to understand as well precisely what happened after the Fancher Train arrived in the Utah Territory, one must turn aside to an earlier day in America, and to a distant section of the country—to the eastern part of the United States—where, a quarter of a century before, the religion popularly known as Mormonism had its origins. For what happened at Mountain Meadows was in some measure at least an act of religious passion, committed by God-fearing men, a number of whom believed they were acting from the most exalted motives. Therefore, to speak of the crime without first taking into account the early history, principles and leadership of the Mormon Church would be as absurd as to speak of the St. Bartholomew's Day Massacre without making reference to France, Catherine de Medici or the Reformation.

The founder of the Mormon Church, and its initial "Seer, Prophet and Revelator," was Joseph Smith Jr., one of the most remarkable leaders to appear on the American frontier during the nineteenth century. This much now can be said with authority, thanks to the advantage of hindsight. Yet there were few among his earliest acquaintances who would have cared to predict such a notable future for one seemingly so lacking in industry, ambition, opportunity and educational attainments.

The future Prophet's parents, Joseph Smith Sr., and Lucy Mack, were both descended from long-established New England

families. In all, they had nine children, including Joseph Jr.,
their fourth child, who was born at Sharon, Vermont, in 1805.

At first the Smiths were fairly well off, but good fortune did not
remain with them long. The difficulty was that Joseph Smith Sr.,
either through ill-luck, idleness or poor judgment—or perhaps
through a combination of all three—seemed unable to earn more
than a marginal living as a farmer; and to make matters worse,
as time went on he became increasingly addicted to chimerical
get-rich-quick schemes and unsound speculations.

After six years of unproductive farming in eastern Vermont, he
decided to invest in a shipment of ginseng, the aromatic root of a
plant that grew wild in Vermont's Green Mountains. His plan
was to export the ginseng to China, where it was highly prized
and where its sale often brought huge profits to American
shippers. Unfortunately, soon after he made his purchase the
price of the root collapsed, and he lost his entire capital.

For the next fifteen years the debt-ridden Smiths lived on at
least six or eight different farms in Vermont and New Hampshire, and during this long, itinerant period, Joseph Sr. eked out a
meager income by performing odd jobs for his neighbors. He was
an occasional well-digger and grew adept at using a divining rod
to locate sources of underground water. Wells, however, were not
all that he dug. Ever tantalized by dreams of sudden wealth, and
at first, perhaps, almost believing some of his own schemes, he
became a "money-digger" and, in return for a small fee, helped
credulous farmers to seek hidden treasure on their land, especially the pirate hoard of Captain Kidd, which was rumored to be
buried somewhere in the vicinity.

At the end of the War of 1812 the western frontier was opened
to settlement, and a wave of emigrants left New England for
Ohio, Indiana and even distant Illinois. Four years later Joseph
Sr. determined to try his luck beyond the Alleghenies. He set out
for Ohio, intending to buy a farm, but traveled no farther than
Palmyra, New York, a town about ninety miles east of Buffalo, on
the route of the proposed Erie Canal. Here he settled, having once
again heard the fatal siren call of easy money—in this case, the
fine tales of fortunes that soon would be made in Palmyra from
the construction of DeWitt Clinton's monumental waterway and
from the appearance of long flotillas of cargo-ladened barges,
shuttingly endlessly between the Atlantic and the Great Lakes.

Joseph Sr.'s decision to take up residence in western New York
was singularly ill timed. Good land was then obtainable in

neighboring Ohio at a moderate dollar and a quarter an acre, but around Palmyra a boom had been underway for several years, and by then real estate prices were reaching their peak. Instead of becoming the owner of a profitable Ohio farm, the elder Smith first settled in rented quarters in Palmyra and then on an undesirable tract of farmland whose value immediately began to decline, so that he became subject to an endless succession of bank loans and the perpetual threat of eviction.

By every account the Smiths, from first to last, remained desperately poor. While still living in town, the Prophet's father opened a "cake and beer" shop in their home and hung out a sign advising that "gingerbread, boiled eggs, root beer, pies and other like notions" could be purchased within. At this time, Lucy Smith added to the family's means by painting and selling oil-cloth table covers, and her husband continued to accept part-time employment as a well-digger and harvest hand, being assisted in these pursuits by William, Samuel, Hyrum and Joseph Jr., the last a tall blond youth just entering his teens.

Eventually two sharply different explanations were offered to account for the elder Smith's never-ending poverty. According to the view of his partisans, the Prophet's father was simply a poor, hard-working farmer who always remained down on his luck through no fault of his own. But among many of the citizens of Palmyra and nearby Manchester, a less-tolerant view took hold, and after the establishment of the Mormon Church and the departure of the Smith family, it was expressed in a number of letters and public declarations. One affidavit, signed by more than fifty people, said that the Smiths had been "particularly famous for visionary projects, and spent much of their time digging for money which they pretended was hid in the earth." The affidavit added: "To this day, large excavations may be seen in the earth, not far from their residence, where they used to spend their time digging for hidden treasure." With so much energy expended on such activities, it could not have been easy for Joseph Sr. and his growing sons to gain even a bare subsistence from their Palmyra farm.

There can be no doubt that as a young man Joseph Jr. patterned himself after his father and shared both his money-digging schemes and his idleness. "Joe was the most ragged, lazy fellow in the place," wrote Daniel Hendrix, a resident of Palmyra, who served as an assistant in setting type and reading proof for the initial printing of the *Book of Mormon,* sometimes referred to as the Golden Bible. "I can see him now in my mind's eye," Hendrix went on, "with his torn and patched trousers held to his form by a pair of suspenders made of sheeting, with his calico shirt as dirty and black as the earth, and his uncombed hair sticking through the holes in his old battered hat."

But there was more to Joseph Jr. than mere dirt and laziness; there also was a winning personality, and a vivid, imaginative mind, though one that was uneducated and poorly disciplined. "Joe had a jovial, easy, don't-care way about him," Hendrix wrote, "that made him a lot of warm friends. He was a good talker and would have made a fine stump speaker if he had had the training." Unhappily, young Joseph lacked any such advantage, and so, before long, he turned his energies in other directions. During his teens he established an extensive reputation as a crystal gazer, who could find lost objects and buried treasure, and now and again he was invited to someone's rural home in Pennsylvania or New York, where he received room and board and a few dollars' pay in return for his special services. In November 1825, a month before his twentieth birthday, he went to Bainbridge, New York, to help an elderly farmer named Josiah Stowel locate a lost Spanish silver mine. It was there, in March of the following year, that he was arrested and charged with being a disorderly person and an imposter.

The future Prophet was brought before a justice of the peace and acknowledged that he had been a practicing clairvoyant for several years. He admitted that he owned a transparent "stone," or crystal ball, "which he had occasionally looked at, to determine where hidden treasures [were] in the bowels of the earth" and, according to the court record, also confessed that he had sought lost property and other valuables for various clients in New York and Pennsylvania. A half-dozen witnesses testified to his treasure hunting on behalf of Farmer Stowel, and finally the court found him guilty as charged.

Scarcely four years now remained before the first printing of the *Book of Mormon* and the founding of the Church of Jesus Christ of Latter-Day Saints; yet until at least this point in his life, Joseph Smith Jr. had shown no discernible interest in spiritual matters; unlike his parents, especially his mother, he had never been concerned with the popular religious questions of the day; and unlike many of their neighbors, he had not partici-pated in the camp meetings and other revivalist activities that at that time were animating, and sometimes convulsing whole communities in western New York, Ohio and New England.

A decade later, when writing his autobiography, the Prophet would portray himself in a very different light. Then he would maintain that at the age of seventeen he had experienced a remarkable religious vision that had greatly influenced and affected him afterward; that in September 1823—more than two years *before* his trial and conviction in Bainbridge—he had been asking forgiveness for his sins one night when the Angel Moroni had appeared to him, announcing himself as a messenger of God. The angel had declared that one day Joseph Smith Jr.'s name would be spoken in many nations, that the Lord had work for him to do and that a previously unknown Bible, written twelve centuries before on plates of gold, was buried in the vicinity. The sacred book's location would be shown to him, and one day, after he had received permission to do so, he would take it from concealment and translate it by means of two miraculous "stones," or spectacles, called the Urim and Thummim, which were buried with the plates. Once translated, the book would disclose the story of the original inhabitants of America—of two races of men called the Nephites and the Lamanites—and would contain as well the everlasting Gospel, as revealed by the Saviour to the ancients.

But this was mere recollection, unsupported by witnesses, contemporary letters or public documents. No testimony of the time spoke of the event nor indicated that the future Prophet reported it, either to his friends or the general public. Nor was there any evidence to suggest that in the years directly after 1823, young Joseph Jr. underwent a change of character and began preparing himself for a religious calling, rather than devoting himself to unearthing treasures from the area's natural hills and Indian burial mounds. Truthfully, if the Angel Moroni did appear to him when his autobiography claimed, it remained a secret that he successfully concealed from the world during the better part of six lean and troubled years.

Joseph Smith Jr.'s publication in 1830 of the *Book of Mormon*, and his assertion that, as God's chosen instrument, he had found the golden plates and translated their mysterious hieroglyphics by means of the Urim and Thummim, soon created a stir around Palmyra, and it wasn't long before a small number of disciples had accepted the self-proclaimed twenty-five-year-old Prophet as their spiritual leader. Both place and time were propitious for the founding of a new religion like Mormonism. During the past two decades New England and the western frontier had been agitated by a great spiritual ferment. Most established churches had been badly shaken, and a few had been torn apart, the Methodists having split into four separate schisms between 1814 and 1830, while the Baptists were dividing themselves into Footwashers, Hard-Shell, Free-Will and Seventh-Day varieties during the same period.

A number of original sects also had sprung to life on the frontier, one of the first and most successful being the Campbellites, or Disciples of Christ, who were organized in Pennsylvania in 1810. At the same time, prophets and preachers of every description began to swarm across the countryside, and eventually Palmyra itself became the geographical center of much evangelical activity, a place where innumerable residents believed literally in hell fire, original sin and redemption through baptism, in the laying on of hands and speaking in tongues, and in the approaching Millennium, an era of a thousand years when Jesus Christ would return to earth and reign in peace and glory.

Some frontier religions were mildly eccentric, while others were extremely bizarre. The Shakers, a celibate sect that regarded its leader, Ann Lee, as the reincarnation of Jesus, became active in New York State, and in 1828 a number of members established a community only thirty miles from Palmyra. Jemima Wilkinson, called the "Universal Friend," believed herself to be the modern Christ and governed a colony of followers twenty-five miles from the Smith family's farm, being aided in her mission by a chief disciple who was known as the Prophet Elijah. Possibly the most flamboyant messiah of all was Isaac Bullard. Clad in nothing but a bearskin loincloth, he led his troop of adherents from Vermont through New York and Ohio and finally south to Missouri, proclaiming a religion compounded of free love, communism and dirt—Bullard often boasting that he hadn't washed in seven years.

Measured against such exuberant competition, the earliest pretensions of the Mormon Church were hardly excessive, and yet, to an extraordinary degree, they offended many free-thinking sceptics as well as orthodox Protestant believers. Perhaps the reason was that while the claims of Jemima Wilkinson, Isaac Bullard and the rest appeared totally absurd to all but their own handful of followers, the claims of Joseph Smith Jr., whatever else might have been said about them, contained at least a semblance of plausibility and therefore were instinctively felt to be a threat not only to conventional faith but also to common sense and reason.

Whether or not this was the case, a band of hostile critics was quickly formed, and a series of questions began to be asked about the golden plates. There was the puzzling problem of why the lost Bible had been written in "reform Egptian" hieroglyphics, as the Prophet insisted, when the original author of the text had been one of the Lost Tribe of Israel and presumably would have written his account in ancient Hebrew or Chaldean? And why had gold been used—it was a practice unheard of among the Jews—rather than the usual papyrus or parchment? There also was the question of the subsequent disappearance of the plates, a particularly disturbing development, since they never actually had been seen by anyone except the Prophet himself and his trio of loyal helpers. These were Oliver Cowdery, an erstwhile blacksmith with a dubious reputation; David Whitmer, a young Dutchman who believed in miracles and witches; and the indispensable Martin Harris, an elderly Palmyra farmer who had been persuaded, over his wife's bitterest objections, to sell their farm in order to pay the cost of publishing the *Book of Mormon*. Harris' mental stability may be judged by the claim that he had talked with several angels, the Devil and Jesus Christ and that he thought the latter "was the handsomest man" he had ever seen, while "the Devil looked like a jackass, with very short, smooth hair similar to that of a mouse." Harris also believed that he once had traveled to the moon, and he later described the trip to Daniel Hendrix, the young Palmyra typesetter, confiding that it "was only the faithful who were permitted to visit the celestial regions."

Among the most serious charges leveled by the Prophet's earliest critics were those of plagiarism and fraud. The assertion was made that there never had been any golden plates, or any celestial revelations about them, but that instead the *Book of Mormon* had been stolen from an unpublished historical novel entitled "The Manuscript Found." Its author was Solomon Spaulding, a graduate of Dartmouth College and a retired Presbyterian minister who had been interested in historical subjects all his life. In 1812 he had settled in Ohio, and within a short time some nearby burial mounds had been opened, revealing various artifacts and a number of human skeletons. Stimulated by the

discovery, Spaulding had written his story and not long afterward had moved to Pittsburgh, where he attempted, without
success, to interest a printer named Patterson in publishing the
work. Despite Patterson's refusal, Spaulding continued to believe
that his novel had great literary merit, and so, until his death in
1816, he read it aloud to friends, neighbors and members of his
family whenever he had the chance.

About 1822 a copy of Spaulding's unpublished work was said to
have been found at Patterson's office by one Sidney Rigdon, a
printer and Campbellite minister, who knew Patterson and may
have been working for him at the time. To Rigdon the manuscript
was a choice curiosity, and he made a copy of it. A few years later
he heard of Joseph Smith Jr.'s crystal-gazing and treasure-
digging schemes, as well as a whimsical rumor that Smith only
recently had launched to spoof his own family, particularly his
naive and pious mother—a rumor that said he had found a
"golden bible" in the surrounding woods, the sacred book having
been guarded by the bloody ghost of a long-dead pirate whose
throat had been slit from ear to ear. Rigdon, the charges went,
had then traveled to Palmyra and together with Smith had
concocted a plan to use *The Manuscript Found,* along with
selected parts of the King James version of the Bible, and certain
theological doctrines of the Campbellites, to found and promote a
new religion.

The charges of plagiarism were denied by Joseph Smith Jr.,
Sidney Rigdon and their followers, and a controversy began that
would not cool until long afterward. To the Mormons, the
authenticity of the Golden Bible was essential, for without it
there would have been neither faith, Prophet nor Church. Smith's
successor, Brigham Young, was aware of this and some fifteen
years later said, in his characteristically blunt and dogmatic
style, "Every spirit that confesses that Joseph Smith is a prophet,
that he lived and died a prophet, and that the *Book of Mormon* is
true, is of God, and every spirit that does not is of the Anti-
Christ." In order to maintain this position, the authenticity of the
book and the revelations concerning it were beyond debate or
compromise.

It was impossible to settle the quarrel to anyone's satisfaction,
but as a practical question, the truth or falseness of the charges
was unimportant. What really mattered was that Joseph Smith
Jr.—either with or without the tutelage of Sidney Rigdon—had
founded a religion that would flourish in astonishing ways; a

religion that would sweep the Prophet and his confederates into a dozen conflicts with real and imagined enemies, and that one day would spur his disciples to great pioneering achievements, as well as to crimes so cruel and formidable that they would have to be concealed, at whatever cost, from the rest of the civilized world.

Chapter 4

THE GROWTH of the Mormon Church was extremely slow at first, and when it became plain that the Smith family's reputation was limiting recruitment around Palmyra, the decision was made to try a different location. Within a year the Church had been transplanted from western New York to Kirtland, Ohio, a bustling frontier town on the outskirts of Cleveland, where Sidney Rigdon had prepared the way for a favorable reception.

The move to Kirtland, Rigdon's birthplace, proved a success. Between 1831 and 1838 the Church established many of its basic tenets and practices, while enrolling hundreds of new disciples. Under the guidance of Smith and Rigdon, there emerged at Kirtland a militant and elaborately organized sect, whose leader claimed to receive frequent revelations from God, and whose members accepted the claim without hesitation. For a time there was a struggle for authority between the two principals, but Smith quickly overcame the fiery and more unstable Rigdon—as he later would overcome all other pretenders—reducing him to a still-potent but nevertheless subordinate role. This left the Prophet himself, supreme among his ardent band of followers, a religious autocrat now capable of assuaging his own long-standing hunger for pomp and public acclaim.

At Kirtland, and later in Missouri and Illinois, all the real power of the Church remained with Smith and his closest associates, although some of the titles and trappings of power were distributed among those in the middle and even the lower ranks. While the Prophet, in actuality, remained an almost unopposed ruler, the nominal head of the Church was declared to be a triumvirate called the First Presidency. This consisted of the Prophet, acting in his supplemental capacity of Church President, and his two Counselors. Eventually the Mormons would assert that the First Presidency held under God not only the keys to heaven and hell but also the right of life and death, with no appeal except to a special assembly of the Church, an assertion that would assume greater significance during later times in the Far West.

Immediately beneath the First Presidency was the office of the Patriarch. No power went with this position, but its holder was permitted to administer certain religious blessings at a fixed fee and so was ensured of a small but regular income. The Prophet, who overlooked no opportunity to assist his relatives, appointed his father, Joseph Smith Sr., to be the first Patriarch, and following the old man's death, one of the Prophet's brothers received the benefice.

Next in rank came the Twelve Apostles, after the Prophet and his two Counselors, the most eminent men in the Church. They often had to deal directly with lesser members, and then they "had the power to inform and discipline other officers, elders, priests, teachers and deacons." From time to time the Twelve Apostles were required to leave home, either to proselytize new disciples by preaching the gospel in distant corners of the world or to fulfill more confidential assignments, and when they left on a mission they invariably carried with them both the Prophet's orders and the full authority of the Church. This was true in the 1830's, and it remained true two decades later, when Apostle George A. Smith, first cousin of Joseph Smith Jr., was sent south from Salt Lake City to the vicinity of Mountain Meadows, with special instructions concerning a party of travelers from Arkansas.

Below the Apostles, and making up the Church's fourth official rank, were the so-called Seventies, bodies of subordinate ministers, who shared with "The Twelve" the task of building up the strength of the Church at home and abroad. Knowledgeable observers sometimes called them the Church's "traveling propagandists" and the "working bees of the community." The Church's fifth and sixth ranks consisted of two priestly orders, the higher, or Melchizedek, whose members dealt with spiritual matters, and the lower, or Aaronic, whose members dealt with material ones. Within these two orders there was ample room for

the typical Saint to serve his Church, while for those who were
exceptionally ambitious or gifted, there were the more-elevated
positions in the Seventies to which they might aspire.

Even before the organization of the Church had been completed
at Kirtland, the Prophet and his·followers began to arouse the
hostility of their non-Mormon neighbors, and only a year or two
after their arrival they found themselves embroiled in a series of
violent disputes. Nor were these troubles at Kirtland the only
ones that occurred. Time and again the same pattern repeated
itself—in Ohio, Missouri and finally in Illinois. First the Mormons were invited to settle in a community where they were
regarded as impassioned but harmless religious eccentrics. Then,
as their numbers and their self-assertiveness increased, and as
their attitudes and beliefs were divulged more freely, they came
to be resented and feared. And finally, as they approached a
majority, and as their strength of arms threatened to equal or
surpass that of their hosts, their presence became intolerable,
and either through indirect coercion or direct force, they were
expelled from the town, county or state which so recently had
extended them a sympathetic welcome.

Sooner or later, after they built their clean, admirable homes,
laid out their neat farms and established a new stake of Zion,
their troubles would begin again. Suspicions would arise and
rumors would circulate. During their first years the Latter-Day
Saints were taxed with innumerable misdeeds and acts of mischief, and with such serious crimes as counterfeiting, fraud,
theft, assault and even murder. A few members deserted the
Church, and these much hated defectors, or Apostates as they
were called by the Mormons, added new charges against the
Prophet, accusing him of secretly advocating polygamy and, in
Missouri, of permitting the formation of a sworn band of assassins, known variously as the Danites, the Avenging Angels, or
the Sons of Dan.

To his many accusers the Prophet gave the same reply: their
charges, without exception, were damnable and false. He and his
disciples were innocent of all wrongdoing. Certainly the Saints
did not condone plural marriage, much less engage in it; they had
not formed a band of assassins; and any assaults or other violence
on their part were merely acts of self-defense or justified retalia-
tion. They were being persecuted for religion's sake, as had

the saints and martyrs of old, in whose holy footsteps they now were treading, in latter-day America.

That the Mormons on occasion were subjected to physical intimidation and mob attack was indisputably true, and it gave initial credence to their claims of innocence. At the same time, it aroused among liberal Americans—especially those living in the East, who were safely removed from the scenes of conflict—a strong sense of compassion for the Mormon cause and for the right of the Saints to worship as they chose. Unhappily, such compassion was not fully justified. Although some of the gravest charges against the Saints were false or exaggerated, a number of them also were true, and ultimately, when the lies of the Prophet and his Apostles were exposed, the disclosures stained the reputation of their Church and, to some degree at least, destroyed the sympathy of their early adherents.

But whether or not the enemies of the Saints misrepresented some of their acts, the fact remained that only the Mormon Church, among several independent sects, aroused such hostility and became the object of such serious accusations. And so a number of puzzling questions were left to be answered. Why were the Mormons, and they alone, "persecuted?" How great a part did their faith play in the matter? Was it chiefly their religious doctrines and their vigorous proselytizing that offended their fellow frontiersmen, or was it their social conduct and, even more importantly, their political actions that incited so strong a response?

At first glance there was little about the Mormon faith itself to stir anyone's animosity. The Church held sacred the Old and New Testaments, as well as the *Book of Mormon,* adhered to the Trinity and shared in common with other fundamentalist sects a belief in miracles, the curing of sickness through a laying on of hands and the phenomenon known as speaking in tongues. Among inoffensive though perhaps more original features of the Church was a particularly strong emphasis on religious education, a rigorous system of tithing and baptism for children after their eighth birthday, because they were deemed to have reached an age of "accountability."

Yet a further inspection revealed certain unique doctrines and attitudes, a number of which were bound to promote ill feeling among many non-Mormons, or "Gentiles," as those who did not belong to the Church were designated. The Mormon faith, from

its earliest days, was an exclusive one. The Saints were taught by
their leaders to believe themselves the world's only true Christians and their Church the only one not guilty of apostasy since
the death of Christ. Marriages performed in a Mormon temple
alone were completely valid; they were "to bind on earth and in
heaven" and would last through all eternity. No one but a
properly annointed Saint could enter the temple, and marriage
with someone of a different faith was prohibited, for indeed, it
would have been no marriage at all. While others on the frontier
also believed in a rapidly approaching Millennium, the Saints
saw no possibility of sharing the glory of that day with anyone
else. When the hour arrived, they alone would come into possession of the entire world, with all its spiritual delights and
material goods, while the rest of the planet's sinful inhabitants
would labor as their servants and at their pleasure, a vision of
paradise from which outsiders could hardly have derived much
satisfaction.

The Mormons freely expressed their views of the future in
every quarter. Remarks made on one occasion during the 1830's
by Apostle Parley P. Pratt were typical of these intemperate
pronouncements. The handsome and eloquent Pratt said in a
public exchange, "Within ten years from now, the people of this
country who are not Mormons will be entirely subdued by the
Latter-Day Saints, or swept from the face of the earth!" Such
insolent predictions might have amused an audience of Boston
sophisticates in Faneuil Hall, but they were unlikely to win the
smiles of many rough Gentiles living on the western border,
where the brethren represented a large and increasing part of the
population.

The Saints' absolute belief in a rapidly approaching Millenium
sometimes tempted them to petty lawlessness, especially to
thievery and other acts against property. For if they were to come
into possession of the world's goods when the Millennium arrived
a few months later, what was the point of delaying now? Why not
expropriate, at the first safe opportunity, a fat hog belonging to
one's Gentile neighbor, or several of his best chickens, or some of
his newly cut cordwood, all of which, this year or next, one
rightfully would possess anyway, as the Prophet and the Apostles
promised almost daily in their sermons?

But there was a more fundamental explanation that accounted
for the Mormons' frequent and widespread criminal behavior, an
explanation rooted in basic doctrines of their Church. Among

other things, the Latter-Day Saints held that there was a Kingdom of God and that to promote its welfare was one of their greatest obligations. In order to accomplish this, and other churchly tasks, ordinary laws did not need to be heeded; and when necessary, what the Gentiles called "illegal acts" were sanctioned by the highest Church authorities, for in such cases the ends always justified the means. The Saints, quite simply, did not believe in the English Common Law, *habeas corpus* or the Bill of Rights, except as convenient expedients; they did not believe in the laws of their local community or of their country, if such laws conflicted with those of the Church; nor would they obey the law except when it suited their long-range objectives or when they were temporarily compelled to do so by superior force. The Saints claimed to possess a "higher law," which came from God and which was received through their Prophet by means of the Bible or by revelation, and this law, and only this law, would they obey, even if it meant denying the rights of their fellow countrymen and defying the Constitution of the United States.

The idea of a higher law evolved and was refined over a period of years. The Apostle Orson Pratt, perhaps the most intellectual of the original Church leaders, eventually explained the matter in his book, *The Kingdom of God*—and at the same time revealed the utterly lawless character of the early Mormon Church. Pratt wrote: "The Kingdom of God is an order of government established by divine authority. It is the only legal government that can exist in any part of the universe. All other governments are illegal and unauthorized. . . . Any people attempting to govern themselves by laws of their own making, and by officers of their own appointment, are in direct rebellion against the Kingdom of God. . . . For seventeen hundred years the nations of the Western Hemisphere have been entirely destitute of 'the Kingdom of God'—entirely destitute of a true and legal government, entirely destitute of officers legally authorized to rule and govern. All the emperors, kings, princes, presidents, lords, nobles and rulers, during that long night of darkness have acted without authority. . . . Their authority is all assumed—it originated in man. Their laws are not from the Great Lawgiver but are the productions of their own false governments."

It should have been clear that men who believed in such dogmas would make poor neighbors and disaffected citizens, and so the Mormons did, during their years in the Middle West. For their concept of society placed them in irreconcilable conflict with all local and national governments; it was a blueprint for license and rebellion, setting the Saints above the law and their acts outside the law; and this, rather than polygamy itself, was the ultimate cause of the bitter struggle between the Mormons and the United States, and it also made possible, at a future date, a theocratic reign of terror which victimized both Gentile and Saint with equal savagery.

Chapter 5

For a decade and a half the Mormons, under Joseph Smith Jr. and Sidney Rigdon, were often on the move, their numbers increasing, along with their political ambitions and the mounting hostility of their various neighbors. During this rootless period the Saints lived in several localities, while their leaders attempted to decide where the Church should make its permanent home. In 1830, after only a few months at Kirtland, the Prophet turned his restless eye to the West, first sending such early missionaries as Oliver Cowdery and Parley P. Pratt to the borders of Missouri, with orders to convert the Indians, or Lamanites, who inhabited the area.

But the Prophet had a more enterprising project in mind than the conversion of the Indians. His ultimate plan, initially mentioned in private just a year after the founding of the Church, was to gather together all the Saints "unto one place," forming an independent nation in western Missouri, at the expense of, and on land to be taken from, the Gentiles. The plan was developed in stages, over several months. In a revelation, dated Kirtland, February 1831, the Prophet reported Christ as promising the Saints: "I will consecrate the riches of the Gentiles unto my people, which are of the house of Israel." Four months after this provocative pledge had been made, in June 1831, as the Prophet led the first small band of Mormon emigrants to Missouri, the Lord, through another revelation, assured the Saints of their right to possess the property of their future neighbors: "If ye are faithful, ye shall assemble yourselves together to rejoice upon the land in Missouri, which is the land of your inheritance, which is now the land of your enemies." It is difficult to understand how the supposedly "peace-loving" Prophet expected such inflammatory rhetoric to promote anything but animosity and conflict, and equally difficult to understand the subsequent complaint of the Mormons that from the very beginning in Missouri they were not the aggressors but rather the innocent victims of unprovoked persecution.

A month later, in July 1831, Smith, Rigdon and the handful of emigrants from Kirtland finally arrived at Independence, Jackson County, Missouri. Independence was a frontier town of some fifteen or twenty log houses, a brick courthouse and two or three stores, which served as the eastern terminus of the Santa Fe Trail. Here, at the laying of a cornerstone for the future temple, Smith publicly announced his fateful scheme. His face becoming strangely incandescent, as it frequently did during important religious rites, and speaking slowly, a single word at a time, the Prophet revealed that the Lord had selected Missouri as the latter-day Zion, the modern Promised Land, and that the site of the New Jerusalem, where the Saints were to gather to build up God's Kingdom, had been designated as this same town of Independence. Smith and Rigdon soon returned to Ohio, but from that July day, strife between the Mormons and the original Missouri settlers was all but inevitable.

The remaining years in Kirtland were not easy ones for the Prophet and his Ohio disciples. Money always was in short supply, and to raise fresh sums, Smith and Rigdon tried several novel expedients. One of the most imaginative was a socialistic scheme of Rigdon's, borrowed from the Campbellites, which became known as the United Order of Enoch. It was established by Revelation, and called upon each convert to legally "consecrate all of his wordly goods" to the Church. Once having done so, however, it did not take long for even the most credulous Saint to realize that he had placed his future in jeopardy, for if the Prophet ever charged him with apostasy and "cut him off" from the Church, he would be stripped of cash, land and home and left utterly destitute.

Understandably enough, the United Order of Enoch did not prove especially popular, and so Smith and Rigdon turned to other means of obtaining money. Eventually they sought to open their own bank but failed to meet the state's requirements and were denied a charter. Undaunted, they formed what they called the Kirtland Safety Society *Anti*-Banking Company, and printed their own unsupported bank-notes, which they used to pay off old and pressing debts. They also began to exchange the worthless paper for coin and other currency and for a variety of goods, much of it belonging to local Mormons.

To aid in the scheme, a number of leading Elders were dispatched to distant cities, where they exchanged Kirtland dollars for legitimate currency; Smith and several officers did well in neighboring Canada, while Brigham Young, who had joined the Church in 1832, gave an indication of his natural business acumen by rapidly disposing of $10,000 in valueless paper among the trusting citizens of the eastern states.

For two or three weeks the Church in Kirtland prospered greatly, but the antibank scheme could not be kept afloat for long. Soon two or three Cleveland merchants began to question the institution's solvency. Local bank-note holders requested payment in coin; their demands could not be met; and, less than a month after it opened, the antibank was forced to close its doors permanently.

Writs then were served on Smith and Rigdon, charging that they had violated the state's banking laws. They were arrested, tried and convicted, and ordered to pay a $1,000 fine. Worse still, the bank's failure had ruined many of the Faithful, and within a short time dozens of disaffected Saints were hurling public accusations at Rigdon, and even at the Prophet himself. Church members brought suits against them, charging fraud and demanding repayment of loans, and finally the Prophet had no choice but to declare them Apostates and cut them off from the Church. Unwilling to risk jail by facing the new charges against him, Smith decided to abandon the Kirtland branch of the Church and, accompanied by Rigdon and Brigham Young, fled from Ohio to Missouri.

By the time the Prophet permanently joined his Missouri flock in early 1838, it had grown to several thousand, and its members had become hardened by six years of adversity, intermittent harassment and near civil war. The Missouri troubles had begun as far back as 1832, a few months after the Prophet had disclosed that the nation's westernmost state was to become the modern Promised Land. Fired by this pronouncement, a party of several hundred Saints had marched from New York, Pennsylvania and Ohio to the vicinity of Independence, their sudden arrival signaling the possibility that the Prophet's disciples might shortly

become a majority in thinly settled Jackson County. Since the
Mormons admittedly voted en masse for all Church-selected
candidates, if this were to happen, the Church certainly would
gain control of the local government.

The original settlers were dismayed at the prospect and insisted that a non-Mormon could expect scant justice under Mormon
rule, a proposition that one day would be thoroughly tested in
Illinois and Utah. For the present, in Jackson County, such an
assertion could not be proved, but the fears that prompted it ran
deep and explained in part the embittered atmosphere that
almost immediately greeted the new arrivals.

There were a number of other reasons why the Saints found so
much hostility in the Promised Land. They were disliked for their
religious practices and for the way they flaunted their own
self-proclaimed moral superiority. In a period of local Indian
uprisings, it was not considered a friendly act to proselytize the
nearby Lamanites and to encourage them to believe that someday
they would succeed in driving all white men, except their
Mormon brothers, out of the state. The Saints were disliked and
envied for their thrift and their remarkable industry and were
feared because they often acted as a single, monolithic entity, in
obedience to the orders of their Elders. They were disliked for
their attitude toward emancipation and for the seditious speeches
they were said to direct against the area's slave population—
Jackson County and neighboring sections of the state having
been settled principally by slave owners and by other southerners
with strong pro-slavery leanings. And finally the Saints were
disliked for the way they boasted that the land was to be theirs in
the near future, without explaining how they expected to obtain
it from the current owners. When a number of Gentiles in the
county did offer to sell their farms to the newcomers, the
Mormons for the most part were either unwilling or too poor to
purchase them, and so it was impossible to employ the best and
perhaps the only means of avoiding a clash.

Violence began in Jackson County when Mormon houses were
attacked with rocks and their windows broken, haystacks burned
and shots fired harmlessly, to frighten the inhabitants into
leaving. These intimidating tactics produced no results, however,
and so a committee of Missouri citizens was formed to compel the
twelve hundred Saints—now more than a third of the county's
population—to halt further immigration, and to resettle in another part of the state.

At first the Mormons refused to negotiate, but eventually, under threats of further violence, they agreed to leave. Instead of doing so, though, they sent emissaries to the governor, Daniel Dunklin, in Jefferson City, asking him for protection.

Governor Dunklin's initial sympathies were with the Saints, but he understood neither the Church's real aims nor the complex nature of the controversy. In all good faith he told the Mormon leaders to seek the help of their local police officers and rashly promised that if such a step failed, the state government then would protect them. Encouraged by the governor's assurances, the Saints flouted the agreement they had made under duress, and set to work to improve their farms and to build new homes. In addition small bands of immigrants, proselytized by the roving Apostles and Seventies, continued to drift into Jackson County from the East in undiminished numbers.

Before long the violence resumed, but now with less restraint. A small Mormon settlement was attacked, some of the men were beaten, and the women and children were forced to seek safety in the woods. Unable to secure effective help from the governor, the Saints began to arm themselves; more than one pitched battle was fought, and on both sides several were killed and wounded.

In time the outnumbered Mormons saw that their cause was hopeless and that temporarily they would have to abandon Zion to the Gentiles. A hasty agreement was made that they would give up their arms and move north to Clay County, across the Missouri River.

During their abrupt and panic-filled departure, many Mormon families suffered both expulsion from their homes and the loss of personal property. For a few days they suffered physically as well, the main party of Saints being herded to the banks of the Missouri during the last weeks of autumn, where its members were compelled to encamp in a heavy rain, some in tents, and others without any shelter whatever. Although they soon received a friendly welcome across the river in Clay County, it made no difference: from that day on the Mormons always claimed that they had been persecuted remorselessly for their religion's sake; their hatred of the Gentiles—and especially anyone from Jackson County—became even more fixed and irrational; and for the first time, the desire for revenge began to smolder in the minds of some of their leaders.

During the following months the governor did his best to restore peace to the western part of the state, and through his

efforts the citizens of Jackson County agreed to indemnify those
who had been evicted. But the Saints had no wish to give up their
"rights" to the Promised Land or their hope of returning. They
refused the offer, demanding instead an additional payment for
damages, which they knew would be rejected. When it was, no
payments at all were made, the Saints kept their claim to Zion,
and affairs in western Missouri remained as troubled as before.

Still seeking a way to placate the Mormons, Governor Dunklin
opened negotiations with the War Department to build a new
arsenal in Jackson County; its establishment would have ensured
the presence of Federal troops, and these the governor could have
used, both to restore the Mormons to their former homes and to
guarantee their safety once they had returned.

But the Prophet himself undermined the governor's efforts;
indulging his taste for military show, he organized a company of
some 150 or 200 volunteers in Kirtland, dubbed it the Army of
Zion and set out for Missouri in support of the western branch
of the Church.

The Prophet and his followers came through the countryside in
loose military array, dozens of armed men, some on foot and
others on horseback, their destination undeclared and their
presence unexplained. Whatever their purpose, they clearly were
not ordinary emigrants, for they had with them neither wives
and children nor wagons piled high with bedding and other
household goods. And so a cry arose that an army was on the
march, a Mormon army of insurrection, heading toward Missouri
and Jackson County, to fight a war with the enemies of the
Church. As they approached the state border, and as ever more
terrifying rumors ran before them, the militias of several Missouri counties took up arms. The governor hastily ordered a truce,
but the damage already had been done. With the appearance of
the Prophet's army, hatred and fear of the Mormons reached new
peaks in Missouri, and any hope of returning the Saints to a
now-enraged Jackson County was gone.

For two years more a tenuous peace was maintained in Clay
County, but eventually feelings there against the Mormons grew
as strong as they had been on the other side of the river. Once
again a public committee was formed, new accusations were
made, and resolutions drawn up, calling for the expulsion of the
Saints. This time, though, the matter was managed more hu-
manely; there was no immediate exodus, and the Saints were

allowed to harvest their crops, settle their accounts and sell their homes without loss.

At the request of the Mormon leaders, the state legislature partitioned sparsely settled Ray County into two divisions, and one of these, newly designated Caldwell County, was set aside expressly for their use. Here the Saints soon gained title to considerable land, some by purchase and some free of charge from the Federal Government; they declared the town of Far West their county seat and, following a plan of the Prophet for building an ideal city, laid it out in broad, open squares, with streets wide enough for several wagons to pass abreast.

The new arrangement was successful at first. Few Gentiles lived near Far West, so that a major source of friction had been removed. The state allowed the Mormons complete political freedom, and the entire machinery of county government came into their hands. Through hard work the Caldwell County Saints quickly prospered, and as one of their leaders wrote not long afterward, "Friendship began to be restored between them and their neighbors, the old prejudices were fast dying away, and they were doing very well, until the summer of 1838." By then, unfortunately, the Kirtland bank had failed, the Church's home in Ohio had been abandoned and Joseph Smith Jr. had crossed the Mississippi, bringing with him, as he might have announced himself—"not peace, but a sword!"

Chapter 6

It was the Prophet's reappearance that changed Missouri into a battleground. After fleeing from Ohio, he arrived at Far West early in 1838, no doubt with spirits deflated over the recent failure of the Kirtland bank and the lawsuits filed against him, many by his own rebellious disciples. But at Far West he soon became his ebullient self again, heartened by the bustling appearance of the town and by the size of the Missouri branch of the Church, which now numbered between ten and fifteen thousand souls.

More eager than ever to gain political power, Smith immediately began to violate the tacit understanding that had been made with the Missouri authorities. Into neighboring Ray, Carroll, Daviess and other counties went dozens of Mormon families, and with the building of each new village and the clearing of each new farm, the scattered Gentile settlers grew increasingly apprehensive.

Extremely provocative was the founding of Adam-ondi-Ahman, or "Adam-on-Diamond" as it soon began to be called, a town that the Prophet decided to build on the Grand River, in Daviess County. To his devout and credulous followers, among them John Doyle Lee, subsequently notorious for his part in the Mountain Meadows Massacre, the Prophet explained that this was the place where Adam had lived after his expulsion from the Garden of Eden, and that because the Saints were God's Chosen People, they were entitled to take up residence there. Such assertions did nothing to calm the Gentile citizens of Daviess County, and to make matters worse, Smith left Lyman Wight, one of his most bellicose lieutenants, in charge of the settlement, an appointment almost certain to ensure future trouble.

Not all the Church's leaders approved of the Prophet's expansionist course. When a serious quarrel developed, Smith and Rigdon finally purged a number of the dissidents, including David Whitmer and Oliver Cowdery, two of the original trio of witnesses to the *Book of Mormon*. Although declared Apostates and driven from the fellowship of the Church, neither man chose to leave Far West. Before long, however, they received an abusive letter demanding that they depart from the county within three days and threatening that they would be driven out by force if they refused to comply. The letter was signed by eighty-odd Mormon Elders, among them Hyrum Smith, the Prophet's most trusted brother, who by now, along with Sidney Rigdon, was one of the Prophet's two Counselors, and a member of the Church's ruling triumvirate, the First Presidency.

Whitmer and Cowdery hastily rode off to Clay County to hire a Gentile lawyer, but on their way back, they met their wives and children fleeing the town. During their absence a group of Saints had surrounded their homes. The armed men were members of the newly formed clandestine organization, the Danites. They had ordered the Whitmers and Cowderys to leave at once, threatening to kill any family members who returned. A hasty inspection told the two Apostates that except for some blankets and a few items of clothing, they had been robbed of all their possessions by their former brothers in Christ.

The Church in later years always denied, with understandable vehemence, the very existence of the Danites or any similar body of men, accusing Gentile enemies of once again making false and malicious charges. Unhappily, the Danites did exist, and to the great harm of the Church, they received both the sanction and encouragement of its early leaders.

During the Missouri days, the Danites had several specific duties to perform. In their capacity of private bodyguards, they were to protect the First Presidency. Serving as a secret police, they were to spy out "traitors" among the membership and then, on orders from their superiors, were to punish such offenders in a suitable manner. Finally, beyond the borders of Caldwell County, they were to serve as an underground guerrilla force, and so were organized into secret companies, with a captain to preside over each band of fifty.

The early Danites swore an oath, pledging themselves to obey the Prophet and the First Presidency "in all things" and to uphold them whether they were "right or wrong." Members agreed that

in times of danger they would communicate with one another
through passwords and signs, and promised never to reveal the
secret purposes of their society. One version of the oath ended by
saying, "Should I ever do the same, I hold my life as a forfeiture,
in a cauldron of boiling oil."

The founder of the Danites was a murderous, bloodthirsty
border ruffian named Sampson Avard. With Smith and Rigdon's
approval, "Doctor" Avard was given a free hand in leading the
Danites, and during the Missouri troubles, he became one of
the most powerful Elders in the Church. He fervently supported
the First Presidency, as he made clear in these inelegant but
candid words: "If I meet one damning and cursing the Presidency,
I can curse them [sic] too, and if he will drink, I can get him a
bowl of brandy, and after a while, take him by the arm and get
him to one side in the brush, when I will get into his guts in a
minute and put him under the sod."

Several weeks before civil war erupted, Dr. Avard sent secret
instructions to his Danite captains which made it clear that the
Church hierarchy now gave its unrestrained approval to theft,
perjury and murder. The message said in part: "Know ye not,
brethren, that it will soon be your privilege to . . . go out on a
scout on the borders of the new settlements, and to take to
yourselves . . . the goods of the ungodly Gentiles? For it is
written, the riches of the Gentiles shall be consecrated to my
people, the house of Israel. And thus you will waste away the
Gentiles by robbing and plundering them of their property; and
in this way we will build up the Kingdom of God. . . .

"If any of us should be recognized, who can harm us? For we
will stand by each other, and defend one another [in] all things.
. . . I would swear a lie to clear any of you; and if this would not
do, I would put them or him under the sand, as Moses did the
Egyptian; and in this way we will consecrate much unto the
Lord."

All during the spring and early summer the Mormon hierarchy
used angry, rancorous sermons to prepare its followers for
conflict with the Gentiles. At last, on July 4, hundreds of Saints
journeyed to Far West to celebrate Independence Day and the
laying of a cornerstone for the new Temple. Before the orations
could begin there was a parade; first came the Mormon foot-
soldiers, then Church leaders and civilians and finally the cavalry, a large, impressive collection of armed horsemen, whose

appearance did little to reassure the non-Mormon dignitaries on the speakers' stand of their hosts' peaceful intentions.

The principal speaker of the day was Sidney Rigdon. Years later the Church would claim that he alone had been responsible for his speech, but in fact it had been composed with the full knowledge and approval of the Prophet and others on the High Council. The address offered an exceptionally fierce and paranoid example of Rigdon's oratory. At one point he said, "Our cheeks have been given to the smiters, and our heads to those who plucked off the hair. . . . We have suffered their abuse, without cause, with patience, and have endured without resentment, until this day, and still their persecution and violence does not cease. But from this day and this hour, we will suffer it no more."

Then Rigdon abandoned the uncongenial role of patient sufferer and, speaking for the Church Militant, hurled a reckless and defiant challenge at its enemies. "We warn all men, in the name of Jesus Christ," he thundered, "to come on us no more . . . for from this hour, we will bear it no more. Our rights shall no more be trampled on with impunity. The man, or set of men, who attempt it, does it at the expense of their lives . . . it shall be between us and them a war of extermination, for we will follow them till the last drop of their blood is spilled, or else they will have to exterminate us; for we will carry the seat of war to their houses, and their own families, and one party or another shall be utterly destroyed."

The Prophet furnished a copy of Rigdon's speech to a newspaper in Clay County, the Gentile population of western Missouri became thoroughly alarmed and civil war had moved a giant step closer. The only way to prevent bloodshed was to place a neutral force between the two hostile sides, but no such force existed in the state, the partisan militia of the various counties being a highly unsuitable instrument for maintaining the peace.

Nor was any help to be had from Washington. On earlier occasions an indifferent or ill-informed Federal Government had stated that it would not intervene in the Missouri dispute; it was Washington's belief that the issues between the Mormons and the original settlers were local in nature and therefore they could— and should—be settled by the state itself, a misconception that would not be corrected for two decades, and then only after a fearful price had been paid in money and lives.

Chapter 7

DURING THE SUMMER and autumn of 1838, the violent struggle for control of western Missouri approached a climax. Early in August, statewide elections were held, and the Church, after five years of neutrality, proclaimed its intention of backing the Democrats against the Whigs, in return for future political favors. The two parties were almost equally divided in troubled Daviess County, and the Mormon vote there promised to be decisive. At Gallatin, the county seat, an attempt was made to keep the Saints from voting; when this happened, thirty club-wielding Danites, led by John D. Lee, clashed with a force of Gentiles and drove them from the polls.

The Election Day fight at Gallatin ended with nothing worse than a few contused heads and some severely bruised limbs, but exaggerated rumors of the incident were quickly carried to Far West, where it was reported that two Mormons had been killed, and that Adam Black, a justice of the peace, was marching on Adam-ondi-Ahman at the head of a Gentile army. Hearing this, Sampson Avard collected 150 horsemen and, with Smith and Rigdon, galloped north to defend the town.

No defense was required, though, because no army was in sight. But instead of returning home peaceably, Smith, together with Lyman Wight and a mob of soldiers, rode on to Gallatin and forced Adam Black to sign a document that the Mormons styled "an agreement of peace."

After the Prophet and his riders had withdrawn, however, a different document was written and circulated. "I, Adam Black," it read, "do hereby certify that I have this day been attacked . . . by one hundred armed men, called 'Mormons'. . . . I was [ordered] to subscribe to an article, which I refused to do, until instant death was threatened me. . . . The above body of armed men [was] commanded by Joseph Smith Jr. and Lyman Wight."

Warrants were issued against Smith and Wight, and the Prophet hired two leading Missouri citizens, General Alexander Doniphan and General David Atchison, to act as their attorneys. The humane Doniphan had been a Mormon sympathizer for several years; while serving in the state legislature he had proposed a bill that had made Caldwell County the Saints' enclave. Now, on Doniphan's advice, Smith and Wight surrendered to the authorities and were released on $500 bond.

Week after week, antagonism mounted sharply in a half-dozen Missouri counties; the two sides continued to arm, there were brief skirmishes and the first prisoners were taken. In Daviess and Livingston counties, the original settlers petitioned Governor Lilburn Boggs for protection, and the new governor, who, unlike his predecessor, was no special friend of the Mormons, sent General Atchison west with four hundred militia, and then General Doniphan with one thousand more.

Early in October the Gentiles of Carroll County drove out a colony of Mormon settlers; fifty wagons carried the refugees back to Far West, and the Prophet announced that their expulsion meant the beginning of civil war.

On both sides hundreds of men now were allowed to express their most savage and brutal instincts, and before long there were numerous outbreaks of theft, arson and assault. John D. Lee, who rode among the Mormon raiders, wrote of his companions: "Men of former quiet became perfect demons in their efforts to spoil and waste the enemies of the Church"—their ferocity no doubt well matched by the Missouri settlers who set out against them.

By mid-October full-scale guerrilla warfare had come to western Missouri, and as the struggle intensified, many Mormon families retreated from the outlying settlements to the security of the two main towns—Far West, in Caldwell County, and Adam-ondi-Ahman, in Daviess County. From these centers the Saints continued to send out swift and effective raiding parties; in Daviess County, eighty horsemen made a spectacular attack on Gallatin and burned to the ground between 100 and 150 houses.

At least one resident of Gallatin, a man named McBride, had

been a good friend to Lee and other Mormons, but during the pillaging he was not spared. According to Lee, "Every article of moveable property was taken by the troops; he was utterly ruined." And then Lee added, thinking to defend the Prophet's reputation, "In justice to Joseph Smith, I cannot say that I ever heard him teach, or even encourage men to pilfer or steal *little* things."

After the raid on Gallatin a new plea went out to Governor Boggs for military protection against Danite arms. At the same time the governor received sworn statements from two disaffected Mormon Apostles, exposing the Danite organization, admitting the Saints' responsibility for the sacking of Gallatin and reporting in full a speech that Joseph Smith had delivered only a few days earlier at Far West. On that occasion the Prophet had said, "If the people will let us alone, we will preach the gospel in peace. But if they come on us and molest us, we will establish our religion by the sword. We will trample down our enemies and make it one gore of blood from the Rocky Mountains to the Atlantic Ocean. I will be to this generation a second Mohammed, whose motto in treating for peace was 'The Koran or the sword!'"

With these developments in mind, the governor dispatched several thousand additional militia to the western counties, at the same time issuing an inexcusable and justly criticized "order of extermination" to his field commanders. The order, echoing Sidney Rigdon's earlier Independence Day speech, said at one point: "I have received information . . . of the most appalling character, which . . . places the Mormons in the attitude of an open and avowed defiance of the laws, and of having made war upon the people of this state. . . . The Mormons must be treated as enemies, and must be exterminated or driven from the state if necessary, for the public peace—their outrages are beyond all description."

Even before this ill-conceived order had been delivered, though, local militia elements already had taken matters into their own hands. Much the bloodiest incident occurred at Haun's Mill, a tiny hamlet on the outskirts of Far West. Here, two hundred militiamen rode up one day and ringed the crudely built blacksmith's shop, which the Mormons had tried to convert into a blockhouse. Aiming at the wide gaps between the logs, the attackers soon had wounded or killed a number of the defenders. Little quarter was given, the Mormons claiming that one wounded fighter who tried to hand over his rifle and surrender was hacked to death by a trooper wielding a corn cutter; another militiaman attempted to spare the life of a wounded young boy, but his companion reputedly said, "Nits will make lice," and shot the youngster through the head.

When the Haun's Mill Massacre was over, another chapter had been added to the brief, rancorous history of the Church—a history not yet ten years old. The incident soon became the subject of poems, hymns and sermons, its savagery considerably exaggerated and its anniversary invariably remembered. Along with the expulsion from Jackson County, it began to serve as a high point in the recitals of innocent suffering and unprovoked wrongs, which the Mormons claimed to have endured for their religion's sake. And along with the name of Missouri itself, Haun's Mill became a catchword by which any congregation of Saints could be aroused to hostile fury and to a thirst for revenge against their Gentile "oppressors."

After Haun's Mill, the end came quickly in Missouri. Overwhelming forces of militia approached Far West and Adam-ondi-Ahman, and the Mormons were compelled to yield, surrendering their arms and promising to leave the state with all due speed. As part of the agreement, a number of leading Saints, including the Prophet, his brother Hyrum, Sidney Rigdon, Lyman Wight and Parley P. Pratt gave themselves up as hostages to the commanding general, Samuel Lucas, "to be tried for their crimes." The same night, according to Mormon accounts, a court martial condemned the Prophet and several others to death, but fortunately General Doniphan interceded on their behalf, and General Lucas, heeding Doniphan's advice, stayed the execution and placed the prisoners in jail. It was then decided that a civil hearing would be held in a few weeks, with Doniphan acting as counsel for the defendants.

Before the hearing, Governor Boggs received reports from his field commanders, including one from General Wilson, the chief officer in Daviess County. "It is impossible for me to convey to you anything like the awful state of things which exists here," General Wilson wrote. "The citizens of a whole county first plundered, and then their houses and other buildings burnt to ashes. . . . I confess that my feelings have been shocked with the gross brutality of these Mormons, who have acted more like demons from the infernal regions than human beings."

There was no question where the marauders had come from or

where they had stored "the wealth of the Gentiles" once it had been seized. In Daviess County, John D. Lee served as General Wilson's guide and later wrote: "Every house in Adam-ondi-Ahman was searched by the troops for stolen property. They succeeded in finding [most of what] had been captured by the Saints in the various raids made through the county. Bedding of every kind and in large quantities was found and reclaimed by the owners. Even spinning wheels, soap barrels, and other articles were recovered."

The civil hearing began a few weeks later, with a number of leading Saints among the prosecution witnesses, including several disaffected Apostles, and the adaptable Sampson Avard, founder of the Danites, who by now had decided to save his own skin at the expense of his former colleagues. The most damaging testimony came from Thomas Marsh, the First President of the Twelve Apostles. In a sworn affidavit he declared: "The Prophet inculcates the notion, and it's believed by every true Mormon, that Smith's prophecies are superior to the law of the land. I have heard the Prophet say that he would tread upon his enemies, and walk over their dead bodies. . . . The plan of said Smith, the Prophet, is to take this state; and he professes to his people to intend [sic] to take the United States and ultimately the whole world."

But by then considerable time had passed, and the passions of many Missouri citizens had cooled, so that their principal desire no longer was to punish all the Mormons, or even the most egregious Church leaders, but simply to rid themselves of these strange, Bible-quoting and utterly intolerable neighbors. Besides, it was clear that violent and illegal acts had been committed on both sides and that in numerous instances the evidence of Mormon crimes would not stand up under fair judicial review. As a consequence most of the complaints were dropped, and a majority of the defendants given their freedom. Only the Prophet, Sidney Rigdon and Lyman Wight were charged with treason; Parley P. Pratt and four companions were charged with murder; and twenty-three others were charged with lesser crimes.

One by one, even these prisoners were released, or else so loosely watched that they managed to escape from custody, until by the following spring, the Prophet alone remained in jail. Finally he bribed a guard, obtained a horse and rode off to Adam-ondi-Ahman, where he joined the last of the departing Saints as they hastened eastward to their new sanctuary in Illinois.

For six months the Prophet had been in a civil jail, but his followers had not been leaderless. At least two of the Apostles had never been captured, Heber C. Kimball, sometimes described by his admirers as "high-spirited" and "jovial," and more importantly, the energetic, wily and enormously efficient Brigham Young. While the Prophet had languished in his cell, Young, assisted by his friend Kimball, had organized the difficult movement of the Saints from Missouri to Illinois. And here they already had settled, and were beginning to build the Church's new home, when the Prophet rode into town for the last chapter of his dazzling career.

Chapter 8

Eﾠ A R L Y   I N   1 8 3 9 the Mormons established themselves at Commerce, Illinois, a tiny hillside hamlet on the east bank of the Mississippi, with a fine view of the river and the surrounding countryside. Soon after arriving, the Prophet decided that the new settlement deserved a more imposing name. Gazing over the water, he was reported to have said, "It is a beautiful site, and it shall be called *Nauvoo*, which in Hebrew means a beautiful plantation." Afterward he remained unperturbed when scholars unanimously agreed that no such Hebrew word existed: Nauvoo his city had been denominated, and Nauvoo it would remain.

At first the Mormons were warmly received in Illinois, a northern state whose inhabitants had scant liking for the slave-holding southerners of Missouri, whom they often referred to as "Pukes." Illinois politicians had their own reason for welcoming the Saints: the Democrats and Whigs were closely balanced, and each party thought it could defeat the other with the help of the refugees. For a time, too, the Church actively solicited Gentile compassion; its recently founded newspaper, *Times and Seasons*, frequently carried lurid accounts of the Saints' expulsion from Missouri and of the Haun's Mill Massacre, and when these stories were reprinted in the general press, many a reader felt, in typical American fashion, a surge of sympathy for the plight of such abused and courageous underdogs.

Before long, though, the people around Nauvoo began to have second thoughts about the newcomers. Unchastened by events in Ohio and Missouri, the Saints remained what they always had been—clannish, self-righteous, engrossed in their own religious pursuits and utterly indifferent to the property or personal rights of anyone else. Soon there were complaints about the Saints' honesty; it was said that Nauvoo was a den of thieves and that no one outside the Church could obtain justice there, because no Saint ever would testify against his brothers in Christ.

Not all these complaints came from the Gentiles. A year after the founding of Nauvoo, John D. Lee attended a religious conference, at which Smith cautioned his more enthusiastic followers to amend their conduct. "We are no longer at war," he said, "and you must stop stealing. When the right time comes, we will go in force and take the whole state of Missouri. It belongs to us as an inheritance; but I want no more petty stealing. A man that will steal petty articles from his enemies, will, when the occasion offers, steal from his brethren too. Now I command that you who have stolen must steal no more."

Another cause of Gentile uneasiness was the rapid growth of the Church and its riverside capital. Month after month new disciples kept arriving at Nauvoo, until by the early 1840's some ten thousand Mormons were living in the town itself or on adjacent farms, an impressive Temple was under construction and the inhabitants of the Beautiful Plantation could rightly claim that they occupied the most populous city in the state.

Such growth was the result of deliberate policy. From the very beginning the Church had been committed to active proselytizing, and now, thanks in considerable measure to the Missouri persecutions, significant numbers of converts, some of them possessing handsome sums of money, were being enrolled in Canada and the eastern states.

But not all the new Saints came from these areas. Several years earlier the Prophet had sent Heber C. Kimball to Great Britain to preach the gospel, and his mission had been well received, especially in Wales and the British Midlands, where many families were desperately poor and at least a third of the population was illiterate.

Once comfortably settled in Nauvoo, the Prophet decided to revive the Church's European efforts. This time the mission to Great Britain was led by Brigham Young, First President of the Twelve Apostles, assisted by Kimball and the Apostles Parley P. Pratt, John Taylor and George A. Smith, the Prophet's cousin. Upon arriving in England, Young established a permanent branch of the Church, set up a printing plant and began to publish a newspaper, the *Millennial Star.* He enrolled thousands of converts and organized a highly effective system of emigration,

so that in 1841, twelve hundred British Saints arrived safely in
Nauvoo, and the following year sixteen hundred were made
welcome there. Heartened by these successes, the ever optimistic
Prophet ordered a copy of the *Book of Mormon* sent to Queen
Victoria, in the belief that she, too, was ready to be converted to
the True Faith. Her Majesty's failure to respond represented one
of the mission's few disappointments in the British Isles.

The importation of foreign converts, the rapid growth of
Nauvoo and the high incidence of petty larceny in Mormon
neighborhoods all served to antagonize the Gentiles in Illinois
and to arose their sense of apprehension. Yet for the most part
these were only minor irritants; it was principally the reckless
behavior of the Prophet himself that brought the Church into
wide disrepute and encouraged a renewal of strife and violence.

Joseph Smith, now in his midthirties, was close to the climax of
his singular life. He possessed substantial political influence in
the state and was eager to augment it. He commanded thousands
and was commanded by none. He had suffered numerous defeats
but after each had managed to emerge unscathed, with followers
more ardently devoted to his cause than they had been before.
Looking back across the past dozen years, it was easy to believe
that the Lord had indeed selected him to carry out great projects
and that there were scarcely any limits to what he might not hope
to accomplish in the days ahead.

Few public figures in the West were more talked about or better
known. At Nauvoo, hundreds of curious tourists, descending from
steamboats, had little difficulty recognizing him—a tall, somewhat portly man with a large, graying head and a beaked nose,
who invariably dressed like someone of consequence, his usual
costume being an expensive blue coat, matching trousers and a
stylish white cravat, with a heavy gold ring glinting on his
finger, and a black cane swinging idly in his hand.

Unlike many of his disciples, the Prophet was no hair-shirt
Calvinist. He enjoyed drinking and made scarcely any effort to
conceal it. Thomas Ford, Governor of Illinois during most of the
Nauvoo troubles, later wrote of the Mormon leader that he
"dressed like a dandy, and at times drank like a sailor and swore
like a pirate." When a visiting English clergyman asked in
dismay how he could permit himself to get drunk, the Prophet
answered facetiously that it was necessary for him to do so once
in a while so that his followers would not worship him as a god. It
was known in Nauvoo that he often drank heavily on days when

he reviewed the militia, and following one such occasion he was heard to say in the pulpit, "Brethren and sisters, I got drunk last week and fell in the ditch. I am awfully sorry—but I felt very good."

Such disarming candor, though, did not extend to all areas of the Prophet's private life. For years there had been rumors that he was excessively fond of pretty, nubile young women, and even during the early Kirtland and Far West days it had been whispered that Emma Smith, the mother of his several children, was by no means the only partner to share his bed. Finally, at Nauvoo, the Prophet finished perfecting his ingenious Doctrine of Plural Marriage and, after asserting that he had received a Revelation from the Lord, which, for the time being, he could not disclose to the world at large, cautiously introduced the subject to a handful of his most trusted followers.

The doctrine called on every male Saint, in the name of high religious duty, to take to himself as many wives as he could. Two categories of wives were contemplated; one, consisting for the most part of elderly women, would belong to him in the next world only and would be "sealed," or married to him, "for eternity." With such "spiritual wives" there would be, of course, no sex or offspring. A man's younger wives, however, would be sealed to him "for time," or for life in this world, as well as for eternity, and these women would cook his food, bear his children and yield him total obedience, in gratitude for the inestimable favor he had bestowed by marrying them. For according to the Doctrine of Plural Marriage, the soul of a single woman could at best attain only a humble position in the afterworld, and with it, hardly any celestial happiness at all. By contrast, a married woman, especially one who had been sealed to an Apostle or some other highly favored Saint, would gain an exalted position in the next world, that would enable her to enjoy the complete delights of Paradise throughout Eternity.

With the Doctrine of Plural Marriage fully developed, and aware of his mounting obligations, the Prophet briskly began to enlarge his circle of wives. Previously at Kirtland and Far West he had in all likelihood contracted three or four secret marriages; at Nauvoo, between 1841 and 1844, he married twenty-five or thirty times more, being sealed to a new wife at the rate of approximately once every six or eight weeks.

From the very beginning plural marriage caused an incalculable amount of misery, anguish and despair. Among its earliest victims were girls like Helen Kimball, daughter of Apostle Heber C. Kimball, who was forced by her father to become an unwilling bride of the Prophet at the age of fifteen. Her case was not exceptional. Over the years a legion of hapless women, young and old, suffered coercion, fear, jealousy and humiliation because of the outrageous demands of polygamy. Nor were women the only victims. Any number of happily married men, who had no desire to take additional wives, were nevertheless forced to do so, under threat of economic reprisal or social ostracism.

Plural marriage, for Mormonism itself, was a pernicious, long-term and many-sided evil. It deepened the Church's inherent clannishness and increased its isolation from the mainstream of Christianity and Christian thought. It drove some of the most humane Saints out of the Church, compelled many of those who retained their faith to lead a secret personal life beyond the law and reinforced the obsessional belief of the Prophet's followers that they were being cruelly persecuted by the non-Mormon world for attempting to live as Abraham and the other Patriarchs had lived in the ancient days. Long before the practice of plural marriage was admitted publicly in 1852, it already had made every church member an object not only of vulgar curiosity but also of widespread ridicule, and from the more belligerent Saints, such mockery could draw only one response—an intensified sense of hostility mingled with an ill-concealed desire for revenge.

But perhaps most harmful of all was the effect of plural marriage on the leaders of the Church. It was true that men like Brigham Young, Heber C. Kimball and George A. Smith were no strangers to questionable plots and schemes; yet before the introduction of plural marriage, their illegal activities at least could have been described as intermittent. Once they began to practice polygamy, however, they became full-time lawbreakers, who were destined to be further corrupted by more than ten years of concealment, lying and deceit. It was hardly a coincidence that among those who first conspired to secretly practice polygamy in the Middle West, there were several of the principals in another conspiracy, organized a decade later in the Utah Territory. Young, Kimball, Smith and the ever loyal and obedient John D. Lee all were introduced to the Prophet's revelation at an early date, and by the time they left Nauvoo, Young had seventeen wives, Smith six, Lee ten, and Kimball an extraordinary thirty-two.

Another early participant in plural marriage was Dimick B.

Huntington, a veteran of Far West and the Missouri expulsion. At Nauvoo, the shadowy, elusive Huntington was a member of the inner circle around the Prophet, and two of his married sisters, Prescindia Huntington Buell and Zina Huntington Jacobs, were soon added to the Mormon leader's roster of brides. In the case of Zina it was Huntington himself who conducted the private ceremony and sealed his bigamous sister to the Prophet as the latter's bride number eight. Huntington, Lee, Smith and Young—polygamists, lawbreakers and, eventually, the unfeeling architects of a truly monumental crime.

Chapter 9

A PRUDENT STRATEGIST, having been forced to flee from Ohio and Missouri, would have acted with caution in Illinois, taking care to remain on good terms with those who made him welcome. But the Prophet never had been noted for prudence; once settled at Nauvoo, he plunged into public affairs in an insolent and capricious way that was certain to alienate his friends while deepening the hostility of his numerous enemies.

The Prophet's first political maneuver took him to Washington, where he placed a grossly inflated claim for damages before Congress and President Martin Van Buren. Neither Congress nor the President was impressed with the merits of the case, and when the claim was rejected, the Saints insisted that they had been victimized by corrupt politicians, accused the United States of unfair treatment and indicated that henceforth they had little need to obey their country's laws, since those laws invariably were used against them.

Back in Nauvoo, the Prophet drafted a city charter, under which the Mormons were to be granted almost complete autonomy from the state and the Prophet himself was to be empowered to run the city with a free hand. The long-term advantages of such an arrangement were evident enough; in addition, there was an immediate and urgent need to secure passage of the charter. Legally the Prophet still was a fugitive from Missouri, and at any moment a posse from that state might ride into town with a warrant for his arrest. Unless he could establish a municipal court in Nauvoo, with the power to declare such a warrant void, he never could feel himself free from the threat of extradition, and a lengthy stay in one of Governor Lilburn Boggs's unwholesome jails.

After considering various means of getting the charter approved by the state legislature, the Prophet decided to accept an offer of assistance from a recent convert, Dr. John C. Bennett, of Springfield. The doctor, a skilled abortionist and formerly a professor of "midwifery" at obscure Willoughy University in Ohio, had only recently moved to Illinois, where he had become secretary of the state Medical Society and quartermaster general of the state militia. For a number of months the two men had been in correspondence, and by now the Prophet doubtlessly realized that the glib, congenial Dr. Bennett was as utterly devoid of political principles and as hungry for political power as he was himself. More important, the doctor was a clever lobbyist, with many useful friends among both Democratic and Whig leaders in the state capital. Quickly a bargain was struck: Dr. Bennett would attempt to steer the Nauvoo charter through the legislature and, if successful, would be rewarded with the highest honors a grateful Church could confer.

The scheme went off perfectly. Both the Whigs and the Democrats were eager to retain the good will of the Saints, and so an act incorporating the City of Nauvoo was passed unanimously, without its having been read by a single member of either house of the legislature.

The rights granted in the twenty-eight articles of the act were extraordinary. The city of Nauvoo was allowed to form its own militia, which became known as the Nauvoo Legion and which operated independently of the state; the city was granted municipal courts with powers superior to those of the state courts; and the mayor and the Common Council were ceded an authority possessed by the executive and legislative branches of no other city in the nation. It was hardly surprising that an exultant Dr. Bennett immediately wrote to the Prophet: "Every power we ask is granted, every request gratified, every desire fulfilled."

Once the city charter had been ratified, Dr. Bennett was handsomely rewarded for the work he'd done. Leaving Springfield he settled in Nauvoo, was appointed a major general and second-in-command of the Legion and was elected to a term as mayor of the city. In addition he was named to the First Presidency along with William Law, an honest, wealthy and able Canadian convert—he and Law succeeding Hyrum Smith and the ailing Sidney Rigdon, as members of the Church's supreme triumvirate.

For almost two years Bennett was the second most powerful man in Nauvoo, a practicing polygamist with several young wives, and the Prophet's closest confidant. Both men enjoyed composing bombastic speeches and newspaper articles, threatening the Gentiles with retribution for their sins; they also enjoyed dressing up in gaudy, gold-braided, blue-and-buff uniforms, high boots, pistols and Napoleonic hats festooned with ostrich feathers, to review the glittering ranks of the Nauvoo Legion, in which every able-bodied Mormon male was compelled to serve, and whose bristling appearance caused visiting Gentiles to wonder what the ultimate purpose could be of such a military display.

Despite Dr. Bennett's rise to eminence, though, the Prophet remained supreme in Nauvoo, his position as spiritual and temporal leader scarcely challenged by his new second-in-command. Yet neither the unflagging loyalty of the Saints nor the growing power of the Legion could entirely relieve Smith of his sense of foreboding or convince him that he ever really was safe from danger. Still fearing that he would be seized by a posse and carried across the river to Missouri, he selected a dozen of the most ruthless Danites in Nauvoo to act as his private bodyguard.

Number seven in the guard was John D. Lee, who considered the appointment a highly gratifying honor, even during those bone-chilling winter nights when it became his duty to stand watch outside a house where the Prophet was visiting one of his wives. Among the other guards were several of the most cold-blood criminals on the frontier; they included two young men, William Hickman and Orrin Porter Rockwell, who eventually would become notorious for the number of men they murdered; and yet, in both Nauvoo and the Utah Territory, the Church found a need for their services, and praise for their deeds.

In 1842 trouble finally erupted between Smith and Bennett, the inevitable result of conflicting ambitions and mutual distrust. It was a woman, though, who caused the immediate break between them. For some time each of the Mormon leaders had kept his eye fixed on Sidney Rigdon's nineteen-year-old daughter, Nancy, with the hope of adding her to his list of wives. Each man suspected what the other was up to and schemed to circumvent him. One day the Prophet found the girl alone and proposed marriage. Forewarned by Bennett, however, Nancy Rigdon refused to accept either the Doctrine of Plural Wives or the Prophet's hand. The following day the Prophet unwisely wrote a letter, renewing his offer, and with this as proof, the girl promptly denounced him to her father.

Until then the monogamous Rigdon had known nothing for certain about the secret marriages contracted by Smith and other leading Saints, although doubtlessly he had heard the rumors and accusations that had been circulating lately in the city. Now his angry voice was raised in the tabernacle against the Prophet, who only a short time before had been similarly denounced by the father of another girl whom he had attempted to seduce.

The Prophet decided that the moment had come to switch the public spotlight from his own affairs to those of his leading associate. He immediately collected a band of witnesses, who eagerly testified to Dr. Bennett's sexual misconduct with numerous women in Nauvoo. Smith then excommunicated Bennett, at the same time piously blaming his now deposed confederate for all of the city's burgeoning scandals.

After leaving Nauvoo, Bennett retaliated by writing a series of generally accurate though vindictive articles for an Illinois newspaper, the *Sangamo Journal*. He denounced Smith for being an insatiable libertine and described in minute detail his irregular domestic arrangements and his sexual excesses. In one article or another, he accused the Prophet of political subversion, treason and murder, asserting that Smith had a personal bodyguard of known assassins, called Danites, and that he was a dangerous and revolutionary "American Napoleon" who had organized his own private army, the Nauvoo Legion, for the purpose of carving out a western empire, which was to include the states and territories of Indiana, Illinois, Ohio, Iowa and Missouri.

Bennett's articles were widely reprinted, especially in Illinois, and proved extremely damaging to Smith; for although Bennett himself obviously was capable of considerable malice and exaggeration, he had indeed been the Prophet's most intimate collaborator for almost two years and certainly knew a great deal about the Church's innermost secrets. As a consequence, his disclosures were believed in many local Gentile circles and sharply increased the bitter animosity felt against the refugees from Missouri.

While John Bennett's articles still were running in the *Sangamo Journal*, a sensational and vengeful crime was committed on the frontier that lent credence to even his strongest accusations. Late one spring evening, at Independence, Missouri, former governor Lilburn Boggs was sitting near a window of his house,

reading by candlelight. Under cover of darkness, an assassin
approached and fired a pistol through the glass, striking him in
the head and neck. Boggs pitched forward and lay unmoving in a
pool of blood, and a few days later, when his death was reported
in Nauvoo, there was considerable laughter and rejoicing among
Mormons of every rank. But the celebration was premature.
Boggs had only been wounded, and although his recovery
remained uncertain for several weeks, he eventually survived
and was restored to health.

From the beginning it was assumed that the would-be assassin
had been a Mormon, and soon the name of Orrin Porter Rockwell
was fixed to the crime. Dr. Bennett was the first to accuse him
openly. He stated that Rockwell, a Danite and member of Joseph
Smith's personal bodyguard, had gone to Independence under the
Prophet's orders and there had committed the attempted assassination. He further charged that several months earlier, at a
secret meeting, Smith had offered a reward of $500 to any
Mormon who would murder Boggs and at the meeting had
declared, "The exterminator shall be exterminated!"

At the time, Bennett's accusations could not be verified, but
years later, two reliable witnesses emerged. One was the universally respected William Law, who had been a member of the First
Presidency at the time of the assassination attempt. "Joseph told
me," he said, "that he sent a man to kill Governor Boggs of
Missouri. The fellow shot the governor in his own house. . . . Joe
Smith told me the fact himself. The words were substantially like
this: 'I sent Rockwell to kill Boggs, but he missed him, it was a
failure; he wounded him instead of sending him to Hell.'" Still
later, when he felt safe from prosecution, Porter Rockwell added
his own evidence. Speaking of the night in Independence, he said,
"I shot through the window and thought I had killed him; but I
had only wounded him; I was damn sorry that I had not killed the
son of a bitch."

While Boggs was convalescing, Rockwell and Smith were
arrested, Rockwell being charged with attempted murder and
Smith with being an accessory before the fact. It was a staple of
Mormon propaganda that Gentile laws afforded the Saints no
protection, but at least in this instance such was not the case;
within a year, both Smith and Rockwell were taken to court, tried
and then released. The Prophet won his freedom in Illinois, on the
ground that he could not be extradicted to another state under the
existing circumstances, and Rockwell was declared not guilty, for

lack of sufficient evidence, by a jury of Missouri citizens who surely would have preferred to see him hanged.

After his acquittal, the Prophet's leadership became even more extravagant and irresponsible. Under his direction the Mormons at Nauvoo passed a number of city ordinances which either conflicted with Illinois laws or violated the Federal Constitution. One ordinance declared gold and silver the only legal tender in the city; another made it a crime for anyone except the Prophet to buy or sell land. If caught indulging in "profane or indecent language," a Gentile visitor might be fined $500 and jailed for six months; and any police officer who came to Nauvoo in connection with the Prophet's old Missouri troubles would be subject to arrest himself and if found guilty by a jury of his Mormon peers, would become liable to a sentence of life imprisonment.

Writing in the *Sangamo Journal*, John Bennett had accused the Mormon leader of being a dangerous political adventurer, and now, following his acquittal, Smith's actions began to confirm Bennett's most sensational charges. In December 1843, Smith presented a petition to Congress, asking that Nauvoo be separated from the rest of Illinois and made a completely independent federal territory. The petition further proposed that the Nauvoo Legion be incorporated into the United States Army, that only the mayor of the city be permitted to employ it and that no state official, including the governor, have any say in the matter. The petition was swiftly rejected by Congress but not before it had cost the Saints their last political friends in the state.

Month after month, a succession of feverish schemes filtered through the Prophet's restless mind. One winter day he called together a number of Mormon leaders and formed a new clandestine organization called the Council of Fifty, referred to in the private journals of John D. Lee by its childish code name— YTFIF. Few Mormon secrets were more closely guarded, but a few facts did become known about the Council; there were fifty Princes; they were to rule over God's Kingdom at some future date; and their first important act was to crown Joseph Smith Jr. King of the Kingdom of God.

Most of the Prophet's plans, however, were concerned with more worldly matters. For a number of months past he had thought of founding a Mormon state somewhere beyond the country's borders and already had discussed with other leaders the possibility of a grand western migration. Now, as tensions mounted higher between the Gentiles and Saints at Nauvoo, he ordered a few families to quietly move up the Missouri River and there to plant enough crops to feed an advance party; at the same time, he sent two dozen men west to Oregon and California, to investigate the prospects of settling in those remote territories.

Oregon and California, though, were not the only distant possibilities he considered. There also was Texas, a new and independent republic, living on precarious terms with its giant neighbor, Mexico. To this promising trouble spot he sent several members of the Council of Fifty, with a bold and larcenous plan—in exchange for "protecting" the new republic and for "standing as a go-between between the belligerent powers," the Mormons would receive empty land on which to settle, the area they desired consisting of the eastern half of New Mexico, a third of Colorado, three fifths of modern Texas, portions of Kansas and Wyoming, and the entire Oklahoma panhandle. The Texans, not surprisingly, rejected the Mormon offer, preferring to keep their own land and counsel and to "defend" themselves with their own arms.

The Prophet had not exhausted his inventiveness, though, and in March 1844, he petitioned Congress to appoint him a general in the United States Army, with special authority to raise 100,000 Mormon troops, who would occupy their own territory in the West and patrol the border from Texas to Oregon, "protecting the inhabitants . . . from foreign aggressions and domestic broils." Congress, unimpressed, refused to consider the petition.

Smith then decided on an entirely new tack—to run in the election of 1844 for President of the United States. He knew that he could not reach the White House himself but hoped that in a few pivotal states he would be able to take away enough votes from either the Whig or Democratic candidate to change the outcome of the election, and if that occurred, he felt certain, the Church would begin to receive the respect it deserved on the national scene. To implement his design, he sent out numerous Elders like Brigham Young and John D. Lee, both of whom reluctantly left Illinois and traveled around the country, electioneering on behalf of the Mormon ticket. The departure of some of the most able Saints came at an unfortunate time, for they hardly had left when a domestic explosion rocked Nauvoo, ultimately bringing the Prophet's career to a bloody end and almost destroying the Church itself.

Chapter 10

BY THE TIME the Saints had spent five tumultuous years at Nauvoo, a clash with their Gentile neighbors had become all but inevitable. For miles around, in Illinois, Missouri and Iowa, thousands of angry, fearful men were ready to rush to arms, either to defend their homes against the Mormon army or, if an opportunity presented itself, to march on Nauvoo and drive the Saints from their river stronghold. At such a precarious moment the Prophet needed the support of every man in the city; instead, through a series of ill-considered actions, especially a number of sexual misadventures, he alienated some of his staunchest followers, including the incorruptible William Law, his most trustworthy counselor.

Law, a wealthy Canadian convert, had been one of the earliest settlers in Nauvoo. With his brother, Wilson, he had purchased land and had built homes and factories, these investments greatly contributing to the city's rapid growth. But Law was extremely devout and had been distressed by the Prophet's worldly concerns, particularly his attempts to monopolize all real estate dealings in the city. Aside from the loss to himself in such a policy, Law thought it highly improper for a man of God to be so preoccupied with material affairs and was shocked when the Prophet threatened to excommunicate any Saint in Nauvoo who bought or sold property without paying him a fee. Law also disapproved of plural marriage and had taken no additional wives. Nevertheless, for more than a year he had refrained from public criticism, trusting that the Prophet would recognize his error and give up the practice of polygamy.

Finally, in an act of gross perversity, Smith tried to add Jane

Law to his list of conquests. When Law learned of the attempted
seduction from his horrified, and no doubt disheveled, wife, he
angrily confronted the Prophet, who drew on a number of Old
Testament precedents to justify his actions. Unappeased, Law
demanded an end to the licentiousness, which he said was
beginning to spread like a plague through the city, and threatened to expose the Prophet unless he went before the High
Council, renounced his sins and promised to repent.

When Smith refused, Law couldn't bring himself to carry out
his threat, still hoping that before too late the Prophet would
change his mind; and he continued to remain silent, for the good
of the Church, even after being warned privately that the
Danites had received orders to kill him—a rumor so persistent in
Nauvoo that Smith finally had to appear before the High Council
to deny it.

But the quarrel continued to fester. Eventually, Law was
joined by several other disaffected Saints, among them Dr. Robert
Foster, who also had discovered that the Prophet, employing the
secret Revelation of Plural Marriage, had attempted to seduce his
wife.

Once again Smith decided that his best defense was to counterattack, and he set out to have Foster tried in court on a variety of
trumped-up charges, only to learn that the dissidents had assembled more than forty witnesses, and could prove that he, and not
the defendant, had been guilty of adultery, polygamy and worse.
So the charges were dropped, and in place of a public trial, Foster,
Law, his wife and his brother were all secretly excommunicated.

An Apostate now, and formally cut off from the fellowship of
the Church, William Law proved a far more formidable opponent
than John Bennett had ever been. He was known in Nauvoo as an
honest man and did not exaggerate his accusations against the
Prophet, once he began to make them public. And unlike Bennett,
Law did not agree to quit either the city or the Church. Instead,
he and his fellow dissidents announced that they would attempt
to return the Latter-Day Saints to their original principles by
purchasing a printing press and exposing the truth in their own
Nauvoo newspaper.

All during the spring of 1844, as Law prepared to publish the
Expositor, charges and countercharges were exchanged between
the two parties. But it was the Prophet who chiefly suffered, for
Law's accusations carried fresh word to the Gentiles that what
John Bennett previously had said was true: Nauvoo had become a

sink of sexual promiscuity and moral corruption; it was a city ruled by an upstart despot; and the Nauvoo Legion was indeed a threat to the freedom of every non-Mormon on the frontier.

Cornered and afraid, unable to clear away the stench from his own name and that of his city, the Prophet, week by week, became more frantic and shrill. Late in May he delivered a frenzied sermon, stridently defending himself against his accusers. "The Lord has constituted me so curiously," he shouted from the lectern, "that I glory in persecution. . . . When facts are proved, truth and innocence will prevail. . . . Come on, ye prosecutors! Ye false swearers! All hell boil over! Ye burning mountains, roll down your lava! For I will come out on top at the last. I have more to boast of than any man ever had. I am the only man that has ever been able to keep a whole church together since the days of Adam. . . .

"God knows . . . the charges against me are false. . . . What a thing it is for a man to be accused of commiting adultery, and of having seven wives, when I can find only one. I am the same man, and as innocent as I was fourteen years ago; and I can prove them all perjurers!"

The first and only issue of the *Expositor* was written in a calm, reasoned style. Without naming the innocent young woman, its leading editorial told how a certain convert had traveled alone from England to Nauvoo, where the Prophet had initiated her into "the mystery of the Kingdom." Three affidavits followed in which the witnesses said they had seen, or had heard read aloud, Joseph Smith's still secret and unannounced Revelation, which gave every Mormon male the privilege of marrying as many as ten wives.

The dissidents also attacked the Prophet's financial manipulations, his attempt to unite church and state, encouragement of bloc voting, abuse of the city charter, and efforts to gain broad, and even national, political power. "We do not believe that God," the *Expositor* said, "ever raised a Prophet to Christianize a world by political schemes and intrigues; but on the contrary, by preaching truth in its own simplicity."

The newspaper's appearance caused a sensation in the Mormon city and its effect was devastating. Those who had heard only an occasional rumor about plural marriage were stunned by what they read—for now it seemed that the rumors might well be true. And those who already possessed several wives were afraid that the surrounding Gentiles would obtain the paper, declare Nauvoo the modern equivalent of Sodom and Gomorrah and storm into the city to drive them from their homes.

For a day or two the desperate Prophet thought of various expedients, including the public condemnation of plural marriage and the blaming of others for his own misdeeds. But such a course held out no realistic hope, for he and many of his strongest supporters were deeply committed to plural marriage, and a retreat from the doctrine now would either destroy the Church or bring ruin to themselves. And so the Prophet, instead of delivering a ringing sermon in the tabernacle, put the *Expositor* on trial before the City Council, where, in a bizarre proceeding, it was agreed that William Law's printing press had "committed libel" and should be destroyed.

Next the Prophet issued a proclamation declaring the newspaper a civic nuisance and ordered units of the Nauvoo Legion to carry out the Council's instructions. The soldiers marched to the paper's office, pied the type and threw it into the street, wrecked the press and made a bonfire of all remaining copies of the *Expositor*. Law and the other dissidents were forced to flee to the nearby town of Carthage, where they published an account of these events and pointed out that the Prophet and his associates clearly had violated the Constitution's guarantee of free speech and a free press.

Hearing of the attack, Governor Thomas Ford went to Carthage to investigate the matter. He talked with the dissidents, learned what had happened at Nauvoo and announced that Joseph Smith and several other leading Saints were to be arrested and brought to trial. He was dismayed to see, however, that the people in western Illinois had not awaited the results of his investigation; the militia already was organizing, and a majority of local citizens seemed eager to take matters into their own hands.

The governor ordered the Prophet and his brother Hyrum to surrender to state officers, who would escort them to Carthage for trial. But the Smiths rightfully feared that they would not be safe in Gentile hands and agreed to come only if accompanied by strong elements of the Nauvoo Legion. Governor Ford refused, feeling certain that such an arrangement would lead to a pitched battle between the Legion and the militia and that then the whole state would rise in fury, descend on Nauvoo and destroy the Mormon capital.

Unwilling to obey the governor, the Prophet elected to flee, and one night, accompanied by Hyrum and the devoted Porter Rockwell, he slipped aboard a waiting skiff, crossed the Mississippi to the Iowa shore and went into hiding. There he received a letter from Emma, his first wife; the letter spoke of his defenseless people and their need for leadership, the necessity of avoiding the appearance of cowardice and the renewed promise of Governor Ford, guaranteeing him a fair trial.

Reluctantly the Prophet and his brother returned to Nauvoo and then went on to Carthage, where they were placed in jail. Soon afterward the governor, a weak but well-intentioned man, paid a visit to the Prophet and assured him that he, his brother, the Apostle John Taylor and the Elder Willard Richards would all be safe where they were. No doubt the governor believed his own words, but the Prophet was shrewd enough to realize that a man like himself, who had preached hatred and revenge for so many years, could hardly expect mercy now at the hands of his enemies.

On June 28, 1844, Governor Ford left Carthage and set out for Nauvoo, to conduct a full investigation of the *Expositor* affair. At first, to ensure the Prophet's safety, he thought of taking him along; but then, unhappily, he changed his mind and decided to leave the prisoner behind, reasoning that none of the Illinois militia would harm Smith and his companions while he himself was at Nauvoo, surrounded by Smith's followers.

But the governor was mistaken. Some of the militia were men who lived close to Nauvoo and had come to hate the Prophet from long and bitter personal experience. They already had reached an understanding with the guards on duty, who had agreed not to interfere. Once they were sure the governor had left, they blackened their faces, took up their rifles and stormed the building, and at their appearance the duty guard melted away.

The attackers quickly reached the second floor, where the Prophet and his companions had barricaded themselves behind the door of their cell. Joseph and Hyrum were armed with pistols, smuggled into the jail the night before, but the other two were armed only with heavy clubs. The struggle was brief; the lynchers shot Hyrum, who died almost at once. The Prophet fired his six-shooter and, when it was empty, flung it away and tried to escape by the window. The sight that greeted him below must have been terrifying—a hundred men with blackened faces, aiming their rifles and gleaming bayonets, waiting to kill him. As he climbed onto the sill, he cried, "Is there no help for the widow's son?" More shots rang out, and he fell, some accounts saying that he died by the time he hit the ground. John Taylor and Willard Richards both survived the attack, Taylor with several wounds, and Richards unharmed except where a bullet had lightly grazed his nose.

The murder of the Prophet was an overwhelming blow to his followers and served to reinforce their already intense hatred of the Gentile world. In Nauvoo, soon after learning of the murders, a typical Saint named Allen Stout wrote in his journal: "I felt as though I could not live. . . . I knew not how to contain myself. . . . And I hope to live to avenge their blood; but if I do not, I will teach my children to never cease to try to avenge their blood, and then teach their children and their children's children to the fourth generation, as long as there is one descendant of the murderers upon the earth."

Chapter 11

ТHE DEATH OF THE PROPHET was followed by several weeks of uncertainty and confusion. From late June until early August a few Elders, particularly Willard Richards and John Taylor, attempted to hold the leaderless Saints together, while a number of parties and pretenders began to assemble at Nauvoo, each claiming the right to succeed the fallen martyr.

Sidney Rigdon received news of the tragedy in Pittsburgh and immediately departed for the Mormon capital. Within a few days word also had reached at least a half-dozen of the Apostles who were then in the eastern states, campaigning on behalf of the Mormon ticket during the preliminary stages of the national election of 1844. As soon as these Apostles, and their President, Brigham Young, learned of Smith's death, they too hastened back to the Mississippi, to take part in the decisive struggle for control of the Church.

At first glance Rigdon seemed the strongest candidate. For a dozen years he had been a member of the Saints' ruling triumvirate, the First Presidency, and during the innovative Kirtland and Missouri days, he had been the Prophet's principal counselor. Nor was this all. To reinforce his position, Rigdon now asserted that he recently had been offered a miraculous vision, indicating that the Lord desired his appointment as guardian of the Church.

Had Rigdon been a popular man, or less evidently eccentric, such claims and credentials might well have carried the day. But unlike Brigham Young, he possessed few impassioned supporters, and his increasingly erratic gestures and speech disconcerted a number of those in the city who were as yet uncommitted to any party or leader. Though Rigdon reached Nauvoo before Young and had several unhampered days in which to consolidate his strength, the outcome still was very much in doubt on the morning of August 8, when a general conference of eight thousand Saints gathered in an open grove overlooking the river, to consider the question of the succession.

Rigdon addressed the conference first. He stood in an open wagon and spoke for an hour and a half, but on this occasion his eloquence failed and his program met with little enthusiasm; his cause was not helped by the proposal he made to lead the Church back east to Pennsylvania, his native state, where during the previous decade the Saints had experienced many of their earliest tribulations.

After Rigdon had finished, Brigham Young arose in turn to address the conference. At this point a seeming miracle took place. The leader of the Apostles was not a tall man, like the late Prophet; he stood but five feet eight inches in height and was of a stockier build. Nevertheless, according to many of the Faithful, as Young stepped out to face the audience in the grove his body appeared to grow taller and leaner, and when he began to speak, he did so in the voice of their murdered leader.

"If Joseph had arisen from the dead," an observer said later, ". . . the effect could hardly have been more startling. It seemed the voice of Joseph himself; and not only that: but it seemed in the eyes of the people as though it was the very person of Joseph which stood before them."

A number of Gentiles refused to accept the miracle, accusing Young of employing certain obvious theatrical tricks that day in the grove, an accusation that continued to circulate for many years, to judge from a sermon delivered long afterward by a loyal supporter of Young, the Apostle Orson Hyde. Said Hyde, describing the event, "We went among the congregation and President Young went on the stand. Well, he spoke, and his words went through me like electricity. 'Am I mistaken?' said I, 'or is it really the voice of Joseph Smith?' This is my testimony: that it was not only the voice of Joseph, but there were the features, the gestures, and even the stature of Joseph before us in the person of Brigham. And though it may be said that President Young is a complete *mimic*, and can mimic anybody, I would like to see the man who can mimic another in *stature*, who was about *four or five inches higher than himself*."

Once the President of the Apostles started to speak, though, it became clear that he had no intention of relying exclusively on either religious miracles or clever theatrical effects to achieve his ends. He already had formed a plan to defeat Rigdon and advance his own cause, and now in the grove he began to implement it.

Young first attempted to shame his audience, and at the same time, without mentioning his name, to discredit Rigdon by implying that he had been guilty of unseemly haste and excessive personal ambition. The chief Apostle expressed surprise that the people, instead of mourning the death of Joseph Smith, had turned to such a mundane affair as the selection of a new leader. For himself, he said, he would far rather have remained in sackcloth and ashes for a month, paying his respects to the dead, than to have appeared before them in such circumstances on a public platform. However, he had felt pity for them in their distress and confusion, and it was this fact, and this fact alone, that had brought him here to speak.

Then Young came to the pivotal point. There was, he declared, a regular, ordained body in the Church which had the duty of learning the will of the Lord on all religious matters, and so he was puzzled why the people had not already delegated the question of the succession to that body: to the quorums of Apostles and Elders. He then proposed that the general conference adjourn, and that a meeting of the quorums—in which he had numerous adherents—be held that afternoon. Young's influence prevailed, and the people, with a docile show of hands, agreed.

A few hours later, Young addressed the assembled Mormon Elders. "I do not care who leads this Church," he said with admirable selflessness, "but one thing I must know, and that is what God said about it." It then turned out that God had intended the Twelve Apostles to lead the Church. "Joseph conferred upon our heads." Young said, "all the keys and powers belonging to the apostleship which he himself held before he was taken away, and no man, or set of men, can get between Joseph and the Twelve in this world, or in the world to come.

"You cannot," Young concluded, "fill the office of Prophet, Seer and Revelator: God must do this. You are like children without a father and sheep without a shepherd. . . . I will tell you who your leaders or guardians will be. The Twelve—I at their head!"

Young's assumption was easy enough to grasp: the Apostles, ordained by God through Joseph Smith, were the only authorized heads of the Church, and neither Sidney Rigdon nor anyone else could change that fundamental—and convenient—truth. So a

simple choice was offered that afternoon to the quorum of
Elders—Rigdon or the Twelve?—and when the decisive vote
came, few men cared to raise their hands for the former. As a
result, the Apostles were able to take command of the Church,
while Young strengthened immeasurably his command of the
Apostles.

From that day on a majority of Saints accepted Brigham Young
as their *de facto* leader, although more than three years were to
pass before he formally succeeded Joseph Smith Jr. as President
of the Church and entered into the office of Prophet, Seer and
Revelator. Nor in 1844 could a single vote by a gathering of
Elders effectively disarm every heresy, or silence every ambitious
rival. For several weeks Sidney Rigdon remained on the scene in
Nauvoo, preaching apocalyptic sermons to anyone who would
listen and repeating endlessly his assertion that he, and not
Brigham Young, was the rightful leader of the Latter-Day
Saints.

Finally the chief Apostle felt secure enough to act. Early in
September, Young accused Rigdon of various crimes against the
Church and convened the High Council to try him. The outcome
was so clearly understood in advance that Rigdon did not appear
in his own defense. Only one Elder spoke on his behalf, while
speeches against Rigdon were made by Brigham Young and his
fellow Apostles Amasa Lyman, Orson Hyde, John Taylor, Parley
P. Pratt and the ever dependable Heber C. Kimball. A vote was
then taken, and the defendant, having been convicted of the
charges, was "cut off," or excommunicated, from the Church, with
the further promise that he would be "delivered over to the
buffetings of Satan" until such time as he might choose to repent.
Shortly afterward the Apostate left Nauvoo, accompanied by a
few dozen followers. He settled in Pittsburgh, where he attempted to form a new Church, but his congregation quickly fell away,
his energies failed and to the relief of Brigham Young, the
once-fiery and threatening Sidney Rigdon lapsed into permanent
silence.

Following the departure of Rigdon, several other schisms arose
to trouble the new leadership at Nauvoo. Among the less dangerous was the defection of Lyman Wight, one of the earliest
Apostles and an active leader during the stormiest days in
Missouri. Wight resented what he called Brigham Young's usurpation and in 1845 led a small group of dissident Saints from
Illinois to the vicinity of Austin, Texas. His followers practiced

polygamy there but still managed to avoid conflict with their Gentile neighbors, perhaps because they made no effort to influence local politics and were honest and truthful in their personal dealings. After Wight's death his followers scattered, a few going to Utah, but a majority taking permanent leave of the Church.

Considerably more menacing was the separatist movement of James Strang, an ambitious Elder who recently had established a Stake or diocese of the Church in the neighboring territory of Wisconsin. When word reached Strang of the Prophet's death he traveled to Nauvoo and informed Brigham Young and the Twelve that Smith had selected him as his successor. A letter from the Prophet to this effect did not greatly impress the chief Apostle, who called it a forgery and denounced Strang as an imposter.

Undaunted by this reception, Strang returned to Wisconsin, where he set about establishing his own independent version of the Mormon Church. He soon realized, however, the value of greater isolation and moved his followers to Beaver Island in Lake Michigan, where he ruled as Church President and then, following his coronation, as the King of Zion.

At Beaver Island the Strangites practiced polygamy, and eventually King Strang acquired five wives. Announcing frequent prophecies and visions, he imitated Joseph Smith's conduct with considerable success, much to the discomfort of the established Church, until finally he quarreled with two of his disciples and was beaten and shot to death. Local Gentile authorities welcomed the chance to remove Strang's followers from their island fortress to the mainland, where the leaderless Strangites soon dispersed, their challenge to Brigham Young and the Church totally extinguished.

The last major schism to arise in the Middle West was the only one to take permanent root. The dissidents in this case were several members of Joseph Smith's family and their supporters, who claimed that the Prophet had conferred the right of succession on his eldest son, Joseph Smith III. According to John D. Lee, "it was understood among the Saints that young Joseph was to succeed his father" after he became old enough to lead the Church. But when the Prophet's mother tearfully pleaded with Brigham Young not to rob the twelve-year-old Joseph of his birthright, the Mormon leader, although agreeing to the justice of her grandson's claim, nevertheless warned "Mother Smith" to remain silent on the subject, because, he said, "You [will be] only laying the knife to the throat of the child. If it is known that he is the rightful successor to his father, the enemies of the Priesthood will seek his life."

In the following years a number of Smith's relatives refused to accept Young's authority, nor did they accompany the majority of Saints on their celebrated western trek. Instead they founded the Reorganized Church of Jesus Christ of Latter-Day Saints and disclaimed all fellowship with Brigham Young and other claimants to the leadership of the Church. Almost alone among various Mormon dissidents, the members of the Reorganized Church refused to practice polygamy and maintained from the start that the Prophet never had advocated or practiced it either. In time Joseph Smith III was placed at the head of the Reorganized Church, which moved first to Iowa and then to Independence, Missouri, where it began to quietly flourish on the site of Joseph Smith Jr.'s New Jerusalem.

By one means or another the various claims and pretensions of Sidney Rigdon, Lyman Wight, James Strang and Joseph Smith III either were noisily discredited or quietly ignored, while month after month at Nauvoo the new leader of the Church patiently gathered power more securely into his own hands. At the same time no one in the city, including Brigham Young himself, could have felt much certainty about the immediate future. It was clear by early 1845, when the state legislature repealed the Nauvoo municipal charter, that the Church no longer was welcome in Illinois or in any neighboring state or territory and that before long the Saints would have to resettle somewhere else. As a result, Young's thoughts, like those of his predecessor, began to turn more frequently to such distant places as Texas, Mexico, Vancouver Island, Oregon and California, places safely beyond the hateful borders and the oppressive laws of the United States. But exactly when the first wagon trains might leave, what trails they might follow or where their passengers might finally alight, no one in Nauvoo could say at first.

Yet even by then, one thing about the future should have been clear enough: in whatever manner he might choose to lead the Saints, Brigham Young was not likely to prove a slavish imitator of the late Prophet. Temperamentally at least, the two men were quite dissimilar. Where Joseph Smith had been a fitful and romantic dreamer, Brigham Young was a practical, keen-eyed man of business. Where Smith had loved to dress in bright gaudy uniforms, Young selected plain dark suits, subdued but rich in appearance.

Unlike his predecessor, Young had no inclination to rule his flock by visionary means, nor to beguile his followers with a steady stream of prophecies; there were enough of the latter, he remarked early in his long reign, to last the Church for the next twenty years. In place of mystery and revelation, Young preferred hard work and carefully assembled facts; in place of exuberance and emotional excess, he preferred diligence and well-made plans. Unless there was a precisely calculated reason to arouse the people, he often chose to let their passions slumber; but at those times when emotions had to be stirred and manipulated, he could become, like many other Mormon Elders, an extremely persuasive orator, capable of steering his audience in almost any direction he desired.

By now a man in his early forties, Brigham Young had gained enough self-knowledge to perceive some of his own limitations. He knew that although the Saints often had followed Joseph Smith because of a passionate attachment that bordered on idolatry, when it came to himself, few of the Saints felt an equally intense devotion. They would obey his commands only if they respected his judgment or feared his power to punish them. At times the flamboyant Prophet had been boisterous and rowdy, and the Saints had delighted in his democratically free-and-easy ways. His successor was outwardly calm, autocratic, at times brutally caustic and always careful of preserving some measure of his dignity. When he wished to, Brigham Young could lead a square dance or deliver an impromptu address to a social gathering with considerable grace and affability; yet he rarely permitted himself to descend completely to the same level as his followers—to indulge in such frivolities as wrestling and other sports—as Joseph Smith Jr. had delighted in doing.

Despite their many differences, however, the two Church leaders did resemble each other in a number of significant ways. Young, like Smith, came from an old but nearly destitute New England family, and his schooling, too, had been severely limited by his father's poverty. After finishing eighth grade, Young had been forced to support himself with a series of odd jobs, working variously as a carpenter, house painter and glazier. Like Smith, he had discovered in the Church both a source of spiritual comfort and an amazing instrument for acquiring worldly advantage, and so, as in the case of the late Prophet, the Church's welfare long since had become synonymous with his own.

In other respects too, there was a resemblance between Joseph Smith Jr. and Brigham Young. Each was parochial, self-righteous and utterly intolerant of any other viewpoint but his own. Each suffered from excessive vanity and considerably over-estimated his own talents as well as the honors and rewards those talents could justly claim from an all-too-frequently indifferent world. Each was a supreme egotist, steeped in his own self-importance, who was convinced of his right not only to lead a vast army of followers but ultimately to rule supreme over all man-kind. To further his own ends—always in the exalted name of religion—each was capable of organizing a great variety of covert misdeeds and open felonies. The attempted assassination of ex-Governor Boggs, undoubtedly commissioned by the late Prophet, already lay several years in the past. What lay ahead were other crimes that would be planned and commissioned by a more-calculating leader, a man utterly without remorse or con-science, who had come to believe, during his service to the Church, that any means were justified in strengthening or defending the true faith, and that to gain revenge from the Gentiles was a grave duty, placed on every Saint by command of the Lord.

Chapter 12

Du r i n g 1845, anarchy slowly spread across much of western Illinois. Military forces had to be interposed between the two hostile sides—the Mormons and the Gentiles—by Governor Ford, and it became clear that there could be no permanent peace in the area as long as several thousand armed and defiant Mormons remained in Nauvoo. What followed was little more than a grim re-enactment of the earlier Missouri expulsions. Once again citizens' committees were formed, inflammatory words exchanged and hurried raids and counterraids made on isolated settlements. Finally the harassed and outnumbered Saints were forced to agree that they would sell all their property in Nauvoo and the rest of Hancock County and begin to leave the state by the spring of 1846.

As the chaos increased, both sides committed numerous crimes with near impunity. The Gentiles were guilty of frequent attacks against Mormon homes and other property, until at last a drunken rabble pushed its way into half-deserted Nauvoo and desecrated the recently completed Temple there, an act for which no apology was offered and for which no satisfactory explanation was possible. The Mormons made highly effective propaganda out of this barbarous episode, piously emphasizing, as always, the many wrongs they were compelled to suffer for their religion's sake, while neglecting to mention any provocation or misconduct of their own.

On their side the Saints were no less ruthless than their enemies. At first, as a practical matter, Brigham Young attempted to restrain his more larcenous followers, realizing that their easily detected thefts would only further enrage the surrounding

Gentiles and increase the size of their volunteer army. Addressing a conference in Nauvoo in late 1844, he said, "Elders who go to borrowing horses and money, and running away with it, will be cut off from the Church without any ceremony. They will not have as much lenity as heretofore."

But once the decision had been made to abandon Nauvoo and leave the Midwest, the leader of the Twelve found less reason to curb his followers or to take the stand to preach against crimes of profit or vengeance. One day, during the autumn of 1845, a particularly vicious incident took place, involving both a local police officer, Sheriff Backenstos, and the Danite Porter Rockwell. Backenstos was not a Mormon, but his brother had married a niece of the late Prophet, and the sheriff was widely known as an extremely ardent partisan of the Saints. The incident occurred outside Nauvoo, when Backenstos attempted to arrest a man long marked for death, Lieutenant Franklin Worrell, the militia officer who had been in command of the Carthage jail on the day of Joseph Smith's assassination. Worrell refused to obey the sheriff's order to surrender and accompany him back to Nauvoo. Instead he and two companions sought to detain Backenstos. The sheriff, following a prearranged plan, immediately turned his horse and fled toward the Mormon capital, pursued by the unsuspecting lieutenant and his fellow troopers. Waiting in ambush along the road was Porter Rockwell. As the sheriff drew near he shouted to Rockwell to fire, and the hidden marksman promptly killed Worrell, though without injuring his companions. When brought to trial for murder Rockwell offered a plea of self-defense and also claimed that he only had been obeying the sheriff's orders, and the jury, for reasons best known to itself, found the defendant innocent of the charges.

Ambushing Lieutenant Worrell did not cause Porter Rockwell to lose favor with the Twelve. A few weeks later he might have been seen among the advance party leaving Nauvoo under the command of Brigham Young, who realized that capable gunmen could very well prove as valuable as Gospel preachers while the Saints were crossing the prairies and establishing the Kingdom of God in the western mountains.

Authorities never have been able to decide the exact date on which Brigham Young selected Utah and the valley of the Great Salt Lake as the future site of Zion. According to Mormon legend, the moment did not occur until some sixteen or eighteen months after the evacuation of Nauvoo, on July 24, 1847, when Young, still recuperating from an attack of mountain fever, gazed down the trail from Echo Canyon toward the valley and the lake and announced prophetically, "This is the place!" Legend, though, can be safely disregarded. Young, a man who enjoyed concealment almost as must as he enjoyed power, might not have chosen to reveal his decision to every member of his own party, but he was far too prudent a leader to have set out across half a continent without first determining both his destination and the route by which he intended to travel.

Possibly Young had decided on Great Salt Lake as early as the summer of 1845, while the Saints still were preparing to leave Nauvoo, but if not, he certainly had reached a final decision six months later, during the winter of 1846. By then he had collected whatever meager geographical information was available and had studied closely the most useful material, particularly Captain John C. Fremont's maps and descriptive account of his western explorations.

The idea of settling in an area remote from civilization had much to recommend it. Prior experience of the Church in Ohio, Missouri and Illinois made it clear that the new Zion would flourish best in isolation, but unhappily a variety of circumstances already had greatly restricted Brigham Young's choice in the matter. By 1846 many parts of Texas had become settled, while the Oregon Territory held out equally little promise, with six or seven thousand Americans recently arrived there, and each year more and more emigrants leaving for the Northwest along the Oregon Trail. Nor had Queen Victoria and the British Government proved responsive to the Mormon scheme for settling Vancouver Island. As for California, it was almost as hopeless as Oregon. War with Mexico had all but begun over its possession, and the future seemed quite plain: perhaps California would become a part of the United States by annexation, perhaps it would declare itself an independent republic on the Texas model, but in either case the region soon would be swarming with thousands of Americans, and should the Saints already have settled there, they would again find themselves surrounded and overwhelmed by an army of hostile Gentiles.

Between California, Texas and Oregon, however, there was empty space—the vast and largely unexplored Utah Territory— occupied by only a few bands of Indians and a handful of mountain men. According to Frémont, the area was isolated, but by no means uninhabitable. Describing Bear River Valley, for example, the explorer had written: "The bottoms are extensive; water excellent; timber sufficient; the soil good and well adapted to grains and grasses suited to such an elevated region. A military post and a civilized settlement would be of great value here; and cattle and horses would do well where grass and salt so much abound." Of Utah Lake, not far distant from Great Salt Lake itself, he had written: "In the cove of mountains along its eastern shore, the lake is bordered by a plain where the soil is generally good, and a greater part fertile; watered by a delta of prettily timbered streams. This would be an excellent locality for stock farms; it is generally covered with good bunch grass, and would abundantly produce the ordinary grains." And a few pages later Fremont concluded that the entire Great Basin was most promising for future settlement.

After studying Fremont's account, it must have been evident to Brigham Young that the valley of the Great Salt Lake offered an excellent opportunity to industrious farmers like the Saints, who would know how to irrigate and work that distant land. And even more important to the Mormon leader was one final consideration: in January 1846 the valley itself, and thousands of square miles of surrounding territory, belonged to Mexico and lay totally outside the geographical boundaries of the United States. For by then it had become the fixed intention of Young and his associates not merely to settle in the Far West but to sever all ties with the Federal Government and to form, without hinderance or restriction, an independent nation of their own.

There is ample evidence that Young and the rest of the Twelve, while still in Nauvoo, covertly preached both separation and treason. During 1845 the Temple had finally been completed in the Mormon capital, and within its inner rooms the people at last began to receive the most important sacraments, or "endowments," of the Church. According to more than one Apostate, the elaborate endowment ceremonies were concerned with political, as well as spiritual, matters. Of his own sacramental indoctrination, the Apostate John Hyde later wrote: "We were sworn to cherish constant enmity toward the United States government for not avenging the death of Joseph Smith, or righting the persecution of the Saints; to do all that we could toward destroying, tearing down or overturning that government; to endeavor to baffle its designs and frustrate its intentions; to renounce all allegiance and refuse all submission. If unable to do anything ourselves toward the accomplishment of these objects, to teach it to our children from the nursery, impress it upon them from the death bed, entail it upon them as a legacy." A number of years later, a litigant against Brigham Young alleged that the endowment ceremonies had included the following oath: "To obey him, the Lord's annointed, in all his orders, both spiritual and temporal . . . and all church authorities in like manner; that this obligation is superior to all the laws of the United States, and all earthly laws; that enmity should be cherished against the government of the United States; that the blood of Joseph Smith, the Prophet, and Apostles slain in this generation shall be avenged."

It was in this spirit that Nauvoo was abandoned and the eyes of the Saints turned to the Far West, and by a curious irony, at almost the same time, another pioneer, Captain Alexander Fancher, also chose to leave Illinois. The captain's destination, however, was not a remote valley in the Utah Territory but a farm in neighboring Missouri, and his principal desire was the commonplace American one of making his way in the world, rather than of destroying his own government and staining his hands with the blood of his fellow men.

Chapter 13

IN FEBRUARY 1846, several months earlier than the date they had agreed to, and during the most bitter part of the winter, the first bands of Mormon refugees abruptly left Nauvoo, crossed the icebound Mississippi and began to establish a camp in Iowa, on the opposite side of the river. Their hasty departure was an error not easily explained. It might have been that Brigham Young planned to reach the Great Basin before the end of the year and so decided that the earliest possible start was necessary; or perhaps his fear of the Gentiles' growing belligerency convinced him that the sooner the Saints began their exodus from Nauvoo, the better.

A different explanation, however, was suggested by an item in the Christmas Day 1845 issue of the *Springfield* [Illinois] *Journal*. "During the past few weeks," the newspaper said, "twelve bills of indictment for counterfeiting Mexican dollars and half dollars and dimes were found by a Grand Jury and presented to the United States Circuit Court in this city against different persons in and around Nauvoo, embracing some of the 'Holy Twelve,' and other prominent Mormons. . . . The manner in which the money was put into circulation was stated. At one mill $1,500 was paid out for wheat in one week. Whenever a land sale was about to take place, wagons were sent off with the coin into the land district . . . and no difficulty occurred in exchanging off [sic] the counterfeit coin for paper." Several months later the Apostles denounced the indictments as a further example of malicious Gentile persecution, but their protests lacked complete persuasiveness, for by then the Twelve had reached Iowa and were safely beyond the jurisdiction of Illinois law.

Whatever the actual cause for their premature flight, it was not long before the refugees from Nauvoo began to suffer acutely. Too little planning had been done prior to their departure. The first camp, across the river at Sugar Creek, soon became overcrowded and insanitary; shelter was inadequate, the snowdrifts grew deeper and food often was in short supply. As a result many fell sick and there were a number of deaths from pneumonia, particularly among the infants and small children. The arrival of spring rains only added to the misery of the refugees, and before the year was over they experienced outbreaks of cholera and "black canker," the latter most probably a form of scurvy, brought on by a lack of fresh fruit and vegetables. Nevertheless, the resolve of the Saints remained firm; the Camp of Israel, as the various refugee companies now called themselves, was going to march west to found a new city of Zion and increase the glory of the Lord, and its members were willing to endure great hardship to accomplish their purpose.

And so, during the early months of 1846, the Mormons began to build a string of auxiliary camps across Iowa, from the Mississippi River to the Missouri. One was established at Richardson's Point, about 50 miles west of Sugar Creek. Here Brigham Young left behind a small, permanent garrison, to ensure that all following parties would find food, firewood, and tools for repairing their wagons. Among the garrison he included a few members of the priesthood, who made certain that the Camp of Israel lived up to its faith, and did not backslide into the familiar frontier sins of gambling, swearing and fornication. The next camp was built at a crossing of the Chariton River, where the first companies planted crops, a small party remained to cultivate them, and subsequent companies came by and took in the harvest. Similar camps were built farther along the way, on Locust Creek, on the Grand River at Garden Grove and at "Mount Pisgah." And finally, at the end of the route, two large camps were established bracketing the Missouri River, one on the east bank where Council Bluffs stands today, and the more important one, called Winter Quarters, on the west bank near the site of present-day Omaha. Brigham Young settled in Winter Quarters with his main party and remained until his departure for Utah the following spring.

While the months slowly passed on the Missouri, Young saw to it that his charges did not fall into sloth or idleness. The Saints built log cabins and dugouts, planted new crops and erected a mill for grinding corn and a council house for holding church meetings. To raise cash, which always was in short supply, some of the Saints made willow baskets and washboards and sold them a few miles to the south, to the hated Pukes, in the nearest Missouri settlements. Religious services were held frequently, and Young, who was partial to dancing, band music and the theater, ordered a number of lively evening entertainments.

At Winter Quarters there was enough work for everyone, even for a humorless, hard-eyed Saint like Bill Hickman, reputedly a former Mississippi River pirate, and, along with Porter Rockwell, one of the most able gunmen in camp. One day a quarrel arose between Brigham Young and a nameless local half-breed, and the latter injudiciously announced that he would separate the Mormon leader from his scalp and perform a war dance over it.

"Brigham sent me word," Hickman later wrote, "to look out for [the half-breed]. I found him, used him up, scalped him, and took his scalp to Brigham Young, saying—'Here is the scalp of the man who was going to have a war-dance over your scalp; you may have one over his if you wish.' He took it and thanked me very much. He said in all probability I had saved his life, and that some day he would make me a great man in the Kingdom. This was my first act of violence under the rule of Brigham. Soon after this, I was called upon to go for a notorious horse thief, who had sworn to take the life of Orson Hyde. I socked him away, and made my report which was very satisfactory."

Such men as Bill Hickman and Porter Rockwell had their uses, but there were occasions when Brigham Young wished to present the Latter-Day Saints in a more angelic light, and then the full activities of his gunmen were concealed or their names purged from the conversation. Doubtlessly this was the case when Thomas Leiper Kane arrived in camp. The youthful Kane was no ordinary visitor, and from the beginning Young realized that the idealistic and well-connected easterner, if handled skillfully, could be employed to the immense advantage of the Church.

Thomas Kane was twenty-four when he came west to Iowa to visit the Camp of Israel. An intellectual, neurotic and snobbish young man, he was, in the words of one historian, "a sentimental humanitarian . . . the kind who loved all good works . . . and obstructed the path of serious reformers." His father was John Kane, the attorney general of Pennsylvania, a leading Democrat and a friend and close political ally of President James Polk. It was hardly surprising that the younger son of such an important politician should have been accorded a particularly tender reception on the banks of the Missouri.

Young Kane's sympathy for the Saints had first been aroused in Philadelphia a few months earlier, when chance one morning had led him to a local Mormon conference. Inside the hall an eloquent Church Elder, Jessie C. Little of New Hampshire, was expatiating on the many injustices suffered by the Faithful, and the impressionable Kane's romantic feelings were deeply stirred. He brought the preacher home as a guest, received further instruction, and two days later informed his family that before long he would travel to Iowa with Elder Little, share the tribulations of the Saints in their encampments and, if at all possible, accompany Brigham Young to the Far West. Almost at once Kane's great excitement led to a nervous collapse, but Jessie Little was able to "cure" him through prayer and prophecy, and after recovering, the grateful young Philadelphian began to devote himself unstintingly to the cause of Mormonry.

Jessie Little, in 1846, was one of Brigham Young's principal agents in the East. At the time he met Thomas Kane he was en route from New England to Washington, with several of Young's schemes for persuading the Federal Government that the Mormons were misunderstood but trustworthy citizens who deserved some form of financial support during their westward hegira. Armed with letters from Kane and Kane's father, Little managed to reach the ear of various representatives, senators, Vice President George Dallas and eventually the President himself.

Surprisingly enough, Little's mission was well received at the White House, though not because President Polk believed in the professed loyalty of Brigham Young and his followers. Political events already were moving swiftly when Jessie Little arrived in Washington. About a fortnight earlier, on May 13, Congress had declared war on Mexico, and the President had ordered Colonel Stephen Kearny to lead an army to Santa Fe, as the first step in America's campaign to seize the provinces of New Mexico and California and possibly portions of the vast Utah Territory as well. On June 2, President Polk met with his cabinet, and it was agreed that a large supply of guns, ammunition and provisions would be shipped by sea from New York to the Pacific, to supply Kearny's men when they arrived on the West Coast. The Colonel's forces were to be composed of several hundred regular army troops and a thousand mounted Missouri volunteers. In addition, according to that day's entry in the President's private diary,

"Col. Kearny was also authorized to receive into service as volunteers a few hundred of the Mormons who are now on their way to California, with a view to conciliate them, attach them to our country, and prevent them from taking part against us." While the President, like the rest of the Gentile world, was misinformed about Brigham Young's exact destination, he was well aware of the true feelings the Mormons held toward the United States.

The next day the President received Jessie Little and was informed that the Mormons were leaving Illinois for the Far West. "Mr. Little said that they were Americans in all their feelings, and friends of the United States," the President later noted in his diary. "I told Mr. Little that we were at war with Mexico, and asked him if 500 or more of the Mormons now on their way to California would be willing . . . to volunteer and enter the United States army in that war, under the command of a United States officer. He said he had no doubt they would willingly do so."

Within a few weeks Jessie Little and Thomas Kane had carried the proposal for a "Mormon Battalion" to Brigham Young, who realized at once how valuable the opportunity was and also how useful it would be to secure permanently the devotion and services of the young easterner, who voluntarily had helped to arrange such an important matter with the White House.

No doubt following Young's instructions, the Saints extended every courtesy to Kane and did their best to impress him with their undeniable virtues. He lived among them, observed their industrious habits, their courageous struggles against poverty and their intense and sincere religious feelings, and having arrived with a strong predisposition in their favor, he found nothing during his visit that lessened his esteem. Afterward in the East he would say of his experiences among the Saints, "Wherever I was compelled to tarry, I was certain to find shelter and hospitality, scant, indeed, but never stinted, and always honest and kind. After a recent unavoidable association with the border inhabitants of western Missouri and Iowa, the vile scum which our own society. . . . 'like the great ocean washes upon its frontier shores,' I can scarcely describe the gratification I felt in associating again with persons who were almost all of eastern American origin—persons of refined and cleanly habits and decent language."

While at Winter Quarters, Kane fell ill again and again was

cured through the agency of Mormon prayer. Perhaps more fully aware of his own frailty, he now gave up all thought of joining the Saints on their western venture and instead elected to return home to Philadelphia by way of eastern Iowa and Nauvoo. Nevertheless, his attachment to the Mormon cause had grown even stronger, and some historians believe, despite Kane's life-long denials, that before parting from Brigham Young at Winter Quarters he became a secret member of the Church. Certainly at that time he received a patriarchal blessing, and a quarter of a century later received another, during a journey through southern Utah. But these minor dispensations were probably nothing more than acts of ecclesiastical gratitude, and in all likelihood Kane never did formally join the Church.

Such a step would not have served the Saints well, and quite possibly Brigham Young discouraged him from seeking membership. As an avowed Mormon, Kane would have become merely one of a hundred Church spokesmen, and much of his unique value would have been lost; but by remaining an ostensibly unbiased Gentile observer, he would be able to exert considerable influence on many important social and political leaders. For Kane himself, nonmembership in the Church promised a number of additional advantages. As a Gentile he might approve publicly of the cleanly habits and fervent piety of the Saints, without being obliged to accept, or to proclaim as revealed truth, any of their singular, and sometimes bizarre, religious doctrines. And what could have been more high-principled, and consequently more soothing to his self-esteem, than to serve a Church to which he did *not* belong—to labor neither for his own material benefit nor for the salvation of his own soul—but for the purely altruistic satisfaction of defending a weak and innocent sect from its ruthless oppressors?

Whether or not Thomas Kane actually joined the Church may always remain a mystery. It is certain, though, that by the time he returned from the frontier and the desecrations at Nauvoo, he was more convinced than ever that the Saints alone were truthful and virtuous, while their critics invariably were bigots, liars, drunkards or self-serving and venal politicians. Kane would soon become, and would remain for the rest of his days, the Church's most effective apologist among eastern Gentiles and its most adroit lobbyist in high government circles. When such an action might assist the Church, he would lie on its behalf with astonishing lack of conscience. He would deny that the Mormons practiced plural marriage, although his Iowa visit must have made the truth perfectly clear to him. And after the massacre at Mountain Meadows had been revealed to an entire nation, Colonel Thomas Kane would refuse to condemn those governing the Utah Territory and would see nothing amiss in continuing to serve his western friends as faithfully as before.

Chapter 14

T HE PROPOSAL to raise a Mormon Battalion, which Thomas Kane and Jessie Little brought from the White House to western Iowa in the late spring of 1846, was not warmly received by the rank and file in the Camp of Israel. Several weeks earlier the Saints had heard of the outbreak of hostilities between America and Mexico, and among the refugees riding in the carts and wagons a new wave of vindictiveness had arisen. Soon afterward, Hosea Stout, a veteran Danite, perfectly expressed the hostile and paranoid feelings of the Mormon host, when he wrote in his diary, "I confess that I was glad to learn of war against the United States. I hoped the war might never end until the States were entirely destroyed, for they had driven us into the wilderness and was [sic] now laughing at our calamities." Clearly, Stout and his companions, if left to themselves, were unlikely to volunteer in large numbers for service in the Far West under newly promoted Brevet General Stephen Kearny.

It was a measure of Brigham Young's astuteness that he immediately grasped the importance of President Polk's unexpected offer, and a measure of Young's authority that despite the almost unanimous opposition of his followers, within three weeks' time he was able to impress five hundred reluctant Saints into Federal service. The "volunteers," many of them accompanied by their wives, and some by their entire families, proceeded from Iowa to Fort Leavenworth, and there were mustered into the United States Army. The Mormon Battalion, as it soon came to be called, then marched with the rest of Kearny's forces to Santa Fe, and during the following months served reluctantly, though without notable incident, while the General thrust his way into California.

The Mormon Battalion no doubt was useful to Kearny, but

despite a subsequent flood of Mormon propaganda, it was hardly
of crucial importance to the success of his California campaign.
Nor did the absence of several hundred Mormon riflemen endan-
ger the Church's westward emigration, as Brigham Young was to
falsely claim a decade later. The truth was quite different, and
none knew it better than Young himself; by forming the Battalion he had greatly increased the Saints' chance of survival, both
on their westward trek and during the first precarious years in
the Utah Territory.

Two considerations led Young to temporarily abandon his
anti-American rhetoric and to adopt instead a policy of guarded
cooperation with the United States. One consideration was political. A few months earlier, when Young and the advance party
had left Nauvoo, the Utah Territory had been a province of
Mexico and the Mormons had believed they were going to
establish the new Zion in a foreign country. Now, with the advent
of war, all such calculations had to be discarded. Within a year or
two the Utah Territory almost certainly would belong to the
United States, and the Saints, having emigrated to the Great
Basin, once again would find themselves subjected to the oppressive laws of their American enemies. There was little time to be
lost, Young realized, in adapting to these changed and unpleasant circumstances, and the formation of the Mormon Battalion
fitted in well with his plans. The Church, by generously providing
five hundred riflemen for service under General Kearny, would
establish future credit with the government in Washington and
simultaneously would strengthen and legitimatize its claims to
millions of acres of empty western land. Looking ahead, Young
hoped that by the time the war with Mexico had ended, the
Mormons in the Great Basin would be able to say that they had
opened a way into the wilderness, settled an area around the
Great Salt Lake, and seized the vast Utah Territory for God and
the United States and that they had done so out of the strong
patriotic feelings they always had claimed to possess, and at the
urging of the President himself.

The second reason for Brigham Young's temporary policy of
cooperation was less complex: the Saints were desperately short
of money, and the White House proposal to form a Mormon
Battalion promised to solve the problem. For one thing, Young
saw that the Church could save itself thousands of dollars by
enrolling five hundred Saints and their relatives in the Army and

letting the Federal Government pay the cost of their transportation to the Far West. In addition, the five hundred would receive
army pay, and though not every penny was destined to be
returned to Winter Quarters, Young made certain that as small a
sum as possible slipped through the fine skein of his ecclesiastical
fingers. When the five hundred volunteers arrived at Fort Leavenworth, they were accompanied by several of Young's agents,
who collected $21,000 of the Battalion's enlistment and clothing
allotments and carried the money off to the Church in Iowa. Later
that year, as the forces of General Kearny were nearing Santa
Fe, another special agent, John D. Lee, was dispatched to the
southwestern city, where he obtained a considerable portion of
the Battalion's back pay for the Church and returned with it
safely to Winter Quarters. It was these exactions that enabled
Young to purchase additional seed, tools and wagons, without
which the Mormons could not have emigrated successfully to the
Great Basin or survived in the mountains once they had arrived.

The mission to Santa Fe was a vital one, and the man selected
by Young to carry it out was no ordinary Saint. John Doyle Lee
had been a steadfast member of the Church for almost a decade.
He had joined the Latter-Day Saints in 1838, during the climax of
the Missouri troubles, had followed Brigham Young to Illinois,
and at Nauvoo had served as one of the twelve Danite bodyguards, whose principal duties had been to protect Joseph and
Hyrum Smith from physical harm and to obey the Prophet's
orders without hesitation.

Some thirty years later, long after the Mountain Meadows
Massacre, Lee wrote a brief account of his life and included
several passages describing his early days in Missouri and
Illinois. He had been one of the first Mormons to practice
polygamy and, in his confessions, explained how he had been
introduced to the Doctrine of Plural Marriage. The curious
episode told more about the character of the Church he served—
and about Lee's own character—than even the penitent author
could have intended. "When I moved to Nauvoo," he wrote, "I had
one wife and one child. Soon after I got there, I was appointed as
the Seventh Policeman. I had superiors in office, and was sworn to
secrecy, and to obey the orders of my superiors, and not to let my
left hand know what my right hand did. It was my duty to do as I
was ordered, and not to ask questions. I was instructed in the
secrets of the Priesthood to a great extent, and taught to believe,

as I did then believe, that it was my duty, and the duty of all men, to obey the orders of the leaders of the Church, and that no man could commit sin so long as he acted in the way he was directed by his Church superiors.

"I was one of the Life Guard of the Prophet Joseph Smith," Lee continued. "One day the Chief of Police came to me and said that I must take two more policemen that he named, and watch the house of a widow woman named Clawson. . . . I was informed that a man went there nearly every night about ten o'clock, and left about daylight. I was also ordered to station myself and my men near the house, and when the man came out we were to knock him down and castrate him, and not to be careful how hard we hit, for it would not be entered into if we killed him."

Lee was in no way disturbed at the prospect of committing such an atrocious crime as long as he could be certain that his orders had come from the proper Church authorities. In this case, though, he suspected that the Chief of Police had not been informed of the Prophet's real intentions, and so, before complying, he decided to investigate the matter for himself. Joseph Smith was not at home, but his brother Hyrum was available for consultation. Lee wrote, "I told him the orders I had received from the Chief, and asked him if I should obey or not. He said to me:

"'Brother Lee, you have acted most wisely in listening to the voice of the spirit. It was the influence of God's spirit that sent you here. You would have been guilty of a great crime if you had obeyed your Chief's orders.'

"Hyrum told me that the man I was ordered to attack was Howard Egan, and that he had been sealed to Mrs. Clawson, and that their marriage was a most holy one; that it was in accordance with a revelation that the Prophet had recently received directly from God. He then explained to me fully the doctrine of polygamy, and wherein it was permitted, and why it was right.

"I was greatly interested in the doctrine. It accorded exactly with my views of the Scripture, and I at once accepted and believed in the doctrine as taught by the revelations received by Joseph Smith, the Prophet. As a matter of course I did not carry out the orders of the Chief. I had him instructed in his duty, and so Egan was never bothered by the police. A few months after that I was sealed to my second wife. I was sealed to her by Brigham Young, then one of the Twelve."

After the death of the Prophet, Lee began to play an increasingly responsible role in Church affairs. He was a member of the

Seventies, which placed him just below the Twelve Apostles in the Church hierarchy. By the evidence of his own private journals, he also was a member of the secret Council of Fifty and therefore a party to many of the most carefully guarded deliberations of Brigham Young and the Twelve. At various times he held important public positions too, serving as "General Clerk and Recorder for the Quorum of the Seventy" and as "Chief Clerk of the Church."

Brigham Young's assumption of power, which drove many Saints into schism or apostasy, did not tempt Lee to follow a similar course. He had believed in the truth of Joseph Smith's mission, and now he simply transferred his trust to Smith's successor. Others in the Camp of Israel might waver in their faith, but not John D. Lee. Others might question the wisdom— temporal or spiritual—of Brigham Young, but not the stocky, gray-eyed, semiliterate frontiersman from Kaskaskia, Illinois.

In earlier days, Lee had yielded blind obedience to the late Prophet, but he had always done so from a distance. Now, with Brigham Young, Lee was on a far more intimate footing, and indeed, for a considerable time, continued to be Young's prótegé. It was Young who sealed Lee to the latter's first polygamous wife, and Young who made Lee his second "adopted son" within the Church. For a few years such adoptions were common among the Saints, their purpose being spiritual rather than legal. The reasoning behind the Doctrine of Adoption was simplicity itself: an important Church leader like Brigham Young or one of the Apostles would eventually die and become a God, and when this happened, his adopted sons and their wives, as well as his own natural children, would be able to assist him in running some portion of the Universe—perhaps a nearby planet—over which his spirit had been granted sovereignty. The doctrine did not prove popular, though, and soon was abandoned by the Church, but this did not lessen Lee's jealous resentment that he only had been Young's second adopted son, while Porter Rockwell, his fellow Danite, had taken precedence over him and had been "sealed" to their leader first.

In Missouri and Illinois, John D. Lee and Brigham Young often had collaborated on items of Church business, and after Young's ascent to power Lee became one of his most trusted captains, a position that he continued to enjoy for a quarter of a century. Lee was eleven years younger than the new Church President and, because of the difference in their ages, quite readily assumed the

part of an eager and dutiful son, who unquestioningly served a
wise and all-powerful father. Lee, whose orthodoxy was complete,
never doubted that his soul's salvation lay in total obedience; he
believed that Young held the Keys to the Kingdom and communicated directly with God, as had Joseph Smith, and that if a man
faithfully followed all Young's commands, whatever those commands might be, his own soul, and those of his wives and
children, would be safe throughout Eternity.

On one occasion he wrote in characteristic fashion to his
spiritual mentor: "I am now, as I always have been, in your hands
and in the hands of the Lord. . . . I have no hesitance in saying
that I believe that I shall be able to accomplish whatever you in
your wisdom may require. . . . Should you [care] to send me a
word of instruction, it will be graciously and cordially received.
With feelings of reverence, I subscribe myself Your son and
brother in the seal of the Covenant forever."

During the early days of 1847, Brigham Young used the money
he had exacted from the members of the Mormon Battalion to
outfit a sizable advance party for the trek to the Far West. John
D. Lee, however, was not enrolled in this initial company of
explorers and pioneers. Instead, to his great disappointment,
Young placed him in charge of a large cooperative farming
venture, some fifteen miles from Winter Quarters, with the duty
of raising needed food stocks for the Church. But Lee did manage
to contribute to the expedition; along with other items he loaned
Brigham Young seventeen fully equipped teams of oxen, and if
his later testimony is to be believed, received no repayment of
any kind for the loan.

The advance party of Mormons left Winter Quarters in mid-
April under the command of President Young. Among the pioneers were Heber C. Kimball, the "Second in Israel," and a
majority of the Apostles, including the scholarly Orson Pratt,
who invented a useful odometer while on the march; Wilford
Woodruff, an Englishman who brought along his fishing rod and
became, in all likelihood, the first sportsman to employ a dry fly
in the Rocky Mountains; and George A. Smith, the late Prophet's
cousin and one of the ablest frontiersmen among the Twelve.

The Mormon company was similar in size to the ill-fated
Fancher Train that departed from western Arkansas almost
exactly ten years later, although naturally enough there were far
fewer women and children in its ranks than would ride with the

later pioneers. The roster of Saints consisted of 143 white men, three Black slaves, but only three women and two children, one of the women a wife of Brigham Young, another a wife of Heber C. Kimball.

Prior to 1847 most travelers, while crossing the Nebraska prairies, had chosen to follow the convenient southern bank of the shallow Platte River. But now, in the hope of finding better forage, and especially in order to avoid contact with Gentile parties, the Mormons decided to follow the northern bank instead, and by doing so, established the central portion of what soon came to be called the Mormon Trail. Such exclusiveness, though, was an unwarranted burden that the Saints needlessly placed upon their own shoulders. One sympathetic twentieth-century historian has said of the Mormons' state of mind, "They remained in deadly fear of persecution . . . and preserved their illusion that innumerable mobbers, politicians, and especially Pukes were after them . . . [although] there is not the slightest evidence that, by the summer of '47, anyone anywhere in the prairies or the Far West intended them any harm whatever."

While traveling westward along the trail, Brigham Young for the first time found himself completely beyond the restraints of Gentile authority, and it was not long before a new and candid note of menace entered into his public speeches, foreshadowing the nature of the regime he intended to form in the Great Basin. William Clayton, the secretary of the expedition, was so struck by one of Young's trailside sermons that he recorded it afterward in his private journal. At one point Young said, "I understand that there are several in this camp who do not belong to the Church. I am the man who will stand up for them and protect them in all their rights. And they shall not trample on our rights nor on the priesthood. They shall reverence and acknowledge the name of God and His priesthood, and if they set up their head and seek to introduce iniquity into this camp and to trample on the priesthood, I swear to them, they shall never go back to tell the tale."

In late July the advance party of Saints reached the Great Basin, and on the twenty-fourth of the month Brigham Young formally declared that Salt Lake was to become the site of the new Zion. According to most official Mormon histories, the outlook was bleak, for the Great Basin was utterly barren and sterile, and it was only God's subsequent beneficence, in helping his Chosen People, that enabled the desert to "blossom like the rose."

But some of the pioneers of 1847 seemingly were unaware of this fiction. William Clayton found himself in late July slightly ahead of the main party of explorers, at the mouth of Emigration Canyon, overlooking the valley of the Great Salt Lake, and in his *Journal* recorded his enthusiasm on that memorable occasion. "While the brethern were cutting the road," Clayton wrote, "I followed the old one to the top of the hill, and on arriving there, was much cheered by a handsome view of the Great Salt Lake lying . . . from twenty-five to thirty miles west of us. . . . The lake does not show at this distance a very extensive surface, but its dark blue shade, resembling the calm sea, looks very handsome. The intervening valley appears to be well supplied with streams, creeks and lakes; some of the latter are evidently salt. There is but little timber in sight anywhere . . . which is about the only objection which could be raised, in my estimation, to this being one of the most beautiful valleys and pleasant places for a home for the Saints which could be found."

And then Clayton, in a more reflective mood, spoke of the future and, at the same time, openly revealed his feelings toward those outside the Church, feelings that doubtlessly were held in common by many of his fellow Saints. "When I commune with my own heart," he wrote, "and ask myself whether I would choose to dwell here in this wild looking country, amongst the Saints, surrounded by friends, though poor, enjoying the privileges and blessings of the everlasting priesthood, with God for our King and Father; or dwell among the gentiles, with all their wealth and good things of the earth, to be eternally mobbed, harassed, hunted, our best men murdered, and every good man's life continually in danger; the soft whisper echoes loud, and reverberates in tones of stern determination; give me the quiet wilderness, and my family to associate with, surrounded by the Saints, and adieu to the gentile world, till God says return and avenge you of your enemies."

Chapter 15

T HE SETTLEMENT of the Oregon question in 1846 and the end of the Mexican War two years later left the United States in possession of a huge, thinly settled western empire that stretched from the Canadian border to the Rio Grande, and from the eastern slopes of the Rockies to the shores of the Pacific. Before long, thousands of pioneers were streaming into this vast region, and as their numbers increased, important changes began to be made in the political organization of the area. California became a state in 1850; Oregon in 1859; Nevada in 1864. But the benefits of statehood were not to be granted so promptly to the Mormon inhabitants of the Great Basin, a fact that hardly was surprising in the light of the Church's open hostility to the American Government, its intolerance of democratic institutions and the truculent words and defiant conduct of its principal leaders. Indeed, it was not until 1896, a full half-century after the establishment of the new Zion, that the last major dispute between the Church and Washington finally was resolved and the state of Utah admitted into the Union.

From their earliest days in the valley of the Great Salt Lake, the Latter-Day Saints proved a trial to the Federal Government, a trial that was to grow more severe with the influx of newly recruited Saints from Europe and the mounting arrogance and ambition of the Church. The truth was simply this: that as early as 1847, a group of disciplined and fanatical enemies of the American republic had placed itself at the crossroads of the Far West, athwart the principal emigration routes between the Missouri River and California, a group whose members could be curbed, or removed from their mountain domain, only at a considerable cost. And so, initially at least, the Government in Washington decided to temporize. Distracted by more-pressing domestic problems—especially the issue of slavery and the increasing prospect of secession and civil war—Washington sought an accommodation with Brigham Young and the distant Saints, and this gave Young the opportunity to establish the Church securely in its final home, to infuse it with greater strength and to complete his own absolute ascendancy over his followers.

Beyond question the Church could not have survived for long in Utah without Young's executive ability, his ruthlessness and his implacable strength of will. The difficulties he faced were truly formidable, and in overcoming them he earned enduring fame as one of North America's most enterprising and successful pioneer leaders. It was no small feat to transport some five or ten thousand Saints from Winter Quarters to the Utah Territory and to make certain that they would have enough food on hand in the mountains to survive until the next harvest. At the same time, an entire city had to be planned at Great Salt Lake, with streets, houses, a Tabernacle, stores, mills and storage facilities; a "bowery" had to be built for outdoor meetings during the warmer months, and a new Temple begun, so that one day the faithful again would be able to receive their endowments. President Young had to deal with these varied concerns, while composing lengthy sermons, settling petty quarrels and making a hundred decisions that would affect the temporal and spiritual future of his people.

Nor was this all. A local government had to be formed at once and put into operation, land distributed, irrigation canals dug, fences put up and farms laid out and planted. The first field parties had to be dispatched, some to build roads, some to search the immediate neighborhood for fresh water, timber and arable land, and some to explore the more remote countryside, in anticipation of the day when additional towns would spring up across the immense territory now claimed by the Church.

The extent of such claims was revealed in March 1849, when the Mormons declared themselves the occupants of a new state, to be called Deseret, the name having been derived from a word in the *Book of Mormon*, meaning "honey bee." Meeting at Salt Lake City, the Saints drafted a state constitution and unanimously elected Brigham Young their governor; his First Counselor in the Church, Heber C. Kimball, became lieutenant governor and a justice of the supreme court; and his Second Counselor, Willard

Richards, was elected secretary of state. The Saints then appointed Almon W. Babbitt their special delegate to Washington and sent him East to petition Congress to admit the state of Deseret into the Union. The proposed state was to include all of modern Nevada and Utah, most of Arizona, and generous portions of Idaho, Wyoming, Colorado, Oregon and New Mexico, as well as a corridor through southern California which was to extend as far as the sea coast near San Diego.

While their petition for statehood was pending in the nation's capital, Young turned his full attention to the problem of populating the huge territory he had appropriated in the name of God and the Church. It was clear that a new army of Saints would have to be raised, but where could this be done? Hardly in the United States and Canada alone, for the latest proselytizing efforts there had proved unproductive, thanks in large measure to the Church's radical social doctrines, its singular reputation for violence, and the persistent rumors of sexual misconduct among its chief priests. In Europe, however, particularly England, Wales and other Protestant countries, the outlook for recruitment seemed more promising. Europeans were not so well informed about the Church, and in addition, they often knew nothing whatever about the harshness of frontier life in the United States. And so a renewed effort began to be made abroad to enroll fresh battalions of the Faithful, who then would be transported across the Atlantic to an East Coast or Gulf port and conveyed across two-thirds of Gentile America to the new Promised Land.

In October 1849, the Perpetual Emigration Fund was founded in Salt Lake City, to assist the poorest of the European converts; money was loaned to them for their arduous journey, and after their arrival at Salt Lake they were obliged to work off their debts to the Church, a proceeding that kept many of them in virtual peonage for at least several years. The "P.E. Fund," as it came to be called, proved its usefulness almost immediately; according to one reliable estimate, between 1848 and 1855, more than seventeen thousand Saints left for the United States from the British Isles, a considerable number of them receiving loans before their departure.

During the same month that he founded the P.E. Fund, Brigham Young assigned a number of leading Saints to foreign missions. The Apostle Erastus Snow left for Denmark, the Apostle John Taylor for France, and the Apostle Lorenzo Snow for Italy, while the following spring the Apostle Orson Pratt was sent to England, to take charge of Church affairs in the British Isles.

Sometimes, in their understandable eagerness to find recruits, the Mormon missionaries were guilty of serious misrepresentations. Writing in the Church's British newspaper, the *Millennial Star*, the Apostle John Taylor promised that European settlers would have an easy time of it, once they had crossed the seas and reached the prairies, a promise completely divorced from the bleak realities of the American frontier. "The way is now prepared," Taylor falsely claimed, "the roads, bridges and ferryboats made, [and] there are stopping places . . . on the way where they can rest. . . . " Another issue of the newspaper carried a rhapsodic description of conditions in the Utah Territory: "The elevated valley of the Salt and Utah Lakes, with the beautiful River Jordan running through it, is the newly established stake of Zion. There vegetation flourishes with magic rapidity. . . . Within one month from planting, potatoes grow to six or eight inches, and corn from two to four feet."

Such cynical huckstering encouraged many impoverished English, Welsh and Danish families to emigrate to the Great Basin, where their increasing numbers supported the Church's demand that statehood—and full self-government—be awarded to the people of Deseret. In Washington, though, congressional memories were not so short, nor common sense so utterly lacking, as Brigham Young and his associates might have imagined. The history of the Saints in Ohio, Missouri and Illinois had not yet been forgotten; in addition, recent travelers' reports from Utah indicated that the Mormons had in no way altered their policies, or improved their conduct, since moving West to a land of their own. As a result, the efforts of special delegate Almon W. Babbitt proved fruitless, the Saints' petition for statehood was denied, and in September 1850, Congress declared Utah a Federal Territory, to be governed by officials appointed by the President and to be subject to the territorial laws of the United States.

Although the immediate campaign for statehood and unrestricted self-government had been lost, the Church's resistance to Federal supervision had scarcely begun. If Congress could not be induced to grant the necessary concessions, there always was the possibility of influencing the executive branch. No longer did the astute and wary Democrat James K. Polk occupy the White House, nor his immediate successor, General Zachary Taylor, the strong-minded hero of Buena Vista and Monterrey, who recently had died in office of typhus. In their place there now sat a lackluster Whig politician, America's thirteenth President, Millard Fillmore, said to be a man of considerable good will, who might be open to accommodation and compromise.

Before the end of the year the matter was tested, and to the Saints' satisfaction President Fillmore turned out to be exactly the sort of obliging national leader they had been seeking. For when the first territorial appointments were announced, it could readily be seen that most of the important ones had been given to prominent Mormons. Seth M. Blair was named attorney general, J. H. Heywood, Federal marshal, and Zerubbabel Snow, one of three supreme court justices.

Of far greater significance, though, was President Fillmore's final appointment—the naming of Brigham Young to be governor of the Territory. Young's elevation united in one person the civil and religious authority and, in effect, transformed Utah into a theocracy, a form of government long feared and detested by a majority of Americans, and expressly forbidden by the Constitution.

Hardly less disturbing was the fact that as governor, Young automatically became commander of the territorial militia, and superintendent of Indian affairs, a development that promised much future mischief. As militia commander, Young would have at his disposal a loyal home-guard, which he could use whenever he pleased in open defiance of the Federal Government; as superintendent of Indian Affairs, he would be in an ideal position to play the same subversive game that Joseph Smith once had attempted in Missouri—a game in which the Saints would win the friendship of the Lamanites, convert them to Mormonism and perhaps even employ them as military allies against the "Americans," manipulating them in whatever ways would prove beneficial to the Church and harmful to the Church's Gentile enemies.

Chapter 16

THE NAMING of Brigham Young and the other Mormons to high places in the territorial government created a political furor throughout much of the country. One of Fillmore's apologists later attempted to explain the President's decision by saying, "In his judgment, conciliation was better than coercion. He thought that by the appointment of some of their important men to an important office in the new territory, the Mormons might be won back to loyal allegiance to the government." There was, however, no mention of the fact that the President had been duped.

The truth of the matter might have remained permanently concealed had not a New York State newspaper, the Buffalo *Courier*, pressed the President strongly on the subject, condemning the appointment of Young and asserting that it posed a threat to good government and the safety of the Territory. The paper questioned Young's moral character and fitness for office and reminded its readers of the many offenses said to have been committed by the Mormon leader, both during earlier times in Illinois and more recently, since his arrival in the West. Stung by these attacks, President Fillmore, in July 1851, forwarded the newspaper articles, and an accompanying letter of inquiry, to his private adviser on Mormon affairs. This, it turned out, was none other than Brigham Young's highly placed eastern friend—and undisclosed confidential agent—Colonel Thomas Leiper Kane.

"You will recollect that I relied much upon you for the moral character of Mr. Young," the President complained in his letter. Therefore, he continued, having been greatly embarrassed politically as a consequence, he now was forced to ask Colonel Kane to state publicly "whether these charges against the moral character of Mr. Young" were true.

Kane immediately rose to Young's defense. "I reiterate without reserve," he reassured the unhappy President, "the statement of his excellent capacity, energy, and integrity, which I made you prior to the appointment. I am willing to say that I *volunteered* to communicate to you the facts by which I was convinced of his patriotism and devotion to the Union. I made no qualification when I assured you of his irreproachable moral character, because I was able to speak of this from my own intimate personal knowledge."

Then Kane went on to answer the main charges against Young. He denied that the Mormon chief had ever participated in any illegal acts at Nauvoo and called the accusation of counterfeiting "a mere rehash of old libels." Nor could Young's devotion to the country be called into question; his patriotism, and that of his coreligionists, had been amply demonstrated by the heroic saga of the Mormon Battalion. False, too, was the current assertion that the Mormons were taxing itinerant Gentiles two percent on the value of any goods they brought into the Territory; the tax applied only to liquor, Kane insisted, and was a credit to the temperance principle of the Saints.

Finally, the Mormons did not practice polygamy now and never had. "The charge," Kane wrote, "connects itself with that unmixed outrage, the spiritual wife story, which was fastened on the Mormons by a poor ribald scamp, whom . . . they were literally forced to excommunicate for licentiousness, and who therefore revenged himself by editing confessions and disclosures . . . to please the public that peruses novels in yellow paper covers." And so Kane, during the summer of 1851—long after his own discovery of the truth at Winter Quarters, and only a year before Brigham Young's belated acknowledgment that the Mormons did indeed practice polygamy—once again lied on behalf of his churchly clients, this time in order to conceal if possible the real character of the men he had recommended for high public office, and the nature of the society they already had begun to build in the Utah Territory.

Yet curiously enough, a considerable amount of reliable information already was available in Washington to anyone who wished to inform himself about conditions in the Great Basin. The discovery of gold near Sacramento, in January 1848, had signaled the end of Utah's almost total isolation; each summer after that, swarms of Americans had hurried West, many of them crossing the continent by way of the Oregon Trail, South Pass and the Humboldt, in a headlong rush to reach the gold fields of California. In 1850 some of the emigrants had suffered delays along the trail and, on arriving at Salt Lake City, were told by the Mormons that it was a grave risk to attempt a crossing of the Sierra Nevadas so late in the season.

At the urging of the Saints, about 325 men had then agreed to spend the winter in the Territory, where they were hired by their hosts to perform a variety of useful tasks, and where, during a residence of several months, they learned about life in the mountains under Mormon rule.

As soon as the western passes were clear the following spring, the emigrants left for California and, on reaching there, scattered to their separate destinations. Before long, though, one of their number, a man named Nelson Slater, decided to summarize their experiences and to present that summary in the form of a petition to Congress, calling for Federal intervention in the Utah Territory. And Slater did just this, after obtaining more than two hundred signatures from those of his fellow emigrants who had not yet traveled too far to be reached. As a result, while President Fillmore sat in the White House and corresponded with Colonel Kane, in an effort to form an accurate picture of conditions in Utah, Mr. Slater's informative memorial on the same subject was circulating through the neighboring halls of Congress.

The California petition contained a host of strong indictments, some, perhaps, too strong to be fully credible back in the East. At the same time, it also contained a series of familiar accusations and, for the most part, seemed distressingly consistent with earlier reports of Mormon misdeeds in Missouri and Illinois. The petition made it clear that for Gentiles at least, there was even less hope of obtaining justice in Utah than there had been at Nauvoo. "Some of the Mormons who hold offices," Slater wrote, "said to certain emigrants, if they should not show favor to their brethren, but should administer impartial justice to emigrants as well as Mormons, they would lose their offices; that they were counselled from headquarters not only to favor their brethren, but also to get away from the traveler passing through their country, his money and effects in every way in which it could be done, from common trade to highway robbery and murder."

The petition offered numerous instances by way of illustration. One case involved an engineer named Custer, who had signed a contract with the Apostle Ezra Taft Benson to build a mill dam on the latter's property for $1,000. After the dam was finished, though, "the debt remained unpaid, for the Mormon courts would not enforce the collection of debts due to California emigrants." Evidently the engineer had been rash in pressing his claims so far and in protesting his ill treatment. "Just before starting for California," the report concluded, "Mr. Custer was shot by the Indians."

A less extreme experience was that of Dr. Whitlock, who lost both of his horses one spring night while making his way out of the Territory. This incident, too, implicated the Apostle Ezra Taft Benson and, more important, revealed that the Mormons already had adopted a general policy of blaming their misconduct, whenever possible, on the local Indians. Dr. Whitlock's loss had occurred one night while he camped near the Apostle's sawmill. "In the morning," Slater wrote, "when he arose, not one of his animals could he find. In the course of the day he found his cattle, but not his horses. It appears his horses had been stolen, and his cattle driven off in different directions some miles in the course of the night, as a blind to prevent the discovery of the theft of the horses, making it appear as if the Indians had undertaken to run off the stock."

Threats and violent speech against the emigrants were common features of life in Salt Lake City according to the California memorial. "Brigham Young, and many of the Mormons," Slater wrote, "are in the frequent habit of using threatening language toward the emigrants. They often talk of cutting off people's heads, cutting their throats, and the like. The following is an instance of this kind: [William] Snow, while sitting as a justice of the peace last winter in the trial of John Galvin for striking a Mormon, said to him (we use his own language), 'If you ever lay hands on another Saint, I will have your head cut off before you leave this city. I thank God that the time is not far distant, and I shall rejoice when it comes, that I shall have the authority to pass sentence of life and death upon the Gentiles, and I will have their heads snatched off like chickens in the dooryard!"

The memorial shrewdly noted that Gentiles were not the only ones in the Territory to suffer injustice and violence; Mormons, too, once they had indicated a desire to leave Utah, and had been declared Apostates, became subject to the confiscation of property and physical assault. "It appears from numerous facts, and from the history of Mormonism," Slater wrote, "that it has ever been its policy to bring down vengeance upon all who forsake it, instead of suffering them, if not pleased with it, to voluntarily and quietly depart. The Mormons seem disposed to compel those who join them, to remain with them. If they will not stay with them, they persecute them to the last extremity; often murdering them in cold blood." It was true that Slater could not present iron-clad, legal evidence to sustain the charge, but interestingly enough, he was far from the last Gentile visitor to the Territory to be told by the Saints themselves of vengeance taken against some recent Apostate.

During the course of their stay in the Great Basin, Slater and the other emigrants collected several stories dealing with the misfortunes of previous Gentile travelers. "A Mormon acknow-leged to Mr. N. K. Hammond," Slater wrote, "that in the fall of 1849, the Mormons killed an emigrant west of the city, near the Jordan Bridge, by tying one end of a long rope around his neck, and fastening the other end to the pommel of a horse, and riding [the horse] rapidly so as to throw [the man] down and drag him upon the ground until he was dead. They then threw him into the Jordan River, not [allowing him] to float into Salt Lake, but with weights fastened, to sink him to the bottom, where he could not be seen by other emigrants."

Not all the forty-niners had been single men, traveling alone. A number were farmers and tradesmen accompanied by their families. The wife of one emigrant stopped at Salt Lake City to visit her sister, a Mormon. There she heard her sister say that some of the "mobocrats"—in this case, the California emigrants—would never get back to the States. According to Slater, some of the emigrants, "having left Salt Lake City for California, were pursued by a company of Mormons on foot. In four or five weeks the company returned with a large number of horses, several carriages, and considerable property."

Slater and his fellow emigrants were convinced there was an organization of "enforcers" who often committed violent crimes in the Territory at the orders of those highly placed in the Church. "In order to carry out their system and accomplish their designs," Slater said, "the Mormons have a class of persons among them, set apart for a specific purpose, and entrusted with a special duty. They are a kind of minutemen appointed to execute any orders which the leaders see fit to give, no matter what those orders are. They are a life-guard to protect the leaders, and a police to pursue and privately dispatch all persons obnoxious to the Mormon Church. Upon these errands they are often sent; these varied duties they often perform.

"The most daring, adventurous, resolute, and hardened characters," Slater wrote, "are generally selected for this purpose. They are usually called 'Danites.' By this name they are known throughout the Mormon community. Whenever they are called upon by the heads of the Church to perpetrate some horrible act . . . they are encouraged and comforted . . . by the leaders, who tell them to go forward and obey the mandates they receive, without inquiring whether their acts are right or wrong; saying also to them, that the responsibility rests upon those who give authoritive commands, and not upon the Danites who execute those commands. The leaders advocate the doctrine that these Danites, in such transactions, have no more responsibility than mere machines; that the leaders, being inspired and constantly under divine influence, are infallibly secured against error in principle . . . and can issue no commands not in accordance with the will of God."

After Slater's petition had arrived from California, it would have been reasonable for Congress or the President to have investigated the matter, and then, for some form of governmental action to have been undertaken. This was not the case, however. Instead, Congress and the President ignored the petition, apparently preferring to place their faith in two comforting illusions— that Federal officials, who already were in the Territory, soon would be able to restore calm and order there; and that Brigham Young, described by his defenders as a fair-minded and humane individual whose character had been besmirched solely for partisan religious and political reasons, now would rise to the full responsibility of the governorship and would moderate his own excesses and those of his followers. So Washington averted its eyes from the distant Territory and hoped that through a combination of tolerance and "benign neglect," the worst of the difficulties with the Saints would shortly be resolved.

Chapter 17

During the late spring and early summer of 1851 the first Gentile officials arrived at Salt Lake City, ready to assume their assigned positions in the territorial government. Acting under the powers that Congress had granted him the previous year through passage of the so-called "organic act," President Fillmore had named Lemuel G. Brandebury chief justice of the supreme court, Perry E. Brocchus an associate justice and Broughton D. Harris secretary of state for the territory; in addition to these principal appointments H. R. Holeman and Henry R. Day were to serve as Indian agent and subagent respectively, under the direction of the governor and superintendent of Indian Affairs, Brigham Young.

Judging from subsequent events, the five Presidential appointees took up their residence in the Great Basin with little or no appreciation of the hazards surrounding them. Justice Brandebury and his fellow officials apparently believed that the people of Utah were ordinary American citizens, distinguished solely by the intensity of their religious convictions, and that United States officers like themselves would be able to perform their proper duties without hindrance, while enduring nothing more inconvenient than the customary rigors of frontier life. It did not take long for the five to discard this pleasing but unrealistic assumption.

Judge Brandebury was the earliest of the Gentile officials to ride into Salt Lake City, reaching the small, neatly laid-out town on the seventh of June, almost a full month before most of the others. According to the report he later submitted to President Fillmore, in collaboration with Judge Brocchus and Secretary

106

Harris, difficulties were placed in his path from the beginning, and instead of the courteous reception he had anticipated he soon began to meet with unlooked for signs of incivility and even insolence. Shortly after his arrival the chief justice decided to pay his respects to Brigham Young, in order to inform the governor that he was ready to enter upon his official duties. With this purpose in mind Brandebury sought out the United States attorney, Seth Blair, a Mormon, and asked him to arrange a meeting with the governor. Blair said he would be pleased to do so, and an appointment quickly was made. On the day of the proposed meeting, however, with only a few minutes to spare, the attorney arrived at Judge Brandebury's quarters to announce that the appointment was off—the governor was "too busy" that day to see him.

Still hoping to establish normal relations with the governor, the chief justice resolved to overlook the obvious affront, and at the urging of Blair, accepted a second appointment, only to see it, too, canceled several days later.

"Satisfied," the justice wrote, "that this was the result of design on the part of the governor, [I] made no further attempt to see him. This conduct of the governor was known in the community, and afforded much merriment to some of the Mormons. We were informed afterward that Mr. Blair made several private applications to the governor to know if he would allow an interview with the chief justice, but he refused, declaring that he did not wish an introduction, for none but Mormons should have been appointed to the offices of the territory, and none other but damn rascals would have come [in their place]."

On July 19, Justice Brandebury's complete isolation came to an end when the territorial secretary, Broughton Harris, reached the city. Almost immediately both Federal officers were invited to attend an important public celebration, commemorating the arrival of the first party of Mormon pioneers in the valley of the Great Salt Lake. The celebration was held in the Bowery on the twenty-fourth of July, with Judge Brandebury and Secretary Harris seated on the platform amid a number of Mormon notables, including the governor, several Apostles and the recently accredited Territorial Delegate to Congress, John M. Bernhisel. It proved an occasion that neither the judge nor the secretary was likely to forget.

One after another, a number of Mormon leaders took the speaker's stand to address the audience. Hatred of the United

States, its laws and its government was the unifying theme, accompanied by elaborate recitals of former persecutions and current grievances. Daniel H. Wells, commanding general of the territorial militia, was one of the main speakers. He began his tirade by recalling the Missouri troubles, the death of Joseph Smith, the expulsion from Nauvoo and the desperate struggles in Iowa during the winter of 1846. Then, producing one of the Church's favorite legends—the story of how the United States had "compelled" Brigham Young and the Saints to form the Mormon Battalion—he thundered at his audience, with more alliterative passion than historical accuracy, "the government of the United States *required* a battalion of five hundred men to leave their families without money, provisons or friends . . . and to perform a campaign of over two thousand miles, on foot, across trackless deserts and burning plains, to fight the battles of their country! Even that country which had afforded them no protection from the ruthless ruffians who had plundered them of their property, robbed them of their rights, waylaid them in their peaceful habitations, and murdered them while under the safeguards of their pledged faith! The country that could have the *barbarity* to make such a requirement, could have no other object in view than to finish, by *extermination*, the work which had so ruthlessly begun!"

No doubt these partisan accusations against the Federal Government, and the effects they produced on the audience, were greatly distressing to that government's representatives, Justice Brandebury and Secretary Harris; so, too, must have been the words of another holiday orator, W. W. Phelps, the speaker of the territorial House of Representatives and a regent of the much discussed, though still nonexistent, University of Deseret. It was Phelps who first confirmed publicly that plural marriage was being widely practiced by the leaders of the Church. Phelps proclaimed that he himself had two wives, others of his brethren had more, Brother Brigham had *still* more, and none of them "dared to return to the United States with [our] families," because the country's "dirty, mean, little, contracted laws would imprison [us] for polygamy!"

Then Brigham Young took the stand. At such times he always dressed somberly, in a black suit, a white or black cravat and black gloves, while carrying in his hand—like the original Prophet—a handsome, gold-headed cane. Recent history concerned the governor on this occasion, particularly the career of the vastly popular military hero and President of the United States, the late General Zachary Taylor. The general, according to Young, had been cruelly hostile to the Latter-Day Saints and deserved the blackest condemnation for his refusal, while President, to grant statehood and liberty to the chosen people of Deseret. The governor's temper grew warmer, and his voice louder, as he reflected on the late hero's sins. Suddenly a new and consoling thought occured to him. "But Zachary Taylor is dead," he cried, "and in Hell, and I'm glad of it!" Then drawing himself up to his full height, he exclaimed even more violently, "And I prophesy in the name of Jesus Christ, by the power of the Priesthood that's upon me, that *any* President of the United States who lifts his finger against this people shall die an untimely death and go to Hell!" The declaration was greeted by enthusiastic shouts of "Amen!" "Good!" and "Hear! Hear!" from all parts of the audience, including the platform, where other Mormon leaders surrounded the two Gentile officials.

Nearly every day after that, for the better part of a month, Judge Brandebury and Secretary Harris found themselves the objects of harassment and intimidation. Without doubt they already had considered the alluring possibility of abandoning their struggle with the governor and returning to the East, when Associate Justice Perry Brocchus, much delayed by illness, finally arrived at Salt Lake City on the seventeenth of August and, almost overnight, precipitated their departure. Judge Brocchus was sincere, naive and well intentioned—precisely the wrong sort of man to plunge headlong into such troubled waters. He possessed a broad streak of patriotic feeling, little imagination and no understanding whatever of the fanatical institution he proposed to deal with, or of the leader who served as its Prophet and President. Though certainly informed by his fellow officers how matters stood in the Territory, the judge nevertheless decided that he could set things right through a candid appeal to what he undoubtedly thought of as "the better instincts of the local citizens." He asked Brigham Young's permission to address the people, and on Sunday, September 6, he delivered a two-hour lecture to a gathering of three thousand Saints.

It is difficult to say what all the subjects might have been that Judge Brocchus dwelled upon or exactly what phrases he might have chosen to employ that day on the speaker's platform. Afterward he was accused, among other things, of having attacked the morality of the Church, the patriotism of its leaders and the virtue of Mormon Womanhood. For his own part, the justice denied the charges, claiming that at every point he had remained tactful, circumspect and inoffensive. It was true, he conceded, that he *had* spoken of patriotism and of the virtue of remaining loyal to one's country, but he had done so only while referring to the exemplary life of their nation's father, George Washington, and while discussing a proposed monument to honor his memory that was to be built in the nation's capital, the stone for which he had been commissioned to obtain from the Saints if they were willing to provide it from their native mountains. As for insulting Mormon Womanhood, or speaking against polygamous marriage in a defamatory way, these he certainly had not done.

However innocuous the judge might have imagined his admonitions and reflections, to the leader of the Saints they represented the gravest sort of danger—a public attack, by a United States official, on fundamental Church doctrine and his own position of authority. And so, that day on the platform, Brigham Young's response was fierce and immediate. According to the Federal officers, "He rose to his feet and denounced the speaker with great violence, as 'profoundly ignorant or wilfully wicked'—strode the stage madly—assumed various theatrical attitudes—declared 'he was a greater man than ever George Washington was'—'that he knew more than ever George Washington knew'—'that he was the man who could handle the sword'—and 'that if there was any more discussions, there would be pulling of hair and cutting of throats!'"

By then even Justice Brocchus must have realized that a Mormon assembly hall was hardly the ideal forum in which to deliver a candid lecture on polygamy and patriotism. "The ferment," he later wrote, "was truly fearful. It seemed as if the people (I mean a large portion of them) were ready to spring upon me like hyenas and destroy me." His fellow officials believed themselves in similar peril. "Those of us present felt the personal danger that surrounded us," they said. "If the governor had but pointed his finger toward us, as an indication of [his] wish, we have no doubt that we would have been massacred before leaving the house. The governor declared afterwards 'that if he had crooked his finger, we would have been torn to pieces!'"

It was now evident to the principal Federal officers that they could serve no useful end by remaining in the Territory. Two weeks after his ill-starred speech, Judge Brocchus dispatched a letter to a friend back East, describing the situation. He announced his intention of departing as quickly as possible and said that on his homeward journey he would be accompanied by Chief Justice Brandebury, Secretary Harris, and Indian subagent Henry Day; their departure would leave Indian Agent H. R. Holeman the sole Gentile official in the Territory. Since delivering his speech, Brocchus told his friend, "the community has been in a state of intense excitement, and murmurs of personal violence and assassination towards me have been freely uttered by the lower order of the populace. How it will end I do not know. I have just learned that I have been denounced, together with the government and officers, in the Bowery again today, by Governor Young. I hope I shall get off safely. God only knows. I am in the power of a desperate and murderous set."

Within a short time it became known throughout the city that the Gentile officers were planning to leave, and for Secretary Harris the disclosure created some last-minute difficulties. The secretary had arrived in the Territory almost two months before, bringing with him $24,000 in Federal funds, to reimburse the territorial government for certain expenses. The money, however, was only to be disbursed if the secretary felt satisfied that the governor had complied fully with Federal laws and regulations. Unfortunately, such had not been the case. Among other things, Brigham Young had committed numerous illegal acts involving the census and the election of officers to the territorial legislature, and as a result, Secretary Harris refused to turn over the money.

The problem quickly came to a head after Young discovered that Harris intended to return to the East, taking the $24,000 with him. The governor immediately launched a full-scale assault, first demanding the money and then threatening Harris with arrest and imprisonment when he failed to yield it up. But the secretary remained firm and in a letter to Young explained the reasons for his refusal, offering seven detailed examples of how the governor had seriously violated United States laws. And a few days later, despite Young's continued threats, Secretary Harris departed from Salt Lake City with the other Federal officers, the $24,000 still safe in his possession.

Chapter 18

THE FLIGHT of the justices and the secretary, and their arrival back East, created a considerable stir in Washington. To explain their actions the officials submitted to President Fillmore a report on their experiences in the Territory, a comprehensive document that offered the President—and those members of Congress who cared to read it—a sobering picture of conditions in the Great Basin.

"It becomes our duty," the officials wrote, "as officers of the United States for the Territory of Utah, to inform the President that we have been compelled to withdraw from the Territory, and our official duties, in consequence of an extraordinary state of affairs existing there, which rendered the performance of those duties not only dangerous, but impracticable, and a longer residence in the Territory, in our judgment, incompatible with a proper sense of self-respect, and the high regard due to the United States. We have been driven to this course by the lawless acts and the hostile and seditious feelings and sentiments of Brigham Young, the Executive of the Territory, and the great body of the residents there. . . .

"To enable the Government," the officials continued, "to understand more fully the unfortunate position of affairs in the Territory, it will be necessary to explain the extraordinary religious organization existing there—its unlimited pretensions, influence and power. . . . We found upon our arrival that almost the entire population consisted of a people called Mormons; and the Mormon Church overshadowing and controlling the opinions, the actions, the property, and even the lives of its members; usurping and exercising the functions of legislation and the judicial business of the Territory; organizing and commanding the military; disposing of the public lands upon its own terms; coining money, stamped 'Holiness to the Lord,' and forcing its circulation at a standard fifteen or twenty per centum above its real value; openly sanctioning and defending the practice of polygamy, or plurality of wives; exacting the tenth part of every thing from its members, under the name of tithing, and enormous taxes, from citizens not members; penetrating and supervising the social and business circles; and inculcating, and requiring, as an article of religious faith, implicit obedience to the counsels of 'the Church,' as paramount to all the obligations of morality, society, allegiance, and of law.

"At the head of this formidable organization, styled 'The Church of Jesus Christ of Latter Day Saints,' stood Brigham Young, the governor, claiming, and represented to be, the Prophet of God, and his sayings as direct revelations from Heaven, commanding thereby unlimited sway over the ignorant and the credulous. *His* opinions and wishes were *their* opinions and wishes. He was consulted by them, upon almost every subject, as an oracle. No man pretended to embark on any kind of business without his permission, or conciliating him by a deferential consultation. In a word, he ruled as he pleased, without a rival or opposition, for no one dared to question his authority."

The officers then summarized the reception they had received in the Territory, and recounted several statements made from the pulpit in their presence, either by Brigham Young himself, by Heber C. Kimball, his First Counselor in the Church, or by the mayor of Salt Lake City, Jedediah M. Grant, shortly to become his Second Counselor—statements attacking the people of the United States, their Government, their officials, and their laws. Such hostile and even seditious attacks, the officers said, were made with calculation, as a matter of deliberate Church policy, for they did much to convince the average Saint that other Americans invariably were his enemies, and that it was the fixed purpose of the American Government to destroy his unique society and faith. Once persuaded of this, and with his fear and hatred of the Gentile world strongly reinforced, he was almost certain to remain loyal and subservient to his churchly rulers.

Of no less concern to the authors of the report was the fiscal misconduct of the governor. At one point they accused Brigham Young of having embezzled United States funds. Only recently, they declared, "Congress appropriated $20,000 to be applied under the direction of the governor and the legislature to the erection of public buildings. The governor no sooner received this money, than he appropriated and used every dollar of it, or a greater portion of it, in payments due by the Mormon Church, and in a few days after its arrival in the valley, it was on its way to the United States in other hands. We were not present at the actual payment, but it was a matter of public notoriety, and talked of by the gentlemen who received it."

The officers understood that despite contrary appearances, the real nature of their quarrel in Utah with Brigham Young had been political rather than social or religious. From the beginning Young had governed the Territory without Federal interference, and he had every intention of continuing to do so. His decision to render powerless the United States courts in Utah had been no fanatic's arbitrary or eccentric whim; it had been made with a plain, practical end in mind—to keep non-Mormon intruders, like Judge Brandebury and Judge Brocchus, from exercising even the slightest power over his Mormon followers. To accomplish this, a crude expedient had been enough. In his capacity as governor, Young simply had refused to appoint any functionaries to the United States courts, so that after their arrival at Salt Lake City the Federal judges had discovered that there was not one officer in the entire Territory authorized to execute a writ or a warrant on their behalf, to summon a jury or to perform the other duties necessary to the normal operation of their courts. The result was that Judge Brandebury and Judge Brocchus had remained without employment, while all trials and legal proceedings continued to be held in the territorial courts, where the governor's wishes were understood in advance and where they were dutifully executed by Mormon judges, court officers and juries.

In their report to the President, the two justices and the secretary referred to a number of violent crimes, including several murders, which were said to have been committed recently in the Territory. Without exception the Mormon perpetrators, although known, had gone untried and unpunished. And what had seemed even worse to the Federal officers was the obvious fact that the rights and safety of the Gentile victims had been of no concern whatever to the governor of the Territory.

Occasionally, too, there were suspicions that the Church itself had been directly involved in a serious crime. One example was Howard Egan's notorious murder of a Gentile named Monroe. "It was reported," the officers wrote, "and believed by many, that the murder was counselled by the Church, or some of its leading members. . . . This rumor received much force from the intimacy between the offender and the leading members of the Church, before and after the commission of the offence. [Egan] was several weeks in the city . . . and it was common talk that he intended to kill Mr. Monroe; he was permitted to go out sixty or eighty miles to meet his intended victim, and none of these men who knew the fact lifted an arm or a voice to prevent the deed. He met Monroe, who was unarmed, invited him out of his camp, took a seat and talked half an hour with him, and then rose up, bid him farewell, and blew his brains out with a pistol! How many other crimes and offences were punished, or passed by, we do not know, for the governor was true to his declaration that 'the United States judges should never try a case if he could prevent it.'"

The Federal officers devoted considerable space in their report to the plight of the emigrants who, each year, in growing numbers, attempted to make their way west along the Oregon and California trails. "The City of Great Salt Lake," the officers wrote, "is an important point on the overland route to Oregon and California, for the emigrant to replenish his stores or to winter, if overtaken by the advance of the season. But the intimidation which is produced by the denunciations and conduct of the Mormon Church and people, upon citizens of the United States passing through . . . is such, as to drive the emigrant upon another route to avoid it . . . [for] no man dare open his mouth in opposition to their lawless exactions, without feeling its effects upon his liberty, his business, or his life. And thus upon the soil of the United States, and under the broad folds of its stars and stripes, which protect him in his rights in every part of the civilized world, there is a spot where the citizen is brow-beaten, and despoiled of his liberties as a free man, by a religious despotism."

Concluding their report, the officers made this final judgment of the Mormons: "These people," they said, "are now living upon the soil of the United States, and drawing their sustenance from it, free of charge. The government is paying their governor, judges, secretary, attorney, marshal, and Indian agents— allowing them to elect their own legislature and a delegate to Congress, and paying them out of the public treasury. They have received twenty thousand dollars for public buildings, and five thousand dollars for a library; and instead of [manifesting] respect and gratitude for these manifold favors, they are inexorable in their hatred, and ready and willing to plot the destruction of their liberal benefactor. . . . We have no doubt the evils complained of will suggest the remedy, and that the Government has the power and the inclination to maintain its dignity, and enforce obedience and respect to the laws, upon every part of the Territory where there is not patriotism enough in the people to do it."

The Federal officers were mistaken in their optimism, though. Even before their report could be examined by the President and Congress, Brigham Young's tireless eastern agent, Colonel Thomas Kane, already had gone to work and within a short time had gathered his allies together for a counterattack. Among them were such political luminaries as ex-Vice President George M. Dallas and Senator Stephen A. Douglas of Illinois, whose eminent reputations did much to assist Colonel Kane's efforts. Skillfully using the lecture hall and the drawing room, as well as the columns of several newspapers sympathetic to the Mormon cause, Kane had little difficulty in discrediting the Federal officers and dispelling any uneasiness the President might have felt concerning conditions in the Great Basin.

The truth was that neither then, nor during the following five years, did either the executive or the legislative branches of the Federal Government possess the interest or the will to deal with such a remote and ugly problem. In order to investigate the charges—and if they were sustained, to mete out punishment to the offenders—it would have been necessary to place the Utah Territory under a military government, with sufficient troops stationed in the area to re-establish public order and to quell any uprising that might occur; far easier to ignore the true state of affairs in the Territory, and from time to time, as the organic law required, appoint new Federal officers, who would head west to the Great Basin and carry out their assigned duties as best they could.

About criminals unpunished and crimes uninvestigated, the President and Congress did not care; the frontier always had been a lawless place, and clearly the Utah Territory was no exception. As for the fate of future emigrants who would have to pass through Mormon country—families of ordinary citizens from the New England or the Middle Atlantic states, from Illinois, Iowa or Arkansas—that, too, was really not a matter of concern to the officials in Washington. *Let the emigrant beware*, had become, in effect, government policy, and it would remain so for half a decade longer, while at the same time, Washington would vigorously encourage additional emigration to Oregon and California. That there were unusual risks to be encountered in the middle of the journey was well understood by officials in the administration of President Fillmore, and in that of his successor, President Franklin Pierce. But what was the point of needlessly calling such a disagreeable fact to the attention of the public and of reminding those Americans who might be thinking of emigrating that they would have to proceed west without benefit of Federal troops or of any other Government protection?

Chapter 19

For Brigham Young and his closest associates the first years in Utah were a time of exhilarating challenge and ceaseless activity. Spurred on by a belief that they were obeying the Will of the Lord and by a conviction of their own moral superiority to the rest of mankind, the President and his men began to explore fully their recently acquired kingdom, while making plans to extend it farther if possible and to fortify it against the Church's innumerable "enemies." At Young's direction several parties of Saints left their homes in or around Salt Lake City and emigrated to other sections of the Territory; they established several small towns and forts to the east, north and west of Salt Lake, a string of similar settlements to the south along the first three hundred miles of the important Southern Trail to California, and a major colony, beyond Las Vegas and the desert, at San Bernardino, in southern California itself. During the same period the Church increased its proselytizing efforts, sending missionaries to such exotic locations as Hindustan and Hawaii—then known as the Sandwich Islands—to Malta, the Cape of Good Hope and the Holy Land, and to many corners of the European continent, gaining in return thousands of new recruits, particularly from Great Britain, Switzerland and parts of Scandanavia. And in 1853 the foundation for a Temple was laid at Salt Lake City, an indication that at least for the time being the pragmatic, flexible leader of the Saints was prepared to build up the Kingdom of God in the Utah Territory, while awaiting the day when the strength of the Gentiles finally would be destroyed, the Millennium would begin and an army of Saints, fulfilling Joseph Smith's prophecy, would return in triumph to Jackson County, Missouri, the Promised Land.

Although Brigham Young was at the heart of every scheme and enterprise undertaken by the Church, and in large measure deserved the credit he received for the Saints' considerable pioneering achievements, it was equally true that he could not have accomplished what he did without the help of a small, well-disciplined band of zealous subordinates, who advanced the Church's interests with enthusiasm and carried out their autocratic leader's dictates without hesitation. For the most part these trusted collaborators had been members of the Church from its earliest days in Ohio and Missouri; they had grown gray and weather-beaten and, in some cases, a trifle portly, in the service of the Lord, and now, entering their forties and early fifties, they held all the important offices in the Church itself and most of the important ones in the civil government.

Each of these veteran Saints had his own particular abilities, and it was an indication of Brigham Young's acumen that he so often could recognize where such talents lay and, as a consequence, was able to employ his followers to the greatest advantage. Dimick B. Huntington, one of Young's numerous brothers-in-law, was an able frontiersman and pioneer. While still a young man he had farmed and fought in Missouri and Illinois and then had marched west to California as a member of the Mormon Battalion. Soon after his arrival in the Utah Territory he had shown an unexpected gift for learning the local Indian dialects and from then on had been assigned to work with different tribes on behalf of the Church. Because of his knowledge and experience, whenever the President wished to conduct an important private negotiation with the Lamanites, and was anxious to keep the matter from becoming public, he invariably called on Dimick Huntington to act as his confidential Indian interpreter.

As able a pioneer as Huntington, John Doyle Lee played a far more varied and important role in Church affairs. For two or three years, while farming near Salt Lake City, he served as a leader in the Church's "Seventies" and as secretary of the secret and immensely powerful "Council of Fifty." Then early in the winter of 1851 he was ordered to leave Salt Lake and settle in the south, where coal and other minerals had been discovered, and where emigration was about to begin. Obedient as always to the commands of the President, Lee complied with scarcely a murmur. Traveling south in the first emigrant train, and working with his immediate Church superior, the Apostle George A. Smith, Lee that year assisted in establishing the walled town of

Parowan in Iron County, 260 miles from Salt Lake City, and the following year went even farther south, exploring much of the area around the Virgin River, which lay beyond the rim of the Great Basin. Eager to build up the Kingdom, Lee later helped found a number of other southern settlements, including St. George and Harmony, introduced the cultivation of cotton and fruit to Utah's "Dixie" and helped to raise food for newly arrived emigrants, principally the Welsh miners who came to dig coal and iron and to work in the local mills. Nor were these the limits of Lee's activities. At one time or another he served as a representative in the territorial legislature, as probate judge, county clerk and assessor, and as farmer to the Indians for the district.

Although Lee was indeed a member of the inner circle of the Church, he occupied a position distinctly inferior to the Twelve Apostles and might have been thought of as a colonel, rather than a general, in the Army of the Lord. The Twelve, almost without exception, either were more highly educated or intelligent than Lee and perhaps because of this, had proved to be more popular and effective leaders. A majority of the Twelve had experienced the old troubles in Missouri and Illinois; some had been Apostles for more than two decades, others only since arriving in the Territory.

Although each Apostle was noted for certain special activities or achievements, all tended to share a number of skills in common—to be capable orators, efficient administrators and experienced pioneers. Parley P. Pratt, one of the original Apostles, was probably the most widely traveled; his eloquence was extremely useful in drawing new members to the faith, and so he usually was absent from Salt Lake City on a mission to some distant part of America.

By contrast, the Apostle Charles C. Rich traveled principally between Salt Lake City and southern California. As a youth, Rich had been a soldier in Missouri; he had risen steadily through the ranks of the Church, and once settled in the West, had become a member of the Twelve. Within a short time he joined with another of the Apostles, Amasa Lyman, in gaining Brigham Young's permission to found a colony in California, and after that his name always was associated with the ambitious enterprise at San Bernardino, on which he lavished so much of his energy and enthusiasm.

Among the Apostles, few had served the Church longer, and

none with more versatility and faithfulness, than the late Prophet's cousin, George A. Smith. In 1847 at Winter Quarters, while
the Mormon host was suffering from malnutrition and scurvy, it
was Smith who had saved many lives by persuading his fellow
emigrants to follow his own example and add pieces of raw potato
to their daily diet. After reaching Utah, Smith held office in the
territorial legislature and also appeared as an attorney in the
local courts; his first case was the successful defense of the Danite
Howard Egan, accused of the willful and premeditated murder of
James Monroe. Selected by President Young to take charge of
Utah's "Dixie," Smith played the major part in the founding of
the distant towns of Parowan and Cedar City and became, in
effect, the one Apostle most intimately concerned with the
southern section of the Territory. And in 1854, aware of his
associate's special talent for such work, President Young added to
Smith's responsibilities by naming him the Saints' official historian and recorder.

Leaders like Smith, Rich and Pratt were the Church's gifted
executives, and their greater abilities helped to distinguish them
from such subordinates as Lee and Huntington. The gulf between
the Twelve and their principal lieutenants was deep and unmistakable; yet at the same time, both groups of men were linked by
a number of common bonds. These included an unthinking
devotion to the Church, an eagerness to "consecrate the wealth of
the Gentiles" whenever there was no risk of apprehension or
punishment, a readiness to obey the President's commands under
every circumstance, and a belief that the Church's laws took
precedence over the laws of the Territory, the nation and even of
mankind. Dangerous bonds that shortly would involve all five
men—either directly or indirectly—in the affair at Mountain
Meadows and leave their names connected forever with that
legendary crime.

Despite the unremitting exertions of President Young and his
small cadre of assistants, the building up of Zion proved a slow
and formidable task. Several familiar problems continued to
beset the Church, among them its unresolved struggle with the
Federal Government for control of the Territory. Though no
doubt a source of considerable amusement in Salt Lake City, the
hasty flight of Justice Brandebury and his fellow officers actually
had settled nothing, and before long their places began to be
filled by a series of new Federal appointees, the first group named

by the departing president, Millard Fillmore, and their replacements by his undistinguished successor in the White House, Franklin Pierce.

As a concession to the special sensibilities of the Saints, and in an effort to mollify their hostile feelings, a majority of the new appointees were chosen from the ranks of the Church, and with a few notable exceptions, all such Mormon judges, territorial secretaries, Federal attorneys, marshals and Indian agents unhesitatingly complied with the wishes of President Young on every conceivable occasion. Among the Gentile officers, too, were a number who gave the Church no trouble; for the most part they either were so flattered or intimidated by the governor that they were willing and even eager to endorse his views publicly and to leave unchallenged his illegal acts and usurpation of power.

A few Gentile officers were not so obliging though, and invariably both the worthy and unworthy among them drew down on their heads the full wrath of the Church. Judges and other officials who insisted that the United States courts should function properly and that the laws of the United States should be obeyed came under close personal scrutiny, and a wealth of obscure "biographical material" was unearthed by Mormon scholarship, and anything to the officials' discredit—whether true or not—received the widest publicity. Occasionally with justice, and always with malice, those Gentile officers who refused to truckle to the governor were vilified as adulterers, carpetbaggers, grafters and drunkards, and branded as unfit to hold public office in a Federal territory where, it was claimed, the inhabitants were morally superior to the rest of their countrymen and where, as a result, crime itself had almost totally disappeared. Still, the offending Gentile officials kept arriving at Salt Lake City, occupied their posts for a time and then departed, only to be succeeded in turn by yet other officials who were equally unwelcome; for there seemed to be no dearth of Americans willing to endure the inconveniences of life in the Great Basin, either because, as the Mormons insisted, they sought financial benefits there or simply because they felt a common, old-fashioned desire to serve their country.

Among the Gentile officials who came to Utah few proved more valuable to Washington—or more trying to the leaders of the Church—than two Indian agents, H. R. Holeman and his successor, Dr. Garland Hurt. In 1851, Major Holeman had declined to leave the Territory with Judge Brandebury and the other Gentile officers; instead, he had chosen to remain behind at his post, and for almost three years after that, by means of letters smuggled out of the Territory, he managed to provide the Federal Government with invaluable information about the subversive activities of Brigham Young and other Mormon chiefs. It was Major Holeman who first disclosed that Young, interested only in the Church's welfare, was misusing his authority as superintendent of Indian Affairs. "His orders," Holeman wrote, "are obeyed with no regard to the consequences, and whatever is to the interest of the Mormons, that is done, whether it is according to the law, or to the interest of the government, or not."

On another occasion the major advised Washington of military preparations that were being conducted in the Territory, of the Mormons' frequent allusions to an approaching war with the United States and of the earnest enthusiasm with which the militia had begun to drill. At the same time he warned that the Saints hoped eventually to turn the Indians into military allies. "It is said upon good authority," he wrote, "that there is an effort being made to form an alliance with the Indians to resist the government, should it be determined to force authority in the Territory."

Major Holeman concluded by saying, "It may be prudent . . . to keep my name secret in relation to these statements. If it was known here that I had [made] such a communication, there is no telling what would be the result. I have heard them boldly assert that, if Brigham was to tell them to cut any man's throat, they would do it without hesitation. I make these remarks to let you know my situation."

After Major Holeman's resignation and departure, his observation post was filled by Garland Hurt, an alert and thoughtful man who soon reported to Washington that he suspected that the Mormons were planning to use a number of widely scattered Indian tribes, in the event of a future conflict with the United States. "At the last semi-annual conference of the Latter-Day Saints," Hurt wrote, "a large number of missionaries were nominated to go and preach to the Indians, or Lamanites. . . . Now, since my arrival in this Territory, I have become satisfied that these Saints have, either accidently or purposely [sic] created a distinction, in the minds of the Indian tribes of this Territory, between the Mormons and the people of the United States that cannot act otherwise than prejudicial [sic] to the interests of the latter. . . . My object in writing is to suggest that the attention of all superintendents, agents, and sub-agents, and all other loyal citizens residing . . . in the Indian country, be called to this subject, and that the conduct of these Mormon missionaries be subject to the closest scrutiny." Considering the sort of letters they forwarded to Washington, it was scarcely surprising that Indian agents Holeman and Hurt were so unwelcome in Utah, particularly since the leaders of the Church were indeed guilty of the illegal and treasonous acts with which they were charged.

In addition to its difficulties with the Federal Government and with numerous meddlesome officials appointed by Washington, the Church in Utah also had to contend with uncertain harvests and the threat of outright famine. During normal years the Saints could grow enough food to feed themselves and to sell their surplus meat and flour at a profit to emigrants passing through the Territory. But sometimes poor weather or swarms of insects greatly reduced their crops, and then they were faced with the prospect of living frugally, or even of going hungry, for there were no nearby markets where they could replenish their supplies.

The Church's self-imposed isolation also contributed to other problems. Separated from the closest midwestern settlements by a thousand-mile barrier of prairies and mountains, the inhabitants of the Great Basin either had to manufacture their own tools, vehicles, furniture and clothing or else import them at highly inflated prices. To conserve their limited supply of money President Young decreed that the Saints should become as self-sufficient as possible and not only raise their own food but produce the many utilitarian items needed in their houses and on their farms. While its members were applying themselves to these tasks the Church's scant capital, with a daring that verged on recklessness, was being committed to the Perpetual Emigration Fund and sent overseas, to subsidize the transportation of thousands of foreign converts from Europe to the new Zion.

In order to survive in their isolated mountain stronghold the Saints learned to adapt themselves to changing circumstances, and whenever fate provided an economic opportunity, the more enterprising among them stood ready to seize it. During the Gold Rush years an alert and industrious John D. Lee did extremely well for himself and the Church; one summer he led a private foraging expedition from Salt Lake eastward to the Green River and the Sweetwater, collecting along the way some of the valuable equipment discarded by the forty-niners in their frenzied rush to reach the gold fields of California; and when Lee returned with his booty of "powder, lead, harnesses, tools, food, clothing, cooking utensils, and almost anything that could be mentioned," it represented a small personal fortune for himself, and a generous gift, or tithing, for the Church. Other Saints, no less devout, also did their best to support the Church's needs; that same year a group of Mormon emigrants from Iowa delayed their passage to Zion long enough to operate a ferry at one of the strategic crossings of the Platte, where they collected $10,000 in tolls from the forty-niners, and then transported the money to Salt Lake City and handed it over to President Young.

For several years the Gold Rush fever provided the isolated Saints with an unexpected bonanza, but when the fever subsided their brief local prosperity subsided too. The forty-niners were followed by better prepared and equipped travelers, many of them farming families who felt no particular need to reach their destination quickly. As a result they seldom found it necessary or expedient to discard expensive possessions by the side of the trail or to trade exhausted horses or oxen for fresh but much less valuable animals. Moreover, while these welcome sources of income were drying up, the Mormons suffered an additional financial loss; because of their rumored abuse of earlier Gentile parties, a number of wagon trains had begun to avoid Salt Lake City and smaller Mormon settlements, and before long, President Young realized that this practice was depriving the Saints of a considerable amount of profitable commerce.

To make up the loss, and to persuade future travelers that they would be well received in the Great Basin, the President temporarily muted his criticism of the Gentiles and, instead, began to advise them how to cross the prairies safely, while also encouraging them to stop at Salt Lake City to purchase supplies. "For the benefit of the traveling public who intend to cross the Plains," Young explained to one midwestern newspaper in 1853, "I have deemed that a few suggestions might be timely and profitable. . . . Arriving among Indians, always be on your guard against surprise; and to enable you to do this, a sufficient number should join together, so that guard duty may not become too burdensome." Then the Prophet, having instructed the Gentiles on how to make themselves secure against Indian attack, was able to turn to commercial matters. "If you take Salt Lake on your route," he suggested, "you can procure many articles there much cheaper than to haul them. Groceries and all kinds of fitting up are expensive, [but] vegetables can generally be obtained, [and] flour, as good as any that can be purchased in the states, can be had in quantity, at a price not to exceed from $6 to $10 per 100 lbs."

The following year Young published a warning to prospective travelers, which, if examined in the full light of the Saints' own conduct along the trails to California, must surely rank as a rare masterpiece of cold-blooded hypocrisy. "From the information brought in by the last California mail," Young wrote in the *Deseret News*, "the emigration on leaving Bear River must be prepared to run a still harder gauntlet, for it is reported that a numerous and well-organized band of *white* highwaymen, painted and disguised as Indians, infest several points on the road, and drive off stock by wholesale, and recent murders are rumored from that quarter." According to Young, the brigands certainly were Gentiles. "It is presumed," he wrote, "that the Arkansas murderer, and a large number of associated outlaws and fugitives compose the robber band; men who have hitherto been in the habit of killing Indians, and probably some whites, for the sake of their stock, and a little booty." What Young neglected to mention, though, were the repeated Gentile assertions that it was the Mormons themselves who long since had adopted the custom of assuming Indian disguise before robbing and murdering parties of innocent travelers on the trails to Oregon and California, assertions that shortly were to be tested, beyond all reasonable doubt, on a quiet, deserted meadow, three hundred miles south of the Mormon capital.

Chapter 20

At the same time that Brigham Young was attempting to attract more Gentile transients to Salt Lake City, he also was engaged in an effort to prevent substantial numbers of his own followers from "turning Apostate" and leaving the Territory. Apostasty was a recurrent problem among the Saints, reaching one of its peaks during the early 1850's, not long after the Church's open espousal of polygamy. That doctrine severely tested the faith of many Mormons, and within a few months of its promulgation a new schism had erupted, led by an extremely unstable Saint named Gladden Bishop. Repudiating polygamy, and proclaiming himself the reincarnated Saviour, Jesus Christ, Bishop began to speak out boldly in public, and although his supporters numbered no more than a few score, their movement, for doctrinal reasons, was considered a grave threat to the orthodox Church. Because of this the verbal assaults soon launched from the pulpit against the heretics were unusually savage, even by the rude oratorical standards that prevailed among the Elders of Utah.

Benjamin Ferris, a Gentile official who was then serving as secretary to the Territory, witnessed much of the strong treatment bestowed on Gladden Bishop and his adherents. "On Sunday, the 20th of March, 1853," Ferris later wrote, "[Bishop] attempted to preach in front of the Council House, in pursuance of a previous notice, but the meeting, though perfectly orderly, was dispersed by the city marshal."

On the same day Brigham Young and other Mormon leaders preached in the Tabernacle. Young's speech, which was widely published afterward, was addressed at one point directly to the

Gladdenites. "I say to those persons: you must not court persecution here," Young warned them, "lest you get so much of it you will not know what to do with it. Do not court persecution. We have known Gladden Bishop for more than twenty years and know him to be a poor dirty curse. . . . I say again, you Gladdenites, do not court persecution, or you will get more than you want, and it will come quicker than you want it!"

Young next described a dream he claimed to have had, in which he'd seen two Apostates creep into the bed on one of his wives; after a brief dialogue, the dreamer had taken a large bowie knife and had cut the throat of one Apostate, saying, "Go to hell across lots!" And a moment later, when Young cried out in the Tabernacle, "Rather than that Apostates should flourish here, I will unsheath my bowie knife and conquer or die!" there was a great commotion among the congregation and many enthusiastic shouts of approval.

In the face of such flagrant intimidation the Gladdenite movement already was foredoomed, but nevertheless, on the following Sunday, the assault against its handful of members continued. Secretary Ferris' account gives a noteworthy picture of that day's activities. "On Sunday, the 27th of March," Ferris wrote, "the subject was again resumed at the Tabernacle by Elder Erastus Snow, in a sermon distinguished by its profanity and brutal ferocity. This was not reported in the *Deseret News*, and the substance of it can only be stated from memory. He began with the most sickening and fulsome adulation of [Brigham Young] . . . after which, by way of lashing himself into a fury, he poured forth a torrent of invective against the Gentiles. He then took up the Gladdenites, and hoped the Lord would curse and destroy them. He plainly told the audience that whoever should be the executioners of divine justice in this case, and slay the Gladdenites, their wives and children . . . would receive a crown of glory. The injunction to assassinate these sectaries was open and undisguised, and repeated in a variety of forms, and what is more to be lamented, was approvingly responded to by the audience. It was a sphere of murder, plain, palable, frightful and sickening. The picture was one which, once seen, can never be effaced from the mind—a *preacher* in the pulpit ferociously enjoining the murder of men, women and children, for a difference of opinion, and 2000 faces intently gazing upon him with fanatical approbation."

The collapse of the Gladdenite movement was immediate and complete, and possibly for this reason there were no later reports of injuries or punishment visited on those who had offended the President. Both before and after the Gladdenite affair, however, there was no lack of such reports, involving less fortunate offenders. All during the 1850's a variety of these stories circulated in the Territory itself, as well as in the East and in California; ugly stories that told of the criminal conduct of Governor Young and other Mormon leaders and of the violent and secret crimes committed at their bidding against those designated as enemies of the Church.

These stories, growing in numbers over the years, did not emanate from an isolated witness or two but from an impressively wide list of independent Gentile and Apostate sources. There had been the affidavits of two hundred forty-niners, signed in California, which had been included in Nelson Slater's early and futile petition to Congress; there had been the extensive report of Justice Brandebury and his fellow officers, compiled after their hasty flight from Brigham Young's mountain kingdom. Journalists and other curious travelers had stopped at Salt Lake City on their way to the Pacific Coast and, after inspecting the scene and talking with the Mormons, had sent off dispatches to eastern papers and magazines, reporting numerous felonies rumored to have been committed in the Territory. And from time to time an informative book, like the one written by Secretary Ferris, was published in Philadelphia, New York or Boston, describing the author's experiences and observations while a resident of the Saints' domain.

Not all Brigham Young's accusers, though, were government officials, journalists or Gentile travelers; some, like young Mary Ettie Smith, were former Saints who had emigrated to the West from Nauvoo and then had lived for a while in the Great Basin, until the conduct of their leaders finally had persuaded them to quit both the Church and the Territory. At the time it was no easy matter to escape from Utah, but the resolute Mrs. Smith succeeded in doing so, and after joining relatives in New York State in 1855, recounted her experiences to all who would listen, before authorizing the publication of a small book, two years later, which described her life as a Mormon in vivid detail and told of the people and the institutions she had left behind in the valley on the Great Salt Lake.

There were, quite naturally, a few minor inconsistencies of date and location in Mrs. Smith's narrative, and occasionally the professional writer who had been asked to prepare it for the press added a false and disconcerting stylistic touch; yet the final result, steeped though it was in melodrama, still carried with it an impression of honesty and truthfulness.

According to the account she gave, Ettie Smith—then Ettie Coray—had been thirteen years old when she had been taken into the Faith, along with her recently widowed mother and several sisters and brothers. Ettie's first husband, Wallace Henderson, whom she had married the same year, proved to be a Danite, and as a result of what she learned from watching and talking with him, Ettie soon began to question the morality of the Church and many of the acts of its then current leaders.

Before long Wallace Henderson announced his intention of acquiring a second wife, and following a period of bitter estrangement, Ettie demanded and received a divorce from Henderson, for she felt that the practice of plural marriage was utterly abhorrent. A year or two later she married Reuben Smith, who worked for a time in the department of Indian affairs, under agent H. R. Holeman. Unlike Henderson, Smith was an unenthusiastic Saint; indeed, he had entered the Territory as a Gentile, and there were rumors in Salt Lake City that he'd only become a Saint in order to gain the permission of the Church to marry Ettie. Eventually Smith was compelled, for his own safety, to flee to California, leaving Ettie behind as an unwilling hostage to the Church.

For five years, both before and after her marriage to Smith, Ettie lived in Salt Lake City. One of her brothers was a clerk, or secretary, to Brigham Young, and the Prophet was on terms of social intimacy with Ettie and other members of her family.

In her narrative, Ettie Smith stated that Brigham Young and several other Church leaders had been responsible for the planning and execution of more than a half-dozen serious crimes, including such felonies as robbery and murder. Ultimately Ettie herself was compelled to become an unwilling participant in their criminal activities, either eliciting information from the proposed victims or helping to allay any fears they might have left for their own safety, it having been made plain to her on each occasion, by the Prophet himself or one of his associates, that a lack of cooperation on her part would lead to prompt and severe punishment in this world and eternal damnation in the next.

Mrs. Smith, two years after escaping from Mormon control, appeared before a justice of the peace in Livingston County, New York, and signed under oath an affidavit in which she accused a number of Mormons of having participated in two of these crimes. The first case involved the robbery and possible murder of a Dr. Roberts, an elderly friend of Ettie's late father, who had known the Coray family during earlier days in Illinois. The affidavit read in part, "This deponent further says, that she was present in the year 1851; when said Brigham Young, governor of the Territory of Utah, 'counseled,' and directed the robbery of Dr. Roberts; and that afterwards she was present, when the said Dr. Roberts was robbed, at night, on the public highway, in pursuance of the instructions of the said Prophet, and Gov., Young; that said robbery was committed by Captain James Brown, now living in Ogden City . . . and Hiram Clawson, of Great Salt Lake City . . . and that she had good reason to fear that Dr. Roberts was afterward murdered by Brown and Clawson, and that she can furnish proof of many other similar crimes."

At another point in her affidavit, Ettie Smith swore "that in the year 1853, she was present when Brigham Young, General [Daniel] Wells and John and Wiley Norton discussed and adopted a plan for the murder of Wallace Alonzo Clarke Bowman, an American citizen, at that time engaged in the Mexican trade . . . and that said Bowman was murdered by direction of Brigham Young; and after the manner determined aforesaid."

The murder itself was committed by John Norton and his fellow Danite James Ferguson, and Ettie Smith's narrative revealed how the crime was arranged and carried out. Referring to her second husband, Reuben Smith, she said, "He had been employed by Major Holeman, Indian Agent for the Territory, to distribute the goods, consisting of beads, blankets, brooches, paints and the like, to some of the tribes; and by accident, a package of the paints used by the Indians had been left at our house. This fact, unimportant in itself, was known to John Norton. Just at night, Norton came to our house with John Ferguson, and asked for some of the paint, and made no reserve in telling us what they wished to do with it.

"The remainder of the story," Mrs. Smith said, "I learned from Norton and Ferguson themselves. They left the city on horseback, and that night, after dark, passed the house where Bowman had put up. Knowing the route he must take from there, they went to

Salt Creek Canyon, where they disguised themselves as Indians, by painting their faces, and putting on blankets and horse-hair wigs."

The wealthy trader, Wallace Bowman, had sent his main party ahead, hoping perhaps to deceive the killers, for by then he certainly must have realized that he had been marked for death, and that a number of Danites already were on his trail. The next morning, accompanied by two Spaniards, he drove his wagon into the canyon, where Norton and Ferguson were waiting in ambush. Each rose up, gave a loud Indian war-whoop, and fired at the trio, and the terrified Spaniards promptly turned and fled back to the city, one of them with a bullet hole through his hat. Bowman was struck by two rifle shots and fell dead in the bottom of his wagon. "Either wound," Mrs. Smith related, "was mortal; one hit him full in the breast, and the other in the forehead.

"The Spaniards," she continued, "upon their arrival at the city, went before a magistrate, at the suggestion of the Mormons, who affected great alarm, and made an oath that Bowman had been shot in Salt Creek Canyon by the Indians, one of them showing the ball through his hat, in confirmation of it; and this statement was credited among many of the Mormons, as among the Gentiles, and is so received to this day by the masses.

"A posse of the police," Mrs. Smith added, "were sent out to look for his body, and for the property, but returned, after a thorough search, without discovering either; and thus the matter was hushed up with the public. No part of his property, which must have been valued at many thousands of dollars, was ever discovered, as far as was generally known."

Ettie Smith soon learned that the body of Wallace Bowman actually had been brought into the city in the victim's own wagon, and was being kept at Norton's house until it could be safely disposed of. Mrs. Smith saw it there and had no difficulty indentifying the dead man. "I clipped from his head a lock of hair with my scissors," she later recounted. "I afterward gave this hair to Dr. [Garland] Hurt, then or afterwards Indian Agent of the Territory. . . . I had afterwards, and at different times, repeated conversations with the actors in this tragedy . . . from whom I gathered what I did not know of my own knowledge. Norton and Ferguson both acknowledged, in my presence, that they killed Bowman in cold blood; and what will perhaps appear singular to my Gentile readers, is [that] they did not consider it a crime. Hiram Clawson, who, it will be recollected, assisted at the robbery, and probable murder of Dr. Roberts, told me that the body of Bowman was given to Drs. Andrews and Williams, well-known physicians of the city, for dissection."

Mrs. Smith was not present as a witness when plans were made to murder a Gentile names Jesse Hartley, but her account of that crime was extremely significant because of the later corroboration provided by the murderer himself. Of Hartley, Mrs. Smith wrote, "He was a man of education and intelligence, and a lawyer by profession. I never knew where he came from, but he was a Gentile when he came, and soon after married a Mormon girl by the name of Bullock, which involved a *profession*, at least, of Mormonism. It was afterwards supposed by some that his aim was to learn the mysteries of the Church, in order to make an expose of them afterwards. At all events, the eye of the Prophet was upon him from the first, and he was not long in discovering, through his spies, good grounds for suspicion.

"Hartley was a fine speaker," Mrs. Smith related, "and he was named by someone, unacquainted with the fact that the Prophet regarded him with suspicion, as a fit person to be appointed missionary preacher among the Gentiles. As is customary in such cases, he was proposed in open convention, when all the Heads of the Church were on the stand; and the Prophet rose at once with that air of judicial authority, from which those who know him best understand there is no appeal, and said, 'This man Hartley, is guilty of heresy. He has been writing to his friends in Oregon against the Church, and has attempted to expose us to the world, and he should be sent to hell 'cross lots!'

"This was the end of the matter as to Hartley. His friends after this avoided him, and it was understood that his fate was sealed. He knew that to remain was death; he therefore left his wife and child, and attempted to effect an escape.

"Not many days after he had gone, Wiley Norton told us, with a feeling of exultation, that they had made sure of another enemy of the Church. That the bones of Jesse Hartley were in the canyons, and that he was afraid they would be overlooked at the Resurrection, unless [Hartley] had better success in 'pleading' in the next world than in this, referring to his practice as a lawyer."

About a year and a half later, when Mrs. Smith was making her way out of the Territory, she met Jesse Hartley's widow at a crossing of the Green River. Mrs. Hartley, she said, "had been a very pretty woman, and was at that time but twenty-two years old. I think she was the most heartbroken human being I have ever seen. She was living with her brother, who kept a ferry there, and he was also a Mormon. We were waiting to be taken over, when I saw a woman, with a pale, sad face, dressed in deepest black, sitting upon the bank, alone. The unrelieved picture of woe which she presented, excited our curiosity and sympathy. Accompanied by my sister, I went to her, and after some delay and the assurance, that although we were Mormons, we were yet *women*, she told us her brief story, without a tear."

Speaking to Ettie Smith and her sister, Hartley's widow said, "I married Jesse Hartley, knowing he was a 'Gentile' in fact, [though] he passed for a Mormon; but that made no difference with me, although I was a Mormon, because he was a noble man, and sought only the right. By being my husband, he was brought into closer contact with members of the Church, and was thus soon enabled to learn many things about us, and about the Heads of the Church, that he did not approve, and of which I was ignorant, although I had been brought up among the Saints; and which, if known among the Gentiles, would have greatly damaged us. I do not understand all he discovered, or all he did; but they found he had written against the Church, and he was cut off, and the Prophet required as an atonement for his sins, that he should lay down his life."

According to his wife, Hartley then attempted to escape, and "set out alone for the United States; thinking there might be at least a hope of success. I told him when he left me, and left his child, that he would be killed, and so he was. William Hickman and another Danite shot him in the canyons; and I have often since been obliged to cook for this man, when he passed this way, knowing all the while he had killed my husband."

A number of years later, in his confessions, "Bill" Hickman recounted his version of the incident, most certainly without any knowledge whatever of Mrs. Smith's earlier description of the crime. The Danite leader wrote: "Orson Hyde being the head of the Twelve, obedience was required to his commands, in the absence of Brigham Young, in all things, whether spiritual or temporal; and, in fact, the man who did not obey, had better leave when he could, especially those who might . . . give any intimation of a dislike to things that elsewhere would be an open violation of the law. . . .

"When we got across what was known as the Big Mountain, and into East Canyon, some three or four miles," Hickman said, "one Mr. Hartley came to us from Provo City. This Hartley was a young lawyer who had come to Salt Lake from Oregon the fall before, and had married a Miss Bullock, of Provo, a respectable lady of a good family. But word had come to Salt Lake (so said, I never knew whether it did or not), that he had been engaged in some counterfeiting affair. He was a fine-looking, intelligent young man. He told me he had never worked in his life, and was going to Fort Bridger or Green River to see if he could not get a job of clerking, or something that he could do. But previous to this, at the April Conference, Brigham Young, before the congregation, gave him a tremendous blowing up, calling him all sorts of bad names, and saying he ought to have his throat cut, which made him feel very bad. He declared he was not guilty of the charges.

"I saw Orson Hyde looking very sour at him, and after he had been in camp an hour or two, Hyde told me that he had orders from Brigham Young, if he came to Fort Supply to have him used up. 'Now,' said he, 'I want you and George Boyd to do it.' I saw him and Boyd talking together; then Boyd came to me and said, 'It's all right, Bill; I will help you to kill this fellow.'

"One of our teams was two or three miles behind, and Orson Hyde wished me to go back and see if anything had happened to it. Boyd saddled his horse to go with me, but Hartley stepped up and said he would go if Boyd would let him have his horse. Orson Hyde said: 'Let him have your horse,' which Boyd did. Orson Hyde then whispered to me: 'Now is your time; don't let him come back.' We started, and about a half mile on had to cross the canyon stream, which was midsides to our horses. While crossing, Hartley got a shot and fell dead in the creek. His horse took fright and ran back to camp."

Hickman then described the aftermath of Hartley's murder. "I went on and met Hosea Stout, who told me the team was coming close by. I turned back, Stout with me, for our camp. Stout asked me if I had seen that fellow, meaning Hartley. I told him he had come to our camp, and [Stout] said, from what he had heard, he ought to be killed. I then told him all that had happened, and he said that was good.

"When I returned to camp, Boyd told me his horse came into camp with blood on the saddle, and he and some of the boys took it to the creek and washed it off. Orson Hyde told me that was well done; that he and some others had gone on the side of the mountain, and seen the whole performance."

To such Danites as Bill Hickman, George Boyd and Hosea Stout, the murder of a Jesse Hartley was of no particular moment and required no explanations or apologies. To many Saints, however, murder still remained a reprehensible crime, an act that could be justified only as necessary under the most extraordinary circumstances. And so, on certain awkward occasions, even the highest Mormon leaders like Orson Hyde and Brigham Young himself felt obliged to dissimulate to their followers, and to conceal the fact that yet another victim had fallen to satisfy the Church.

"When supper was over," Hickman said, concluding his description of the Hartley incident, "Orson Hyde called all the camp together, and said he wanted a strong guard on that night, for the fellow that had come to us in the afternoon had left the company; he was a bad man, and . . . intended stealing horses that night. This was as good a take-off as [Hyde] could get up . . . it was all nonsense, [but] everyone that did not know what had happened, believed it."

Or else, Hickman might have added, if they did not believe it, they certainly had enough good sense to keep their doubts to themselves.

Chapter 21

Because most violent crimes in the Utah Territory were committed against obscure and powerless individuals like Jesse Hartley and Wallace Bowman, they usually passed unnoticed in the outside world, but the Indian attack on Captain John Gunnison's party of surveyors proved a far different matter. In this case the victims either were United States soldiers or civilian employees of the Federal Government, and their explorations in the West already had aroused considerable public interest, so that when news of the ambush was reported by local authorities, it immediately caught the attention of the entire country.

From the very beginning suspicions were voiced that the Mormons had organized the attack for their own ends and that Captain Gunnison, despite his earlier services on their behalf, had been ruthlessly sacrificed to current Church policy. A graduate of West Point, Gunnison first had visited Utah in 1849 as a member of Captain Howard Stansbury's exploration party, which that year had come to the mountains to make a topographical survey of the Great Basin. Having completed its assignment, the expedition then had spent a sociable winter in the valley, and two years later, in 1852, after returning home, Gunnison had published a book of his observations, a work considered extremely favorable to the Latter-Day Saints.

The Church, according to Gunnison, had undergone a complete metamorphosis since President Young had led his followers to the mountains a few years earlier. "This sytem," he wrote, "is not what it was in its first decade. Once it was aggressive, now it is on the defensive—then it was violent, now it is politic. The thousand mile wall of space uninhabited, hems it in, and renders it harmless. The industry of its supporters makes it useful to the country. They are more than an army against the Indians on the west. The weary traveler to the land of Ophir shares in their hospitality."

The next year Washington decided that Gunnison should test that hospitality a second time; the captain's orders were to return to the mountains and there to survey various routes for a transcontinental railroad that would run between Missouri and California. Perhaps Gunnison himself, remembering the pleasant reception accorded him on his previous visit, did not fully appreciate the risks that might be involved in his new assignment, but certainly few informed officials in Washington could have been deceived. The Government knew all too well that Gunnison's reappearance in the Territory would be viewed with intense hostility by Brigham Young, who never had taken the trouble to conceal his inflexible opposition to any attempt to build a railroad through his empire, for as both the Church and Washington clearly understood, the introduction of such a line would quickly end the Saints' almost complete isolation and with it at least some of the immense control Young wielded over his followers. Only one question remained unanswered: Would the governor cooperate with a Federal survey or attempt to disrupt its activities?

Having received his orders, Gunnison acted swiftly, gathered together a party of thirty-seven soldiers and civilians and in early summer left St. Louis for the Rocky Mountains. Proceeding westward, the expedition spent late August and all of September crossing what is now central Colorado, where the captain's experience and judgment preserved his men from harm, although at times, as one member of the party observed, he had to deal with Indian tribes "even more hostile" than the one encountered a few weeks later, with such tragic results, in the Great Basin.

Leaving Colorado at the beginning of October, the survey party made its way deep into Mormon country, successfully exploring long miles of rugged mountains and valleys, despite the inability of Captain Gunnison, on more than one occasion, to persuade any of the local Indians to act as guides. But then, most fortuitously, two Mormon brothers named Potter agreed to serve with the expedition, quite possibly having received instructions from Salt Lake City that they were to do so, and perhaps because of their timely appearance the captain decided to spend a few extra days in the field, inspecting the area around Sevier Lake, before yielding to the threat of approaching storms and retiring to the Mormon capital for the winter.

At this point the true course of events became more difficult to follow. According to the story that Brigham Young later told the eastern press, Captain Gunnison went to Fillmore City on the twenty-third of October to exchange a money order for $500 in gold. While the captain was at Fillmore, a Mormon resident purportedly warned him of the danger of an Indian attack, explaining that a month earlier an unruly party of Gentile emigrants, taking the southern route to California, had wantonly murdered a brave of the Pah-Vant tribe and that the victim's sons had sworn to avenge their father's death by killing the next Americans, or "Mericats," to appear in their midst. No evidence of this murder was produced afterward, nor did the survivors of the expedition later recall that their leader had received any such warning.

If Young's story could be credited, Gunnison now began to act with uncharacteristic rashness. On the following day he divided his small party into two sections and, despite the possibility of an Indian ambush, left behind most of his men and arms and set off with only eleven companions, including one of the Mormon guides, William Potter, to explore the land around Sevier Lake. That evening, according to Young, without taking the trouble to post an adequate guard or to select a safe campsite, Gunnison and the rest of his party carelessly bedded down for the night, completely unaware of a large band of Indians nearby who had come to the area to hunt ducks. In the morning these same Indians, realizing that they were undetected, had decided on the spur of the moment to exact their revenge; using bows and arrows they'd attacked without warning, and killed and robbed eight of the twelve men in camp, including Gunnison and Potter, four of the soldiers managing to escape the ambush unharmed, after being pursued on foot for several miles.

Such was the governor's story—which differed considerably from the testimony of the survivors. For example, Gunnison's men said that on the afternoon before the ambush the captain and the rest of the party had been fully aware of the presence of Indians in the neighborhood, as their numerous signal fires had been seen near the lake and along the Sevier River. No one had considered them particularly menacing, for there was no reason to; but as an ordinary precaution, when the party had bivouacked that evening the captain has posted an all-night guard, with each man, including Gunnison himself, standing a watch. And just after sunrise the next morning, the clever, obviously well-planned attack was launched not only with a storm of arrows but also with a considerable amount of rifle fire, although the Pah-Vants were said to have few if any rifles of their own.

In addition, unfriendly critics of Brigham Young were quick to point out another oddity: that the attackers had stolen the notebooks and scientific instruments of the survey party, when in ordinary circumstances no Indians would have recognized their value and so would have limited their plunder to such familiar items as food, blankets and clothing. The governor, for reasons of his own, made no effort to answer this dark innuendo, choosing only to say that as soon as he had learned of the massacre he had done what he could to restore peace to the area; that in order to recover the stolen property he had dispatched Dimick Huntington, the Indian interpreter, from Salt Lake City to the vicinity of Sevier Lake, and that before long Huntington had succeeded in recovering, from some friendly braves of the Pah-Vant tribe, all but one of the expedition's missing instruments and all the notebooks. Nowhere in his account did the governor convey a sense of regret over the fate of Gunnison and the others, nor did he indicate that he planned to inquire further into the matter in order to apprehend and punish the offenders, even though one of the victims, William Potter, had been a member in good standing of the Church.

The aftermath of the Gunnison Massacre was no less singular than the crime itself. From the outset Washington correctly assumed that Brigham Young's investigation would be dilatory and ineffective and that no arrests were likely to be made; therefore, President Pierce ordered Colonel E. J. Steptoe to lead three hundred artillerymen and dragoons west to California and, while en route, to halt in the Great Basin until such time as he could investigate the massacre and bring the murders of Captain Gunnison to justice.

Once at Salt Lake City, though, Colonel Steptoe soon learned how little a Federal officer could accomplish without the good will and cooperation of Brigham Young. Eventually, having found no other recourse, the colonel was reduced to the absurdity of consulting with the governor and asking advice from the very man he had crossed half a continent to curb and perhaps even to arrest. In answer to his queries, Young solemnly told the colonel that the Indians alone had been responsible for Gunnison's death and that if the Federal Government wished to gain custody of the murderers, suitable presents would have to be given to two chiefs of the Pah-Vants, Kanosh and Walker, after which the chiefs, in exchange, would yield up the worst of the offenders. Why Young, as superintendent of Indian Affairs, had neglected to take this obvious step himself, remained a question that the colonel undoubtedly was too diplomatic to raise and that, in any case, would scarcely have elicited an illuminating response from the Lion of the Lord.

Heeding the governor's advice, Colonel Steptoe proceeded south and offered appropriate gifts to the chiefs, receiving in return six members of the Pah-Vants who supposedly had been the most active participants in the massacre—three young braves, two squaws and an old man almost totally blind. A Federal grand jury was then impaneled, and after the squaws and the old man had been declared innocent of the charges and given their freedom, the three young braves, Ankle Joint, Sandy Hair and White Tree, were indicted for first-degree murder.

Considering that he was a responsible public official, Brigham Young's conduct now became most curious indeed. Before the trial could begin he privately instructed one of his ablest followers, Albert Carrington, to act as an attorney and demand the release of the prisoners on a writ of *habeas corpus*. A Gentile official, supreme court justice John Kinney, after hearing the plea, found no justification for releasing the three Indians and allowing them to escape trial by fleeing to the mountains, which they no doubt would have done; as a result, he denied the writ, but not before the country had been treated to the interesting spectacle of a territorial governor, sworn to uphold the nation's laws, covertly attempting to prevent the courts from performing their proper function.

In March 1855, at Nephi City, a Federal court was convened, with Justice Kinney presiding, and the trial of the three Pah-Vant braves finally began. The evidence seemed clear enough to a majority of the correspondents representing the nation's press, and their expectation was that the defendants would be speedily convicted of premeditated murder for their participation in the Gunnison Massacre. The defense evidently did not impress the correspondents, although it was conducted by Almon W. Babbitt, said to be the most eloquent of Mormon public speakers. Babbitt, acting on this occasion as Brigham Young's mouthpiece, offered a novel plea on behalf of his clients: that the Indians could not be convicted of Gunnison's murder or, indeed, of any wrongdoing at all, because at the time of the massacre the Pah-Vant tribe had been at war with the United States—an ingenuous argument that Brigham Young and his followers would soon adapt to other circumstances, and offer on their own behalf, as one of the principal justifications for a larger subsequent massacre.

After the witnesses had been examined and the attorneys had delivered their speeches, Justice Kinney summed up the case for the jury, informing the twelve Mormons seated in the box that only two findings were possible in the light of the evidence— either a verdict of not guilty or one of murder in the first degree.

The justice, however, was mistaken. By then Dimick Huntington, Brigham Young's useful Indian interpreter, had traveled from Salt Lake City to Nephi, bringing word from the capital that President Young did not wish his followers to return either a verdict of first-degree murder or one of not guilty. What Brother Brigham required of the twelve Saints in the jury box was a verdict of manslaughter, which would give the three braves, Ankle Joint, Sandy Hair and White Tree, a brief term of no more than three years in jail. When the jury concluded its deliberations, to the astonishment of assembled court officials and members of the press, its verdict was indeed one of manslaughter.

In much distress, Justice Kinney—often characterized as a Gentile official who invariably enjoyed the most cordial relations with the Saints—now turned to address some agitated words to the crowded courtroom. "The learned judge," one correspondent later wrote, "in dismissing the jury, stated that it was customary for the court to indulge in some remarks, as seemed fitting to the occasion. He said that a special term of court had been called, for a trial of great moment to the people of the Territory, and of great interest to the people of the United States. That the case for the United States had been clearly made out, but the jury, contrary to the law, the testimony, the instructions of the court, and in violation of their solemn oath before God, had returned a verdict of manslaughter. Although the Grand Jury had other business to present, he felt it his duty to say, that in view of these facts, the court *had no other business there, and was therefore adjourned.*"

Not long afterward the three braves apparently escaped from confinement and disappeared into the mountains, and on that final note, the story of the Gunnison Massacre came to a close.

Eight years had now elapsed since Brigham Young and the Saints had reached Great Salt Lake, determined to establish the Kingdom of God in the Utah Territory, and during these years serious charges had never ceased to be made against the Mormon leader and his principal confederates. In response to the clamor, Young had not deviated an inch from his original position—that his detractors, without exception, were liars, bigots and mercenary politicians of the most corrupt stamp, and that he and his innocent followers were yet again being defamed and persecuted for their religion's sake.

The familiar litany gained the Saints little credit in the East, and perhaps because of this a more plausible explanation for the Utah troubles was advanced by Mormon apologists like Colonel Thomas Kane. That a certain amount of lawlessness existed in Mormon country Kane did not deny, but after all, the frontier always had attracted a lawless element, and it was his opinion that compared with similar regions in Oregon and California, the Land of the Honey Bee actually was a place remarkable for the sober and orderly conduct of its citizens rather than for the number of its criminals and the magnitude of their crimes. Glossed over by Colonel Kane and similar idealists were the grave and specific accusations made against Brigham Young and the Church, none of which, it was true, ever had been legally proved nor ever could be so long as Mormon juries alone were impaneled in the Territory and while the Prophet himself remained in control of the Territory's courts.

And so the ninth year of Brigham Young's unrestrained rule began, bringing with it a brief and fearful epoch that reached its savage climax in a single extraordinary crime, a crime spawned by almost three decades of lawlessness, by a thirst for vengeance deliberately fostered as a matter of calculated policy and by the barbarous conviction—still so familiar in our own century—that the members of other societies and faiths were morally inferior beings and therefore had no right to justice, to freedom or even to life itself.

Chapter 22

For Captain Alexander Fancher, his wife Elizabeth and their eight children, and for several other frontier families in northwestern Arkansas, 1856 turned out to be a busy and decisive year. By this time the captain had returned from the West with an enthusiastic account of what he had seen in California; soon discussions began to be held with friends and relatives concerning the prospects for farming and trade beyond the Sierra Nevadas, and the desirability of organizing a wagon train to protect lives and property from Indian attack while on the long journey they would have to make across prairies, deserts and mountains.

One by one, about fifteen or twenty families, including the Bakers, the Mitchells, the Millers, the Dunlaps and the Camerons, agreed to join the proposed party, and having indicated a readiness to leave the following spring, husbands, wives and their older children all turned to the innumerable tasks that had to be completed before the day of departure. For men who were the heads of large families, like Alexander Fancher, William Cameron and "Uncle Jack" Baker, there were many strenuous days of planning and negotiation. Within a year's time buyers had to be found for houses, farmland and other real property; tents, stoves and additional pieces of field equipment had to be acquired to use on the journey; tools and firearms had to be put into good working order; new wagons had to be commissioned, and old ones carefully repaired, so that there would be few serious breakdowns along the hundreds of miles of rough trails that lay ahead.

During the autumn, seed had to be set aside for future

plantings in California and livestock culled of those animals that would be unable to keep up with the train. Money had to be collected, either in the form of paper bills that could be sewn inside blankets, petticoats or the lining of a coat or skirt, or else in the form of gold and silver coins that could be hidden almost as easily, and kept equally close at hand, as William Cameron demonstrated when he concealed his fortune within a hollowed-out portion of the family wagon.

By harvest time the women in the party were working at least as diligently as the men. A supply of food to last their families several months had to be gathered, prepared and stored. In every family, household possessions had to be sorted out and a division made between those items that could be taken on the trip, and those that had to be sold or given away; new clothing for eight, ten or a dozen family members had to be fitted and sewn, and old clothing stitched, patched and mended; and all the while the ordinary demands of life went on without interruption.

It was an active and exhilarating period in the lives of those who shortly would leave in the Fancher Party, as well as a period that called for sober reflection. Even such experienced pioneers as the Fanchers, the Camerons and the Bakers must have realized that this time they were embarking on a venture unlike any they had previously undertaken and that once the journey to California had been completed, it was doubtful if they would ever again return to their former homes or see those friends and relatives who had chosen to remain behind. And so the year closed on a note of expectation, mingled with a sense of approaching change and loss; a busy and decisive year, but essentially a conventional one, for the Fanchers and their numerous companions from northwestern Arkansas.

The year 1856, however, was anything but a conventional year in the distant Utah Territory. For the inhabitants of Deseret it was the beginning of a period marked by increasing social and political turmoil and by Brigham Young's decision to raise the moral standards of the Latter-Day Saints through a religious revival, afterward known as the "Mormon Reformation," a frenzied exercise that gave free rein to some of the darkest forces within the Church and eventually produced a number of acts that could only be described as bizarre, ferocious and horrifying.

Several considerations impelled Young to launch the Reformation when he did; perhaps the strongest was the fact that now, for

the first time since he had led the Mormon host into the valley of
the Great Salt Lake, he found himself subject to sharp and
frequent criticism from some of his most loyal followers. One
major source of discontent was the area's faltering economy and
the continued poverty of the average, hard-working Saint. Another was the current shortage of food in the Territory; the
previous summer a vast plague of grasshoppers had destroyed
thousands of acres of crops, and as a result, by the spring of 1856,
even such staples as potatoes and flour had fallen into short
supply, and among some of the poorest Mormon families conditions of near famine were said to exist.

Before many months had passed, the Saints suffered a fresh
calamity that did little to enhance the President's reputation for
wisdom or infallibility. Several years earlier the Church had
begun to experience a considerable financial strain, due in no
small measure to Young's ambitious and costly policy of transporting to Utah, through the efforts of the Perpetual Emigration
Fund, thousands of impoverished recruits from Denmark, Great
Britain and the rest of Europe. Unhappily, by 1855 the Church no
longer was able to meet all its financial obligations, and the
President saw that he had no choice but to reduce expenses. One
obvious way to do so was to bring future emigrants to Zion at a
cheaper rate, and with this in mind, Young decided to implement
a scheme he had devised a number of years before, the so-called
"handcart" method of crossing the western plains and mountains.

Afterward, like any other nimble-footed politician whose plans
have gone awry, Young tried to place the blame for the handcart scheme on others—in this instance, on certain of his
subordinates—but the attempt was as ignoble as it was unjust. In
a letter dated September 30, 1855, Young had written to Elder F.
D. Richards in Liverpool, "We cannot afford to purchase wagons
and teams as in times past. I am consequently thrown back upon
my old plan—to make handcarts, and let the emigration foot it."

Young had crossed the prairies and mountains three times
himself and well understood how much additional suffering his
plan was likely to bring, even under the most favorable circumstances, to those in the emigrant trains who either were extremely young, in poor health, or frail and elderly. But the building up
of Zion demanded painful sacrifices from the Faithful, and Young
shut his mind to the less palatable implications of his plan.
"Fifteen miles a day," he wrote to Elder Richards, "will bring
them through in 70 days, and, after they get accustomed to it,

they will travel 20, or even 30, with all ease, and no danger of giving out, but will continue to get stronger." Then Young concluded with this curiously ambiguous observation: "The little ones and sick, if there are any, can be carried on the carts, but there will be none sick in a little time after they get started."

In February 1856 a descriptive circular appeared in Liverpool, announcing the handcart scheme. Under the new arrangement, the P.E. Fund offered to transport a Saint to Utah for the sum of nine pounds, with half-fare charged for any infant less than a year of age. The vehicles were to be two-wheeled carts, made chiefly of wood, the only iron in their construction a thin tire. Each cart was to have two projecting staffs of hickory or oak, joined by a wooden crosspiece, and the owners were to place themselves between these shafts, in the manner of draught animals, prior to hauling their vehicles along the trail.

And so it was that during the summer of 1856 the emigrants from Europe arrived at Iowa City, where they were formed into separate companies for the twelve-hundred-mile westward trek to Zion. The first company or two left early enough and encountered only such hardships as might have been anticipated by anyone familiar with their equipment, the distance of the journey and the nature of the country through which they proposed to walk. A Gentile traveler returning East from Oregon that summer described one of these comparatively fortunate parties: "We met two trains," he wrote, "one of thirty and the other of fifty carts, averaging about six [people] to the cart. The carts were generally drawn by one man and three women each, though some carts were drawn by women alone. There were about three women to one man, and two-thirds of the women were single. It was the most motley crew I ever beheld. Most of them were Danes, with a sprinkling of Welsh, Swedes, and English, and were generally drawn from the lower classes of their countries. Most could not understand what was said to them. The road was lined for a mile behind the train with the lame, halt, sick, and needy. Many were quite aged, and would be going slowly along, supported by a son or daughter. Some were on crutches; now and then a mother with a child in her arms and two or three hanging hold of her, with a forlorn appearance, would pass slowly along."

Those in the final emigrant companies fared much worse. Because of poor organization and planning no carts were ready for them when they arrived in Iowa, and as a result, they were forced to delay their departure several weeks. Eventually the carts were delivered, but unfortunately, since they had been made of green wood, they did not hold up well on the trail. Having been issued no axle grease, the emigrants soon were compelled to use their meager allotment of bacon as a substitute. Food was short from the start, hastening the onset of disease; while the companies still were crossing Nebraska the daily allowance of flour for each adult Saint was reduced to ten ounces, with four ounces issued to children eight and younger; occasionally sugar, coffee and rice were dispensed as a supplement, until the supply of these items gave out.

The weather turned colder after the travelers left the plains, and the first snows came earlier than expected, slowing their advance and then trapping them at various points among the mountains. By the time news of their plight reached Salt Lake City and a rescue party could be sent to their assistance, it was too late to avert a disaster. Many of the exhausted, half-starved emigrants lost fingers or toes because of frostbite; worse still, out of one company of 400 people, 67 died along the trail, a considerable number frozen to death for lack of blankets and clothing. In a later company fatalities rose even higher before the last gaunt survivors trudged through Emigration Canyon and entered into the capital city of Zion.

Chapter 23

THE HANDCART AFFAIR reflected little credit on Brigham Young's leadership, and undoubtedly the Prophet felt that public attention should be immediately focused on a more desirable subject, preferably one that would emphasize the spiritual imperfections of the average Saint rather than the administrative shortcomings of his ecclesiastical superiors. Clearly a suitable distraction of this kind was needed, and it could scarcely have been a coincidence that within a short time the Mormon Reformation had been fully launched. Beginning slowly and then gathering momentum, the movement engulfed in turn the capital, lesser towns and remote outposts and villages, until at last the furious lust to punish and purify had swept into every corner of the Kingdom, often with the most appalling results.

Although Brigham Young was responsible for the course of the Reformation and could at any time have curbed its excesses or brought it swiftly to an end, it was Jedediah Grant, the mayor of Salt Lake City and Young's Second Counselor in the First Presidency, who in the popular mind was thought to have initiated the revival and whose name became inextricably linked with the extreme fanaticism of the period. Referred to on more than one occasion as "Brigham's sledge-hammer," the grim, spell-binding Grant hardly cut an engaging public figure, at least in the judgment of Gentile and Apostate journalists. A itinerant correspondent for the *New York Times*, having observed him speaking in the Tabernacle, described Grant as "a tall, thin, repulsive-looking man, of acute, vigorous intellect, a thorough-paced scoundrel, and the most essential blackguard in the pulpit."

Whether a blackguard or not, during the autumn of 1856, before his unexpected death from a fever, Grant, along with various Apostles, his fellow Counselor Heber C. Kimball and the Prophet himself, took to the speaker's stand with increased frequency and zeal, demanding on each occasion confession, repentance and rededication from the backsliding Faithful, whose faults it now was publicly announced had brought famine and other recent disasters to the Territory and whose wickedness had caused the delay, and perhaps the permanent postponement, of the Millennium. According to one eyewitness, "All were called upon to confess their sins, and to make known to God's servants the crimes of which they were guilty. The most extravagant language and bitter denunciations were uttered against the Saints, and strict, unquestioning obedience to the priesthood was commanded in all things, [along] with the consecration of body, soul and property to the Church."

By deliberate policy the fanatical contagion was allowed to flood out of Salt Lake City in every direction. "Elders were sent to various settlements," the same observer reported, "whose duty it was to excite people to confess their secret sins and reveal their private conduct to them and the bishops. Teachers were appointed in every ward and block, whose duties were to pry into every secret and learn the private history of every family. Men, women, and children were asked the most indelicate questions about private actions and secret thoughts. Husbands were asked inconvenient questions about relations with their wives, and wives about their husbands, by rude and ignorant teachers, and 'counsel' was given accordingly. Girls were counselled to marry into polygamy to old men, 'that they might be saved,' for young men were 'not tried' in the kingdom and could not 'save' the girls; and in many instances young women were forced to break off engagements with young men whom they loved, to gratify a bishop's preference, a missionary's feelings, or a great elder's desires. . . .

"A catechism was printed by authority of Brigham Young, and a copy of it was put into the hands of every missionary, elder, bishop, and teacher, who catechized with unblushing effrontery every member of the Church. Those refusing to answer were cursed and reported at the bishops' meetings as worthy to be disfellowshipped, and those who honestly told their feelings were likewise reported to the authorities. . . . Polygamy—notwithstanding the claims of the Utah writers—had not pre-

vented illicit intercourse among the sexes. No house of professional prostitution publicly opened their doors invitingly to
the Saints, but secret confessions showed that private evils
existed in the cities of the professed Saints which were not
surpassed by the inhabitants of many cities of 'Babylon'. . . .
Thefts, rougishness, cheating and lying were divulged, which had
been carried on for years."

Of all the incredible aspects of the Reformation, none was more
singular or sensational than the so-called Doctrine of Blood
Atonement, a dogma whose very existence was passionately
denied by the early Church and its most vociferous defenders.
The doctrine, as promulgated by Brigham Young and his close
associates, assumed that certain sins, like adultery or incest,
were so heinous that they could be "atoned for" only if the sinner
had his throat cut and gave up his life; as a consequence, it
became an act of "loving kindness" to shed the sinner's blood, in
order to save his soul from eternal damnation, a form of ritual
murder which, according to Young, had been implicitly endorsed
by Christ himself in the Gospels.

During the Reformation the doctrine was openly preached in
the Salt Lake City Tabernacle, a fact that could not be disputed,
thanks to the Mormons' indiscreet custom of publishing numerous sermons of the Prophet and other high-ranking Church
officers soon after their public delivery. Yet it would be a mistake
to assume that the Doctrine of Blood Atonement was first
conceived in the autumn of 1856, or that it burst into life
spontaneously while the Reformation was in progress. The truth
was that Young and his intimate collaborators, steeped in their
own original and perverse brand of Puritanism, long had accepted the validity of such a dogma and long had yearned for the day
when they would be at liberty to punish and shed blood without
restraint, not merely to save the souls of their errant followers, as
they themselves sincerely believed, but also to temporarily as-
suage, through the most brutal acts of suppression and violence,
their own subconscious rage against the rest of mankind.

Over the years this vengeful, thinly disguised desire to punish
and inflict pain on others had run like an ugly, menacing thread
through many of the public utterances of Brigham Young and
other Mormon leaders. One winter, a half-dozen years earlier,
there had been a shortage of corn among the Saints, and John D.

Lee, at that time often in the Prophet's company, noted in his
private journals what Young had said about the matter. "If those
that have [corn] do not sell to those who have not," the Prophet
had warned his followers, "we will just take it and distribute [it]
among the poor, and those that have and will not divide willingly,
may be thankful that their heads are not found wallowing in the
snow."

As early as 1852, while a resident in the Utah Territory, the
unfortunate explorer Captain John Gunnison had become convinced that certain high Mormon officials believed in the Doctrine
of Blood Atonement. "Witnesses are seldom put on oath in the
lower courts," Gunnison wrote, "and there is nothing known of
the 'law's delay,' and the quibbles whereby the ends of truth and
justice may be defeated. But they have a criminal code called 'The
Laws of the Lord,' which has been given by revelation and not
promulgated, the people not being able quite to bear it, or the
organization still too imperfect. It is to be put in force, however,
before long, and when in vogue, all grave crimes wll be punished
and atoned for by cutting off the head of the offender. The
regulation arises from the fact that 'without shedding of blood
there is no remission.'"

Quite independently, other Gentile and Apostate observers had
noted from time to time the frequent employment of violent
words—and occasionally the commission of violent acts—by
various Mormon officials. Nelson Slater, in his early petition to
Congress, had written: "Brigham Young and many of the Mormons are in the frequent habit of using threatening language
toward the [Gentile] emigrants. They often talk of cutting off
people's heads, cutting their throats, and the like." And later in
the same year, Judge Brocchus and his fellow officers had
described an angry tirade of Brigham Young's, delivered to an
audience of two thousand followers, which had ended with the
Prophet's declaration "that if there was any more discussions,
there would be pulling of hair and cutting of throats!"

As early as March 1854, Jedediah Grant had delivered a
memorable sermon on sin and punishment in the Salt Lake City
Tabernacle, during which he candidly confirmed his belief in
Blood Atonement and in the desirability of murdering both the
enemies of the Church and those Saints who had broken their
sacred covenants. "Then what ought this meek people who keep
the commandments of God do unto [the covenant breakers]?

Grant had asked rhetorically. "'Why,' says one, 'they ought to pray to the Lord to kill them.' [But] I want to know if you would wish the Lord to come down and do all your dirty work? . . . When a man prays for a thing, he ought to be willing to perform it himself. . . . I wish we were in a situation favorable to our doing that which is justifiable before God, without any contaminating influence of Gentile . . . laws and traditions, that the people of God might lay axe to the root of the tree, and every tree that bringeth not forth good fruit might be hewn down. . . . Putting to death the transgressors would exhibit the law of God."

And finally, two years later, in March 1856, as complaints began to arise concerning the shortage of food and other troubles in the Territory, Brigham Young took to the speaker's stand and warned his discontented followers of what lay ahead if they did not change their ways. "The time is coming," he said, "when we shall take the old broadsword, and ask, 'Are you for God?' and if you are not heartily on the Lord's side, you will be hewn down!'"

By September there had been no improvement, and having decided to set off the Reformation, Young publicly explained and endorsed the Doctrine of Blood Atonement. Addressing an audience in the Tabernacle on the twenty-first of the month, he declared, "There are sins that men commit for which they cannot receive forgiveness in this world, or in that which is to come; and if they had their eyes open to their true condition, they would be perfectly willing to have their blood spilt upon the ground, that the smoke thereof might ascend to heaven as an offering for their sins, and the smoking incense would atone for their sins. . . .

"I know," Young continued, "when you hear my brethren telling about cutting people off from the earth, that you consider it is strong doctrine; but it is to save them, not to destroy them. . . . There are sins that can be atoned for by an offering upon an altar as in ancient days; and there are sins that the blood of the lamb, of a calf, or of turtle doves cannot remit, but they must be atoned for by the blood of the man."

And on the same day, Jedediah Grant offered his opinion on the subject, in words that avoided any ambiguity: "I say there are men and women here," he told the congregation, "that I would advise to go to the president immediately, and ask him to appoint a committee to attend their case, and then let a place be selected, and let the committee shed their blood."

Improbable as it may seem, such committees actually were

formed and ritual murders actually committed against a number of repentant and unresisting Saints. In his confessions, written long afterward, John D. Lee described at length one well-remembered case; it involved a Danish emigrant, Rosmos Anderson, who at the time had been living with his family at Cedar City, far to the south of the Mormon capital. Anderson had a young stepdaughter, and the two fell in love, but unfortunately the girl also was desired by Philip Klingensmith, the local bishop. "At one of the meetings during the Reformation, Lee said, "Anderson and his stepdaughter confessed that they had committed adultery, believing when they did so that Brigham would allow them to marry." The sinners' request was denied, but at first no harm seemed to have been done; for, having confessed their sins, they were rebaptized and restored to full fellowship in the Church.

Before long, though, a special council, headed by Bishop Klingensmith, was appointed to try the stepfather for his transgressions, and without being given a chance to defend himself, or to make a statement, he was condemned to death for violating his covenants. "Klingensmith went to Anderson," Lee wrote, "and notified him that the orders were that he must die by having his throat cut, so that the running of his blood would atone for his sins. Anderson, being a firm believer in the doctrines and teachings of the Mormon Church, made no objections, but asked for half a day to prepare for death. His request was granted. His wife was ordered to prepare a suit of clean clothing, in which to have her husband buried, and was informed that he was to be killed for his sins, she being directed to tell those who should enquire after her husband, that he had gone to California."

The bishop and three of his helpers then dug a grave in a deserted field near Cedar City, and about midnight, went to Anderson's house and told him to make ready to obey counsel. "Anderson got up," Lee said, "dressed himself, bid his family goodbye, and without a word of remonstrance, accompanied those that he believed were carrying out the will of the 'Almighty God.' They went to the place where the grave was prepared; Anderson knelt upon the side of the grave and prayed. Klingensmith and his company then cut Anderson's throat from ear to ear and held him so that his blood ran into the grave.

"As soon as he was dead they dressed him in his clean clothes, threw him into the grave and buried him. They then carried his bloody clothing back to his family, and gave them to his wife to wash, when she was again instructed to say that her husband was in California. She obeyed their orders."

During the course of the Reformation, not every Saint was as obedient to the counsels of the Church as Rosmos Anderson, a fact vividly demonstrated by the notorious case involving an innocent couple and Warren Snow, the elderly bishop of the town of Manti. According to Lee's confessions, the bishop of Manti already had a number of wives, when a blond, buxom young woman of the town happened to catch his fancy. Snow courted her assiduously, only to be refused on the reasonable ground that several months previously she had become happily engaged to a young Saint in the town, with whom she was deeply in love.

This rejection in no way discouraged the elderly bishop, who told the girl, Lee wrote, "that it was the will of God that she should marry him, and she must do so; that the young man could be got rid of, sent on a mission, or dealt with in some way, so as to release her from her engagement—that, in fact, a promise to the young man was not binding, when she was informed that it was contrary to the wishes of the authorities."

The girl, however, still refused to break off her engagement and marry Bishop Snow, even after weeks of intense urgings by various members of the local Church hierarchy and by her own parents as well. In the face of such resistance the bishop then changed tactics, calling on the young man himself, and commanding him to give up his fiancé. But the young man, in his turn, refused. At this point, according to Lee, "he was promised Church preferment, celestial rewards, and everything that could be thought of—all to no purpose. He remained true to his intended, and said he would die before he would surrender his intended wife to the embraces of another.

"This *unusual* resistance of authority by the young people," Lee wrote, "[only] made Snow more anxious than ever to capture the girl. The young man was ordered to go on a mission to some distant locality, so that the authorities would have no trouble in effecting their purpose of forcing the girl to marry as they desired. But the mission was refused by the still contrary . . . young man.

"It was then determined that the rebellious young man must be forced by harsh treatment to respect the advice and orders of the Priesthood. His fate was left to Bishop Snow for his decision. He decided that the young man should be castrated; Snow saying,

'When that is done, he will not be liable to want the girl badly, and she will listen to reason when she knows that her lover is no longer a *man.*'

"It was then decided," Lee continued, "to call a meeting of the people who lived true to counsel, which was to be held in the school-house at Manti, at which place, the young man should be present, and dealt with according to Snow's will. The meeting was called. The young man was there, and was again requested, ordered and threatened, to get him to surrender the young woman to Snow, but true to his plighted troth, he refused to consent to give up the girl. The lights were then put out. An attack was made on the young man. He was severely beaten, and then tied with his back down on the bench, when Bishop Snow took a bowie-knife and performed the operation in a most brutal manner, and then took the severed portion from his victim and hung it in the school-house on a nail, so that it could be seen by all who visited the house afterward.

"The party then left the young man weltering in his blood, and in a lifeless condition. During the night he succeeded in releasing himself from his confinement, and dragged himself to some haystacks, where he lay until the next day, when he was discovered by his friends. The young man regained his health, but has been an idiot, or quiet lunatic, ever since."

The affair was almost over—but not quite. "After this outrage," Lee said, "old Bishop Snow took occasion to get up a meeting at the school-house, so as to get the people of Manti, and the young woman he wanted to marry, to attend the meeting. When all had assembled, the old man talked to the people about their duty to the Church, and their duty to obey counsel, and the dangers of refusal, and then publicly called attention to the mangled parts of the young man, that had been severed from his person, and stated that the deed had been done to teach the people that the counsel of the Priesthood must be obeyed." And then, Lee added, "the young woman was soon after forced into being sealed to Bishop Snow."

In Lee's account of the affair, Brigham Young exhibited great anger when first informed of the bishop's conduct, although apparently the Mormon leader—and governor of the Territory— soon was able to master his powerful emotions and turn to more practical considerations. "Brigham Young was very mad," Lee wrote, "but afterward did nothing against Snow. He left him in charge as Bishop of Manti, and ordered the matter hushed up."

As time passed, the religious turmoil of the Reformation began to be matched by a similar political frenzy; United States officials were subjected to public insult and threatened with physical harm, and before long the uneasy truce between the Church and the Federal Government had broken down completely.

In the Mormon view of things, any number of recent Gentile "provocations" amply justified the Church in taking up arms and renewing the old, bitter conflict with Washington. Within the past few months the Saints had once again petitioned Congress for statehood—"motivated solely by the highest feelings of patriotism"—and yet their earnest, well-meant petition had been peremptorily denied. In addition, President Pierce once again had appointed a new set of officers to the Territory, and according to Brigham Young's assertion, these corrupt time-servers had come to Utah with no other purpose than to plunder the defenseless Saints of their money and land, while flagrantly denying them their just and equal rights as American citizens. What then was more reasonable than to drive these venal office-seekers from the Kingdom of God and to reassert the intention of the Latter-Day Saints to follow God's laws and rule themselves?

No doubt adding considerable fuel to the Prophet's anger, frustration and desire for revenge was the increasingly bleak political outlook that the Mormons faced. During recent months disapproval of the Saints had increased sharply throughout the rest of the nation, thanks chiefly to reports describing their violent crimes, their subversive dealings with the Indians, their harassment of government officials and especially their clamorous flaunting of the Doctrine of Plural Wives, for of all the Mormons' various offenses, it was polygamy, rather than assault or theft, subversion or even murder, that most deeply affronted the moral sensibilities of mid-nineteenth-century America.

The results was that by the summer of 1856 the Church had never been so lacking in Gentile supporters, nor had its spiritual pretensions been so universally scorned. In June the two leading political parties held their nominating conventions, and from neither gathering could the Mormons draw much satisfaction. The Democrats, meeting in Cincinnati, the Queen City on the Ohio, were torn by dissension over the slavery question, and although a majority of the delegates ostensibly favored the Doctrine of Popular Sovereignty for the territories—and by extension, perhaps, the right of the Saints to practice polygamy in Utah—any Mormon observer with the least knowledge of the party's leaders would have put little trust in Democratic support.

From the newly formed Republican party and its Presidential candidate, the noted western explorer Colonel John C. Frémont, it was all too evident that only the worst was to be expected. A plank in the party's election platform accurately stated that the Constitution gave Congress sovereignty over all Federal territories, and then went on to declare, with a savage bluntness well calculated to win the votes of millions of monogamous northerners, that it was "both the right and duty of Congress to prohibit in the territories those twin relics of barbarism—polygamy and slavery."

Unquestionably anti-Mormonism was on the rise, and as an indication of this, a bill was soon introduced into the House of Representatives which would have made polygamy illegal anywhere in the United States and its territories. Even more outrageous, from the Prophet's point of view, was the gradual—and allegedly cynical—abandonment of the Mormon cause by the Saints' former political champion and protector, Senator Stephen A. Douglas of Illinois. Exactly when the senator decided to turn away from his former friends is far from clear, but by 1856 his voice in the Senate no longer could be depended upon by Brigham Young and the Church, and by the following year, when Senator Douglas delivered a major speech in Illinois on territorial affairs and other matters of contemporary interest, it was certain that their former ally had changed into an implacable foe.

Recent reports from the Utah Territory, the senator said, seemed to indicate that a state of utter lawlessness existed there; that a substantial majority of its inhabitants were aliens who voted and held public office in violation of the Constitution; that every Saint was bound by strong and dreadful oaths to obey the commands of Brigham Young in all things; that the Church had formed treasonous alliances with several Indian tribes; and that it had organized Danite bands to rob and murder American citizens.

"Under this view of the subject," the senator told his audience, "I think it is the duty of the President . . . to remove Brigham Young and all his followers from office, and to fill their places with bold, able, true men; and to cause a thorough and searching investigation into all the crimes and enormities which are alleged to have been perpetrated daily in that territory under the direction of Brigham Young and his confederates, and to use all the military force necessary to protect the officers in the discharge of their duties and to enforce the law of the land."

Faced with so broad and grave a challenge to his authority, a more rational leader might have drawn back and sought an accommodation with his numerous and powerful enemies; but Brigham Young, after enjoying almost a full decade of dictatorial power, had become too self-willed, too vain and too imperious to accept any accommodation except one temporarily forced on him by overwhelming necessity. Therefore, the Prophet turned his back on compromise and, instead, loosed his followers against every Federal official under his jurisdiction, until he succeeded, within a few months, in driving almost every United States officer from the Territory.

Among those who came to feel that it no longer was healthy to remain in Utah were two Gentile justices of the supreme court, W. W. Drummond, and George P. Stiles. Drummond, a seemingly dissolute and intemperate man, and certainly a fiery enemy of the Church, often had clashed openly with Brigham Young and his associates, and although some of his accusations had indeed been exaggerated or unfounded, later events nevertheless tended to prove, after Drummond's retirement to the safety of Illinois, that a majority of those accusations had been all too true.

Drummond's fellow justice, George P. Stiles, was an Apostate Saint, and because he had left the Church he was regarded with particular animus by President Young and the Mormon hierarchy. To make matters worse for Stiles, it had become evident that he soon intended to decide against the Church, and for the Federal Government, in the critical question of court jurisdiction; as a consequence, a Mormon mob, incited by Hosea Stout, the acting United States attorney, and by several other well-known Danite leaders, invaded Stiles's courtroom and threatened the judge with injury or death unless he decided the case in the Church's favor. Some days later, while Stiles was absent, another mob broke into his private office, stole the records of the United States District Courts and set fire to the judge's law books, correspondence and other personal papers.

When Justice Stiles returned to his office and saw the destruction, he naturally assumed that the Federal records had been burned, along with his own property. Choosing to resist no longer, he fled to the East, where he made a full report of the crimes committed against him and his court. His disclosures further discredited the Mormons, and although Brigham Young and various Church apologists later tried to make capital of the fact that the records of the district courts actually had *not* been destroyed, the conduct of the mobs and the treatment accorded to Justice Stiles proved all too clearly that in Utah the rule of law—if indeed it ever had prevailed—by now was nothing more than a thing of the past.

For several months, despite intense harassment, a small number of Federal officers, including the surveyor general, David H. Burr, refused to desert their posts for sanctuary in California or the East, hoping against hope that sufficient help would arrive so that they might remain in Utah until the end of their tours of duty. Early in 1857, as winter finally drew to a close, Burr dispatched an official letter from Salt Lake City to Washington, indicating how desperate their condition had become. "The United States courts," he wrote, "have been broken up and driven from the Territory, and the Utah courts, with their usurped power, will not recognize the United States laws. . . . The fact is these people repudiate the authority of the United States in this country, and are in open rebellion against the general government."

As for himself, Burr said, "For the last three months my friends have considered my life in danger. . . . I have been cursed and denounced in their public meetings, and the most diabolical threats made against me. . . . Several houses of 'apostate Mormons' have been pulled down, and at one time an attack was contemplated on the office, to destroy its contents, and 'wipe me out.' [But] I got notice of it in time, and kept well guarded."

After interminable months of silence, Burr and the few remaining Gentile officials were eagerly awaiting the next mail and news from the East. "If it should bring us no tidings or assurance of protection from the United States," the surveyor general said, "every Gentile officer may be compelled to leave the Territory. We find our position a critical one. We are by no means sure that we would be permitted to leave, for it is boldly asserted we would not get away alive.

"The same threats have been made against disaffected Mormons. We were inclined to think them idle menaces, until a few days since, when three men were killed at Springville, sixty miles from this place, for making the attempt. They were shot, their throats cut, and their bowels ripped open. Another party was fired upon, and three of them wounded, one of them seriously. These outrages are perpetrated by Mormons, and we have every reason to believe by the orders of Brigham Young. No efforts are made by the authorities to bring the perpetrators to justice." This letter of Burr's, the last official one he wrote before his flight to the East, was dated 28 March 1857. On the following morning, well over a thousand miles away, the unsuspecting Fancher Party, having assembled for the summer's journey, with horsemen in the lead and women and children riding in the wagons, set off unhurriedly toward the neighboring Indian territory, and an eventual passage through Mormon country, to California.

Chapter 24

ALL DURING the spring and summer of 1857, thousands of travelers could be seen making their way slowly across the open plains and through the narrow mountain passes of western America, following two or three well-worn trails to Utah, Oregon and California. Most members of this annual emigration were peaceable pioneers—farmers, traders, artisans and laborers—who long had dreamt of finding a better life in the fabled lands of the West, and who now were putting their dreams to the hard test of reality.

But this year travelers of a different sort were scattered among the stream of ordinary settlers. The United States had elected a new President, James Buchanan, who shortly after entering office had decided that a decade of insolence, subversion and even open defiance was quite sufficient and that henceforth the laws of the United States were to be obeyed in the Utah Territory and the authority of the United States was to be supreme. To bring about this desirable but elusive goal, a Gentile governor was to be appointed to succeed Brigham Young, and an army of some 2,500 men was in the process of being assembled to accompany him to Salt Lake City, with a few advance units already on the march, including companies of the Fifth and Tenth Infantry regiments, and a battery of the Fourth Artillery. Also heading West were twenty-five or thirty trains of cattle, driven chiefly by youthful, inexperienced civilian teamsters, only recently hired in several southern and border states; the animals they drove were to be delivered to the Army at Salt Lake City, where they would furnish the soldiers with fresh meat during the winter months while the expeditionary force was carrying out whatever occupation duties the situation might call for.

Among the hundreds of anonymous military and civilian parties inching their way across the prairies, the Fancher Train almost alone could have been singled out and identified, thanks to its unusual size and the evident prosperity of its twenty or twenty-five families; indeed, at least one sharp-eyed fellow voyager, an army doctor en route to join his unit, did recall a year later that he had spent several pleasant hours in the train's company and that he had especially noted an elegant carriage—stags' heads emblazoned on its panels—in which a number of the ladies from Arkansas had been riding. Yet for the most part the Fancher Party attracted little attention and proceeded along the trail with no great stir, much as smaller and less prosperous parties did, and because of this, and because all the papers in the train itself were subsequently destroyed, in later times no one could say for certain exactly when the Arkansas travelers might have reached a particular landmark or exactly how they had fared at each and every turn of their westward trek.

On the other hand, a number of contemporary explorers and adventurers passed over the same terrain and then wrote voluminously of their impressions, and from these accounts it is easy enough to judge what sort of country the Fanchers and their companions must have journeyed through after leaving Fort Smith, and what sort of common pioneering experiences they undoubtedly met with while on their travels.

At first the Fancher Party either headed directly north to Leavenworth, Kansas, one of the starting points at the eastern end of the Oregon Trail, or else set off north by northwest and followed the Arkansas River upstream before turning north and passing across a hundred miles or so of unmarked prairie, to reach the Platte River and the Oregon Trail somewhere in the neighborhood of Fort Kearney, Nebraska; along both routes the land was rather flat though sometimes broken by successions of low hills, with plentiful grass for the party's cattle, and stretches of thick and attractive woodlands. Small game and birds were in good supply, especially prairie hens, and the men of the party, being excellent marksmen, no doubt were able to add more than one tasty dish to the usual bill of fare.

Once they were at the Platte, conditions began to change; the ground by the riverbank became rutted with wheel tracks left by earlier emigrants, and the trail itself grew crowded with a steady flow of travelers; grass for the cattle was harder to find, and now and then it was thought expedient to make a short excursion away from the river in order to obtain additional forage.

A few years before, a young adventurer from New England, Francis Parkman, had followed the same route along the Platte and in his classic narrative, *The Oregon Trail*, had described the country that travelers had to traverse as they journeyed from Fort Kearney to Fort Laramie, Wyoming, some four hundred miles to the west. "During the whole of our trip," Parkman said, "we [passed] up the middle of a long sandy plain, reaching like an outstretched belt nearly to the Rocky Mountains. Two lines of sand hills, broken often into the wildest and most fantastic forms, flanked the valley at the distance of a mile or two on the left and right. . . .

"Before and behind us, the level monotony of the plain was unbroken as far as the eye could reach. Sometimes it glared in the sun, an expanse of hot, bare sand; sometimes it was veiled by long coarse grass. Skulls and whitened bones of buffalo were scattered everywhere; the ground was tracked by myriads of them, and often was covered by circular indentations, where the bulls had wallowed in hot weather. The river itself [was] a thin sheet of rapid, turbid water, half a mile wide, and scarcely two feet deep. Its low banks . . . [were] of loose sand, with which the stream [was] so charged that it grated on the teeth in drinking."

Because of their early departure from Fort Smith, the Fanchers and their companions already had advanced so far west along the Oregon Trail that they did not encounter the northward passage of the buffalo herds, as the huge animals arrived by the thousands in early July, to feed and water at the Platte; consequently, the hunters of the party had no chance to add fresh buffalo tongues and steaks, or dried buffalo meat, to the train's gradually dwindling food supply; happily, however, this also meant that none of the party's cattle were stampeded, to become permanently lost among the buffalo herds, a common misfortune on the plains which could, at a single stroke, cost a careless or inexperienced party much of its capital, its best means of locomotion and its principal reserves of food.

While the Fancher Train was making its way steadily through Kansas and Nebraska toward the distant barrier of the Rockies, the summer advanced and the days grew hotter; often, though, by late afternoon the weather suddenly would change, and then the travelers would find themselves subject to a prodigious and chilling storm. At one point in his narrative, Parkman described a hard day's ride across the plain, and then the swift approach of a typical midsummer's deluge. "The sun beat down on us, with a sultry, penetrating heat," he wrote, "and as our party crept slowly along . . . the horses hung their heads . . . and the men slouched in the easiest position in the saddle. At last, toward evening, the old familiar black heads of thunder-clouds rose fast above the horizon, and the same deep muttering of distant thunder . . . began to roll hoarsely over the prairie.

"Only a few minutes elapsed before the whole sky was densely shrouded, and the prairie and some clusters of woods in front assumed a purple hue beneath the inky shadows. Suddenly from the densest fold of the clouds the flash leapt out, quivering and quivering again down to the edge of the prairie; and at the same instant came the sharp burst and the long rolling peel of the thunder.

"A cool wind filled with the smell of rain, just then overtook us, leveling the tall grass by the side of the path. . . . We rode pell-mell . . . leapt from horseback, tore off our saddles, and in a moment each man was kneeling at his horse's feet. The hobbles were adjusted, and the animals turned loose; then, as the wagons came wheeling rapidly to the spot, we seized upon the tent-poles, and just as the storm broke, we were prepared to receive it. It came upon us almost with the darkness of night; the trees which were close at hand, were completely shrouded by the roaring torrents of rain."

Such violent storms were a considerable annoyance on the prairies, but when proper measures were taken there was little to be feared from them; the arrival in camp of an Indian hunting party, however, was a different matter. While it was true that an "official" peace existed in 1857 between the United States and the Indian tribes of the plains—the Pawnee, Sioux, Cheyenne and Arapaho—emigrant parties still found themselves subject to harassment and attack, and no traveler ever could be certain that a seemingly friendly band of braves might not turn, without warning or apparent provocation, into a fiercely hostile one.

Difficulties between the whites and the Indians usually arose over questions of property. To the Indians of the plains every stranger was a potential enemy, and as a consequence, they believed they had a perfect right to rob him if they chose. This meant that whenever a brave visited a camp or wagon train he felt no hesitation in appropriating any unguarded item that happened to strike his fancy—a horse, some cows, a gun or just a blanket or two—and if he was caught during the transaction, the

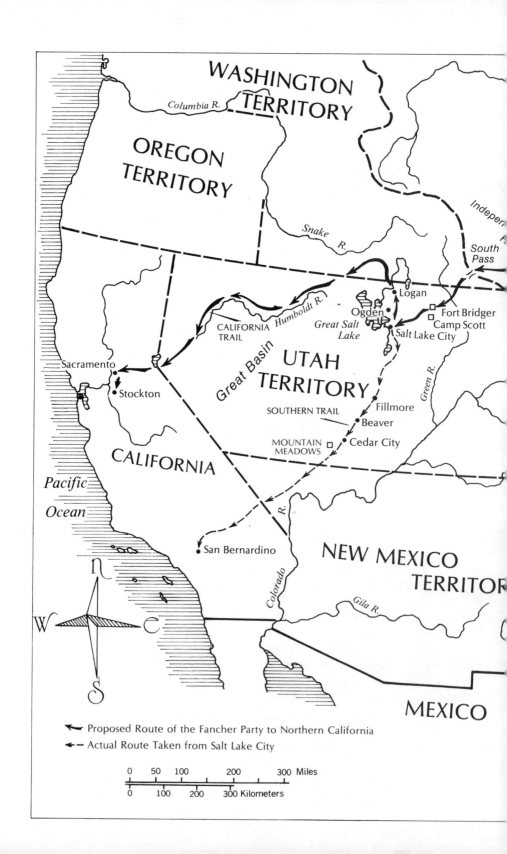

WASHINGTON TERRITORY

Columbia R.

OREGON TERRITORY

Snake R.

South Pass

Indepen

Logan

Fort Bridger
Camp Scott

Ogden

Great Salt Lake

Salt Lake City

CALIFORNIA TRAIL

Humboldt R.

Great Basin

UTAH TERRITORY

Sacramento

Stockton

SOUTHERN TRAIL

Green R.

Fillmore

Beaver

MOUNTAIN MEADOWS

Cedar City

CALIFORNIA

Pacific Ocean

R.

San Bernardino

NEW MEXICO TERRITOR

Colorado

Gila R.

N
W   E
S

MEXICO

← Proposed Route of the Fancher Party to Northern California
←– Actual Route Taken from Salt Lake City

0   50   100   200   300 Miles

0   100   200   300 Kilometers

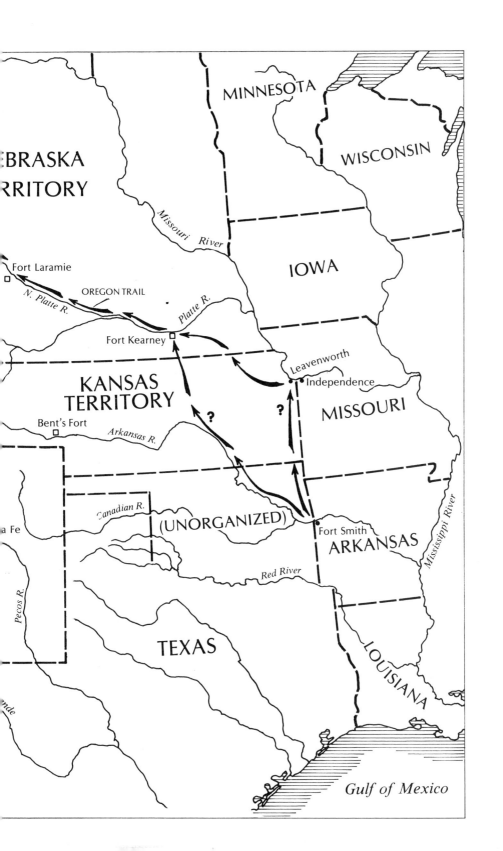

MINNESOTA

WISCONSIN

BRASKA
RRITORY

IOWA

Missouri River

Fort Laramie

OREGON TRAIL

N. Platte R.

Platte R.

Fort Kearney

Leavenworth

Independence

KANSAS
TERRITORY

MISSOURI

Bent's Fort

Arkansas R.

?

?

Canadian R.

(UNORGANIZED)

Fort Smith

ARKANSAS

a Fe

Pecos R.

Red River

Mississippi River

TEXAS

LOUISIANA

nde

Gulf of Mexico

spirited resistance of the emigrants was all too likely to result in bloodshed.

Because of its size and the vigilance of its leaders, there never had been much likelihood that the Fancher Train would experience great difficulty with the Indians whom they met along the trail, and judging from contemporary reports, such turned out to be the case, the party traveling without incident from Fort Kearney to Fort Laramie and beyond; nevertheless, danger always was near at hand on the prairies, especially for small, inexperienced parties, and sometimes ignorance or carelessness cost the unlucky traveler dearly. In July 1857, John L. Ginn, an itinerant southern journalist with a strong desire to visit California, having agreed to work as an expressman or a teamster for William McGraw's shipping company, began to make his way across the plains, a few weeks behind the Fancher Party. Guarded by more than eighty armed men, the large wagon train in which Ginn traveled was not attacked, but a smaller company just ahead was less fortunate. One evening its members unwisely allowed a band of Cheyenne to wander freely about their camp, and encouraged by this, the braves attempted to loot the wagons and to run off some of the cattle; within minutes, according to Ginn's account, a pitched battle broke out, and before it was over several men in the company had been seriously wounded and a hapless Bostonian named Sanburn had been killed.

Without doubt there were times when the sudden appearance of an Indian hunting party caused considerable excitement among the members of the Fancher Train, but such encounters certainly were not the only highlights of their long journey from the prairies to the mountains. New and curious sights were to be discovered on every side as the train crossed the grassy plains and the dry, almost treeless uplands, rode past famous Chimney Rock, made camp for a day or two near the little Army Post of Fort Laramie and for the first time beheld the full and extraordinary grandeur of the Rockies.

For the children especially, there was a fascinating profusion of wildlife to be seen and heard along the way, including timber wolves and coyotes, mule deer, pronghorns, elk and bear, an endless variety of birds and many curious reptiles and insects. On one occasion in his narrative, Parkman described a number of the creatures that he saw during a single journey not far from Fort Laramie. "There was an abundance of insects and reptiles," he wrote. "Huge crickets, black and bottle green, and wingless grasshoppers of the most extravagant dimensions, were tumbling about our horses' feet, and the lizards without number darting like lightning among the tufts of grass. . . ."

During late June and early July the Fancher Train made its way toward the northwest, along the North Branch of the Platte, through increasingly mountainous country; then, near the famous outcropping known as Independence Rock, on which a generation of emigrants already had scrawled its names and salutations, the trail turned due west and began to follow the Sweetwater River toward its source. At South Pass, the funnel through which all emigrant traffic was obliged to travel, the train crossed the Continental Divide and began to move southwest in the direction of Salt Lake City, where soon there would be, according to long-standing Mormon solicitations and advertisements, an opportunity to restore the animals of the train and to purchase fresh supplies.

By now the Fancher Party had completed well over half of its proposed journey, and thus far, good fortune had unfailingly accompanied it; none of the wagons had broken down seriously enough to cause a delay, the cattle were thin but in reasonably fit condition, and even the frailest members of the train—the infant children and the pregnant and nursing mothers—remained in excellent health.

There were no striped customs' barriers across the trail, but at some invisible border point—perhaps along the Sweetwater, perhaps beyond South Pass on the Green River or at Pacific Springs—the Fancher Train left the familiar world behind and entered a new realm, a dangerous private kingdom, through which, in the summer of 1857, all Gentile emigrants, especially the more wealthy ones, traveled at exceptional risk.

While the Fancher Train was journeying across America's heartland during the spring and early summer of 1857, Brigham Young, in his mountain headquarters at Salt Lake City, was coolly examining the political landscape, calculating the strength and determination of his adversaries and drawing up plans to meet what promised to be the most serious crisis of his tempestuous and spectacular career.

Rumors were legion in the Mormon capital, but at best the tide of events seemed to be running against him. His own actions, particularly his renewed assault on the Federal courts and his expulsion of the Federal officers—the second time within a mere

six years that such officials had felt compelled to flee from
Utah—had greatly increased the likelihood of a ruinous clash
between the Church and Washington and had all but guaranteed
that a powerful contingent of Federal soldiers soon would attempt to enter the Territory and take up permanent residence
there. It was a most unhappy turn of affairs, though doubtlessly
Young was incapable of recognizing the decisive part that he
himself had played in the matter. What he *did* recognize was a
single, imperative fact: that before long his almost unrestricted
freedom to reign over the vast Mormon kingdom would be
challenged as never before. In response to this, he determined
that whatever else might prove to be true during the months
ahead, at the end of the approaching struggle he—and he
alone—would remain the actual ruler of the Territory, although
it was all too likely that by then he no longer would enjoy the title
of governor and, with it, the gratifying pleasure of being referred
to as "His Excellency" in the local press.

Unlike a majority of his impassioned followers, the President
of the Latter-Day Saints could be a realist as well as a fanatic,
and although he might indulge now and again in the old-time
rhetoric, which gleefully proclaimed that God was on the
Church's side and that one Mormon could easily dispose of a
thousand Gentiles, in his own mind Young well understood that
such words were nothing but bombast and that his untrained and
ill-equipped militia had as much chance of defeating United
States Army troops in open battle as he himself had of drinking
up the waters of the Great Salt Lake.

This awareness of the Church's military weakness, however,
did not mean that Young intended to surrender meekly or,
indeed, to surrender at all. It simply meant that from the very
beginning the Mormon leader decided to play a waiting game, to
roar defiance at every opportunity and then to see how steadfast
Washington might be in its efforts to replace him. Should the
Government prove firm, then countermeasures could be taken;
their precise nature would depend on the situation that developed
between the two opposing sides.

It was Young's astute assumption that the ultimate outcome of
the conflict would be decided not by a pitched battle fought
somewhere in the Great Basin but by the force of public opinion
operating in Washington and the rest of the nation. Having
decided this much, he began to evolve a two-fold strategy. In
order to win renewed favor in the States, the Church would be
obliged to pose as a small, resolute David, bravely defending the

personal rights and perhaps even the very homes of its members, against a monstrous Goliath of oppression—the Army of the United States. Regaining a measure of good will in the Gentile world, however, would by no means guarantee success, and so, alternate tactics would have to be employed. These would include widespread and unconcealed public resistance to the authority of the Federal Government and quite possibly some form of guerrilla warfare against the advancing troops as well. The object of such drastic measures would be to persuade Washington's "corrupt and cynical" politicians that they had a great deal to gain from a reasonable compromise, for while the Utah Territory certainly could be occupied by a large standing army, as every senator and representative understood, the cost of doing so, both to America and to their individual constituents, would be truly staggering. Once this painful economic lesson had been demonstrated, maximum concessions could be wrung from Washington and a settlement reached that would be satisfactory to the Church and also to the Church's President.

As a first step in implementing this strategy, Brigham Young decided to put his followers on a more disciplined military footing, and early in April, well before the start of the so-called "Mormon War," he issued orders reorganizing the territorial militia along geographical lines. Still known as the Nauvoo Legion, the force now was divided into thirteen military districts under the overall command of its long-time chief, Lieutenant General Daniel H. Wells. Ammunition and arms began to be collected, musters and drills were held and soon the drums of war were pounding furiously.

From the speaker's stand in Salt Lake City came an uninterrupted stream of the crudest invective directed against the Federal Government and the rest of the outside world. Warnings were endlessly repeated that the United States was plotting to destroy the Church and that before long a vengeful enemy army would appear in Utah for the purpose of murdering Brigham Young, Heber C. Kimball and other Mormon notables. Once this had been accomplished the Gentiles would be free to destroy Mormonism by driving the leaderless Saints into the Wilderness, where, unlike the ancient and original Israelites, they would perish in misery to the last man. Over and over again the rank and file was exhorted to remain loyal to Brigham Young and to obey his commands in every circumstance, both for the sake of the Church itself and for the benefit of their own souls, since they could hope to enter Heaven only with the approval of the

President and through the powers that he alone possessed.

Few opportunities were missed to stir up additional hatred against the Gentiles and to reinforce the average Saint's obsessive belief that all non-Mormons were his mortal enemies. And so, during the early spring, when the much beloved Apostle Parley P. Pratt came to an untimely end, the Church hierarchy immediately seized on the incident for its own propaganda purposes. Two years earlier, while in California on one of his frequent missions for the Church, Pratt had won the affections of a woman named Eleanor McClean and, having converted her to Mormonism, persuaded her to abandon her husband and return with him to Utah as his twelfth wife. Hector McClean, a San Francisco customhouse official, soon learned of his wife's intentions; unable to deter her from leaving, he did manage to keep her from taking along their three young children, and after her departure he sent the children to Louisiana to live with Eleanor's parents, at the latter's suggestion.

Some months later, with Pratt's connivance, Eleanor McClean conceived a plan for recovering the children; appearing in Louisiana, she swore to her parents that she had given up Mormonism and wanted only to live with her family in their former faith. Shortly afterward, having successfully lulled her parents' suspicions, Eleanor seized the children and set off for Salt Lake City, her course directed by Pratt, who recently had come to the South. McClean, informed by his in-laws of the abduction, sped to New Orleans and was able to trace Eleanor—and Pratt—to Houston, and then to Fort Gibson, near Van Buren, Arkansas; here he recovered the children and had Pratt arrested and put in jail. But there was no law under which the Mormon could be held for long, and in a day or so Pratt had regained his liberty and had started back toward the Northwest and safety. McClean, however, still consumed with rage, hastily rode after Pratt, and using the Church's own code of "Mountain Justice," first stabbed and then shot the man who had destroyed his home and committed adultery with his wife. News of the Apostle's death quickly reached Salt Lake City, where the martyr was eulogized from the pulpit, his death lamented and the Gentiles excoriated for once again having wantonly murdered one of the noblest of the Saints without any cause or justification.

Throughout the spring and early summer the hierarchy's fiery exhortations and pronouncements continued. Finally, on the twenty-fourth of July, during a three-day celebration at Big Cottonwood Lake commemorating the tenth anniversary of the Saints' arrival in Utah, Brigham Young dramatically announced to his followers that a Gentile army was indeed advancing on Zion, as rumors so long had suggested; that the Nauvoo Legion would bar the enemy from entering the Territory; and that the Saints would defy their Gentile foes, while he, Brigham Young, would remain their governor until God decided it was time for him to yield the post. Pending such a celestial decision, no Gentile appointee from Washington would be able to take office and rule in his stead. In addition, Young declared, from that day on the Territory would sever all ties with the rest of the country and become the independent state of Deseret, where no repetition of the Haun's Mill Massacre or the Expulsion from Nauvoo could ever recur. Deeply stirred by such rhetoric, his followers drew closer together and prepared, each in his own sphere, for the suffering, sacrifices and glory that lay ahead.

Incredibly enough, however, many of Young's public utterances by now had become little more than elements in a shrewd, elaborate and complex charade, designed equally to deceive the Prophet's own followers and his political adversaries. For in late July, if not before, the Mormon leader had gained vital and comforting intelligence from the East—intelligence that told him that a favorable accommodation almost surely could be arranged between the Church and Washington.

It is not certain how the good news was carried west to Salt Lake City; perhaps it was brought there by the Apostle George A. Smith on his return from the nation's capital, where earlier that year he had collaborated with the Mormon delegate to Congress, John M. Bernhisel, in a fruitless attempt to gain statehood for the Utah Territory; perhaps Bernhisel sent the secret tidings that Colonel Thomas Leiper Kane had been working overtime on the Church's behalf; or perhaps it was Kane himself who sent the reassuring word that the Federal Government now appeared to be amenable to reason and compromise and that in early June, President Buchanan, beset by unexpected and serious political difficulties within his own party, had taken Kane's private advice and had appointed Alfred Cumming to be the new governor of the Territory. Cumming, a man who, Kane could assure Young, would be most favorably inclined to the Mormon cause.

Through Kane's efforts victory already seemed near at least for the Church itself. But still, the charade had to continue, as only Brigham Young, and perhaps a few of his most intimate collaborators, really understood; for in the past the laws of the nation and of mankind had been broken more than once by the Mormon hierarchy, and unless its members now could outface Governor Cumming and his accompanying army, they might all be prosecuted for their crimes, and in courts controlled by others than themselves, might even be convicted and jailed or executed. And so Brigham Young was compelled to roar defiance and prepare for guerrilla warfare, even while knowing that the official who was slated to succeed him in office had been selected by Young's own confidential agent in Washington and that the Church itself—though perhaps directed by a different Seer, Prophet and Revelator—surely would survive under the new territorial regime.

On the twenty-fourth of July, while Brigham Young addressed two thousand of the Faithful at Big Cottonwood Lake, the Fancher Train was making its way slowly down the last section of the trail to Salt Lake City, a mere ten days' distance away. Not long before, at a remote locality called Pacific Springs, the travelers had been joined by two fellow emigrants, Frank E. King and his wife. At first it was the Kings' intention to remain with the Fanchers all the way to California, but soon Mrs. King fell sick, and once they had arrived in Salt Lake City, the couple decided to remain behind, while the main party proceeded on its journey.

According to King, the Fancher Train was truly a large one; in the company, which was made up principally of several Methodist families, there were approximately sixty men, forty women and fifty children; about twelve of the men were mounted on horses, and the rest traveled in the wagons or on foot.

They arrived at Salt Lake City on the third of August, 1857, just over ten years after the first party of Mormons had entered the Utah Territory. On the former occasion, one of the Mormons, William Clayton, had written these words in his *Journal*: "Give me the quiet wilderness, and my family to associate with, surrounded by the Saints, and adieu to the gentile world, till God says return and avenge you of your enemies."

Ten years had elapsed, and clearly there was to be no return to Missouri and the New Jerusalem. But now Brigham Young, claiming that the Saints were at war with the Federal Government, was ready to sanction what many veterans of Nauvoo and Missouri so ardently desired—the long-awaited opportunity to exact revenge.

Chapter 25

FOR NEARLY THREE DECADES the Latter-Day Saints had been accused of innumerable crimes, ranging from petty theft to premeditated murder, but with the local courts almost invariably in their own hands, there rarely if ever had been an opportunity to determine the truth of such charges; now, in the summer of 1857, Brigham Young and other important members of the Church hierarchy began to devise an ambitious, elaborate, cold-blooded crime that eventually proved impossible to conceal and that so patently had been organized by the Saints themselves that its disclosure tended to confirm even the worst accusations previously made against them.

Church apologists always have clung to a comforting absurdity—that the Mountain Meadows Massacre was planned independently by one or two minor aberrant Mormon leaders far from Salt Lake City and that despite the overwhelming suspicions pointing in his direction, Brigham Young was far too clever a politician ever to have sanctioned an act so damaging to the Church, the President of the Saints actually having been unaware of the conspiracy against the Fancher Party, the wealthiest company ever to appear in the territory, until well after the crime was over and the political damage done. The truth, unhappily, was quite different; in this instance—and by no means for the first time—Young's natural astuteness was overcome by rage and greed, the adroit politician unwisely yielding to the criminal fanatic.

During the 1850's, when the Fancher Train arrived in Utah, conditions were such that no large-scale crime could possibly have been planned and executed without Brigham Young's full

knowledge and participation. The Territory was a private kingdom ruled by a single despot whose submissive underlings lived
in constant fear of his anger or disapproval, a fact amply testified
to by a variety of commentators, including some of the very
apologists most anxious to prove Young's innocence. In his
important study of the early Mormons, titled *The Rocky Mountain Saints*, Thomas Stenhouse, a knowledgeable Apostate, included this telling description of the way that Brigham Young
ran the Territory and kept himself informed of his followers'
activities. "No person could enter business without consulting
him" Stenhouse wrote, "nor would anyone ever think of leaving
the city to reside in any other part of the country without first
having his approval. Merchants who went East or West to
purchase goods, had to present themselves at his office, and report
their intention of going to the States at such a time—if he had no
contrary orders to give them. Some, no doubt, may have sought
his counsel on their proposed undertakings and journeys believing that his superior wisdom could aid them, but in his own mind
he claimed that the Saints should do nothing without his knowledge and approval. That oft-reiterated expression, that it was his
right to dictate and control everything, 'even to the ribbons that a
woman should wear,' or 'to the setting up of a stocking,' was the
truthful illustration of his feelings.

"A ball even could not take place," Stenhouse continued, "until
he was consulted upon the propriety of dancing . . . and before
the invitations were issued, the list of the invited was read to
him, and he erased or added names at his pleasure. Before any of
the married brethren could make love to a maiden with a view of
making her a second, third, or tenth wife, he was expected to go
and obtain Brigham's permission."

That Young's domination was absolute, Stenhouse confirmed in
these words, written during the early 1870's, some fifteen years
after the assault on the Fancher Train: "No one today, even in
Utah, can form any idea of the thorough control Brigham Young
had over the people. Nothing was ever undertaken without his
permission—he knew of everything." In such a state, under such
a leader, was it even remotely conceivable that two or three
subordinates in a distant section of the Territory would take it
upon themselves to commit a crime of truly monumental propor-
tions, robbing and murdering, for the benefit of the Church, the
members of a large passing company, and to do this without the
prior knowledge, guidance and approval of Young himself? To

most observers the answer quite simply was no—it was *not* conceivable—despite all manner of disclaimers and denials subsequently offered on the Prophet's behalf.

From the moment the train reached the vicinity of Salt Lake City, a number of curious circumstances began to surround the Fanchers and their companions, perhaps the most noteworthy being the unusual failure of the Church's own newspaper to publish any report of their arrival. The matter was noted by an exceptionally fair-minded Mormon author, who confessed that the implications of this omission were highly significant. "It had been the habit of the *Deseret News*," she wrote, "to print the lists of emigrant companies who camped near Great Salt Lake City, but for some strange reason the Fancher Company from Arkansas was not listed. This in itself," she aptly concluded, "was ominous." And so it was, for it clearly indicated that the Church hierarchy already had decided to victimize the Fancher Train, eliminating whenever possible evidence of its passage through the Territory, and therefore, as a logical first step, had ordered the paper's editor, Albert Carrington, to omit any reference to the train's appearance near the capital.

Criminal conspirators all too seldom leave behind a nicely detailed account of their plans and proceedings, and in this particular, the authors of the Mountain Meadows Massacre were no exception; yet despite a lack of official documents on the subject, and the destruction of certain private papers as well— including a number of pages from John D. Lee's personal journal, which afterward was commandeered and disposed of by the Prophet himself—it still was a relatively easy task for investigators to learn the identity of the principal conspirators, the part each was expected to play in the affair and the general outline of the conspiracy as it initially took shape in the offices of the Church.

The plot against the Arkansas travelers began to form no later than the end of July or the first day or two of August, about a week or so after the Mormons' annual celebration at Great Cottonwood Lake, on which occasion Brigham Young had boldly "declared war" against the United States and had revealed that henceforth Deseret, if an invading army crossed its borders, would consider taking whatever measures might prove necessary to defend itself. Within ten days of these pronouncements the Fancher Train had made its way through Emigration Canyon

and by the third of August was safely encamped not far from Salt
Lake City; here the train's principal families long had anticipated purchasing much-needed supplies from their Mormon hosts
while they refreshed their horses and cattle prior to resuming the
journey to California. In this hope, however, they were disap-
pointed; for although it was true that the Saints now were enjoying a bumper crop, the members of the train were nevertheless
informed that war between Deseret and the States was imminent
and that when it broke out, the Mormons would need the entire
harvest for themselves; as a consequence, both at Salt Lake City,
and afterward at various towns and villages along the trail, the
increasingly hostile Saints, obeying Brigham Young's orders,
refused almost without exception to sell any food whatever to the
Fancher Company, although there was no indication that the
policy was extended to individual Gentiles then in the area. What
purpose the Prophet expected to achieve by this singularly cruel
and unusual tactic never became entirely clear; perhaps his aim
simply was to reduce the emigrants' strength so that they would
be unfit to resist a future attack; perhaps he hoped to goad the
Arkansas travelers into some angry, ill-considered act that would
serve as a pretext for ordering out the Nauvoo Legion to "punish"
the offenders; or it might have been that the orders were issued
from Salt Lake City, not so much to serve a logical plan, but
rather to satisfy a spirit of malice and a desire for revenge.

Because of the extraordinary size of the Fancher Train it must
have been immediately evident to the Prophet and his associates
that what they were about to undertake was no routine act of
pillage or violence and that if the affair was to be brought to a
successful conclusion, an exceptional amount of forethought and
planning would be required. Put more plainly—it was one thing
to ambush with impunity a single individual or a small party of
three or four men traveling along the road, and quite another
matter to rob and dispose of a numerous, well-armed company
and to do so without being exposed to the world as the actual
agents of the crime. Therefore, at least three critical questions
had to be considered at once: Where could the attack best be made
without the troublesome presence of Gentile witnesses; Was
there sufficient time to organize the assault; and Who were the
attackers to be?

In addition, it was most unlikely that so extensive an ambush
could be kept indefinitely from public notice, as might easily
happen in the case of a smaller party; the difficulty was that

among so many travelers there almost certainly would be several whose relatives were awaiting them in California, and when the train failed to reach its destination, they would become alarmed and raise a considerable hue and cry. Of one thing, though, Brigham Young was certain: no matter how the affair was conducted, it was essential that afterward nothing should remain to link the Church—or its President—to what the Gentile press all too eagerly would label an ignoble and barbarous crime.

By the third of August, Young had begun to put into motion the machinery necessary to carry out his plans. The first step was to select a suitable site for attacking the Fancher Train and running off its livestock, and this the Prophet did promptly and with seeming confidence. Some 320 miles south of the capital, along the Southern Trail to California, just at the Rim of the Great Basin, lay a narrow strip of open, well-watered grassland known as the Mountain Meadows. It was in many respects the ideal location for what the Prophet had in mind. Here, in a remote corner of the Territory, far removed from the prying eyes of strangers and talebearers, was the last place that westbound travelers could rest their horses and cattle before setting out on the arduous trek across the desert to southern California. If the Fanchers and their companions decided to take the southern route, rather than the Northern Trail to California, then surely during their journey south from Salt Lake City they would spend several days at Mountain Meadows, as almost all the emigrants did who came that way. While the Fancher Party was relaxing at the Meadows the surprise assault could be launched, and then, if everything went well, it would not be long before the fiery traditions of Nauvoo and Missouri had once again been revived and "the wealth of the Gentiles consecrated to the True Church."

There always was the chance, of course, that a few of the emigrants would escape the ambush and succeed in making their way across the desert to California, where undoubtedly they would report the incident in full. And so, to make sure that none of the Saints could be identified as participants in the affair, Young decided to fall back on an expedient that Mormon critics long had insisted was a favorite one of the Church and that, they said, certainly had been employed several years earlier in the notorious Gunnison Massacre. Young's idea was simple enough: let most of the attackers be Indian braves, drawn from tribes loyal to the Church, and let an utterly trustworthy Mormon serve as their leader in the field, after he had assumed the familiar role of "white Indian" by disguising himself in feathers, blankets and red paint.

It long had been the conviction of many observers that a considerable number of Saints who lived in the vicinity of the Southern Trail had been actively engaged in thievery and murder for some years past and that by now these assassins, or Danites, on receiving orders from Salt Lake City that they were to do so, were quite prepared to attack any party of travelers who happened to pass their way; indeed, since the start of the Reformation the criminal activities of the southern Saints had become so open and commonplace that three or four months *before* the arrival of the Fancher Party, in May 1857, a description of the lawless conditions then prevailing along the Southern Trail to California had been published in a front-page story of the *New York Times*.

The *Times* account, written by a resident of Salt Lake City, included the story of a former soldier named John Tobin, who once had served with the Gunnison Expedition; later, embracing the Faith, Tobin had returned to Utah, where he had helped to train elements of the Nauvoo Legion and purportedly had lived on terms of considerable intimacy with both the Prophet and one of his daughters, Alice Young. Eventually, however, dissension had set in, and Tobin, abandoning the Church in late 1856 or early 1857, had been declared an Apostate and "turned over to the buffetings of Satan." The former soldier, judging his life to be in danger, decided to leave for California and soon set out from Salt Lake City with three companions, choosing to take the Southern Trail through Fillmore City, Parowan, Mountain Meadows and Las Vegas, to San Bernardino.

One night Tobin and the others made camp at a spot about seventy-five miles south of Parowan; here they planned to await the arrival of the mail train from the north, which they then could join, for safety's sake, during the remainder of the journey to California. "The place they selected for their camp," the *Times* informant wrote, "was at the face of a perpendicular ledge of rocks in the vicinity of some bushes. About four o'clock in the morning, the moon shining brightly at the time, the attacking party crept up and fired down from the top of a rock. Tobin was shot in the head, a ball entering close under his eye, passing diagonally through the nose and cheek, and lodging in his neck.

He was also shot in five other places and left for dead. The other men escaped into the bushes, one of them, however, having been shot in the back of his neck, and another having had two fingers shot off. When the party returned to the camp, they found that Tobin was still alive, and with the assistance of the mail party, who soon overtook them, they carried him along with them. . . .

"There is no doubt," the *Times* account continued, "but that the attack was planned in this city, and that orders were sent from here to execute it. It was said publicly by the Mormons, immediately after the party left the city, that they would not live to get through to California." And then the observer concluded, "The Mormons here, in speaking of this transaction, wink their eyes to each other and say, '*The Indians are very bad on the lower road.*'"

Obviously at this time the Southern Trail was infested with its share of cutthroats and fanatics, and it must have occurred to Brigham Young, who in many respects was a cautious man, that should his Indian allies fail to carry out the ambush satisfactorily, it might prove useful to have a number of such impassioned Saints available in the neighborhood, to complete the task.

Having determined the site of the ambush and the general composition of the attacking force, Young was ready to alert those Saints who were to take part directly in the scheme and help to draw the lines tight around the proposed victims. Two of the conspirators were the Apostles Charles C. Rich and George A. Smith, each of whom was assigned a significant role in the proceedings. Both Apostles were thoroughly familiar with the Southern Trail, and because Apostle Rich happened to be in the capital at the beginning of August, Young no doubt consulted him about certain fine points of geography and the suitability of Mountain Meadows as the location for the proposed attack.

Apostle Smith, on the other hand, already had left Salt Lake City for a tour of the southern settlements, a number of which he had helped to establish during the past ten years. While traveling along the Southern Trail, and through even more remote parts of Utah's "Dixie," Smith was to deliver sermons designed to increase even further the southern Saints' already extreme hostility to the United States and their fellow Americans. Such had been the original object of his travels, but the Apostle certainly had not journeyed far from the capital before being informed of the Prophet's plans for the Fancher Train and being told what instructions he was to give to his old friend and fellow pioneer

John D. Lee, who had been chosen to lead the Indians in the field.

Exactly when Lee first heard of the affair is far from certain. Most probably he did not learn many important details until late in August, after a private discussion of the subject with Apostle Smith, for only by then would it have been decided which tribes seemed willing to participate and the circumstances under which Lee was to approach them. In any event, the necessary arrangements eventually were made, and Lee was told of his appointment as ambush leader.

The reasoning behind Young's choice was plain enough: John D. Lee was the perfect man for the job. The Prophet's second adopted son was then living far to the south, only a few hours' ride away from the Mountain Meadows. Lee was presently serving as Farmer to the Indians, was familiar with the neighboring tribes and knew most of their chiefs with at least some degree of intimacy. Even more important, his fidelity to the Church and his intense personal devotion to Young were beyond doubt or question. Because he already had proved his reliability on numerous occasions, it was only reasonable to assume that once again the veteran Danite could be depended upon to carry out orders and to tell no tales.

The scheme was so elaborate and far-flung that sooner or later a number of other Saints also had to be informed of the proposed ambush and given their parts to play in the crime. At Salt Lake City, the Prophet's brother-in-law and favorite Indian interpreter, Dimick B. Huntington, was apprised of pending events, no doubt by the Prophet himself; while far to the south, several civil and military leaders, then living in Parowan and in other towns along the Southern Trail, were alerted to their added responsibilities by the touring Apostle George A. Smith. Among these southern officials were William Dame, Isaac Haight, Philip Klingensmith and John Higbee, four men who knew of the proposed ambush well before the initial attack and who afterward were linked inextricably to the commission of the crime, despite a fourfold flood of protests and perjuries.

At least one other Saint had a fundamental part to play in the scheme, and therefore, on the fourth of August, while the Fancher Party was still at Salt Lake City, Brigham Young took pen and paper in hand and wrote a brief, guarded, official letter that was dispatched from the President's office. The letter was addressed to Elder Jacob Hamblin, a Saint of proven loyalty, who recently had been successful in missionary work among the Pah-Ute Indians of the Santa Clara and Virgin rivers and who, interestingly enough, then occupied the only house within several miles of Mountain Meadows.

The letter began with a terse and significant announcement. "You are hearby appointed," the Prophet wrote, "to succeed Elder R. C. Allen (whom I have released as President of the Santa Clara Mission). I wish you to enter upon the duties of your calling immediately."

Allen's dismissal and Hamblin's appointment, coming as they did on the fourth of August, were all too revealing. Clearly it was the Prophet's view that the dismissed Elder, either because he lacked energy, skill or discretion, was unfit for the work ahead, while his successor could be counted upon to perform a variety of useful tasks, among them the essential ones of gathering a number of important tribal chiefs and bringing them to Salt Lake City for a conference with the Prophet, and afterward, of keeping silent about whatever private arrangements might have been made.

The letter to Jacob Hamblin then offered one or two bits of platitudinous advice and one observation that was extremely meaningful. "Continue," the Prophet wrote, "the conciliatory policy toward the Indians, which I have ever recommended, and seek the words of righteousness to obtain their love and confidence, for they must learn that they have either got to help us, or the United States will kill us both." The "help" that Young had in mind, of course, would be required during the immediate affair at Mountain Meadows and during later acts of murder or insurrection, and for a veteran Saint like Jacob Hamblin, there was no difficulty in concluding that such was the case.

Although for many months longer Brigham Young would claim that he still was governor of the Territory, in his August 4 letter to Hamblin he acknowledged that a duly authorized replacement even then was heading West to succeed him. "The government," he wrote, "have at last appointed an entire set of officials for the Territory. These Gentry are to have a bodyguard of 2,500 of Uncle's Regulars. They were to start from Fort Leavenworth July 15th. . . . The current report is that they somewhat query [sic] whether they will hang me with or without trial. There are about 30 others whom they intend to deal with."

And then the Prophet, who already had issued orders to his

subordinates that no food was to be sold to the Fancher Party,
wrote to Hamblin: "Grain is abundant, and our cities are alive
with the hum of industry. All is peace here, and the Lord is
eminently blessing our labors."

After writing to inform Jacob Hamblin of his promotion, the
Prophet was free to consider two final problems. The first involved number of questions that inevitably would be asked—and
asked insistently—by every critic of the Church as soon as the
fate of the Fancher Party became known in California and
the eastern states. On what grounds could anyone believe, the
questioners would demand, that the Mormons really had had
nothing whatever to do with the ambush at Mountain Meadows?
If, indeed, they had not been involved, and had not incited the
Indians to attack the train, then what had made the Indians go on
the warpath? And why had the Indians chosen to attack this
particular train, rather than any other?

The Prophet realized that if the Church were to successfully
maintain its pose of innocence, some sort of explanation would
have to be provided. As a consequence, he began to fabricate, for
immediate circulation, the outlines of several highly discreditable stories about the Fancher Train, and eventually at least two
of these tales, with additional elaborations, gained wide acceptance throughout the southern part of the Territory. According to
the most popular version of one tale, the emigrants were a
particularly vicious lot; several of them had witnessed or participated in the recent murder of the beloved Apostle Parley P. Pratt
back in Arkansas and, upon entering the Saints' domain, had
exulted openly over his tragic demise and then had threatened
similar treatment to any other Mormon who happened to dis-
please them. After that, certain members of the train had
behaved with even less restraint, until at last, passing farther
along the trail, they had wantonly poisoned a drinking well,
known to be used by a neighboring tribe of Indians. As a result,
several Indians had fallen sick, more than one had died, and a
band of braves, swearing vengeance, had followed the train south
until early one morning they had seized their opportunity and
ambushed the murderous emigrants from Arkansas.

On even the briefest reflection, though, this tale did seem a
touch too fanciful and overdrawn, especially since any number of
eyewitnesses were ready to swear that the Fancher Party had

been made up of ordinary, sober, God-fearing citizens rather than mindless criminals or devils incarnate, and so another tale quickly was contrived to replace it. This time, it was said that the Fanchers and their companions, though innocent of any evildoing themselves, unwisely had fallen in with a rough set of "Missouri Wildcats," and these swaggering, blasphemous cutthroats—some claiming to have driven the Saints from the Promised Land of western Missouri two decades earlier, and others boasting of having murdered Joseph and Hyrum Smith back in Illinois—first had so antagonized the Saints that they had refused to sell the train any food and then had so provoked and injured the Indians that an ambush naturally had followed. Why the leaders of the Fancher Party would have chosen to jeopardize their own safety by allying themselves with such disreputable and undesirable companions was never made clear, and indeed, Gentile investigators later found no evidence that a group of so-called Missouri Wildcats ever had traveled with the Fanchers, save, perhaps, in the collective imagination of the Church. Nevertheless, these and other maladroit rumors and fancies began to circulate in the Territory even while the Fancher Party remained in the vicinity of Great Salt Lake, creating the sinister impression, so little desired by the Saints, that from the very start the Arkansas emigrants had been marked out for special attention.

Of far greater concern to the Prophet, however, than any mere question of public opinion, was the second and remaining problem, which still confronted him on the fourth of August. It was, in fact, so crucial a problem that unless he could find a way to solve it, there would be no ambush at Mountain Meadows and all his calculations would have been made in vain. Because the distressing truth was that if left to themselves, the leaders of the Fancher Party had no intention of taking the Southern Trail to California, but were determined—*as they always had been*—to take the much more frequently traveled, shorter and more convenient Northern Trail; this would leave the members of the train hundreds of miles closer to Stockton, and to other locations in central California, where they intended to settle.

In later times the Church never denied that one day in early August Apostle Charles C. Rich approached the members of the Fancher Train and conferred with them about their travel plans and their itinerary. So much undoubtedly was true, but the rest of the Church's version of that vital meeting was remarkable only for its calculated and total deception. For according to the Mormon account, it was Captain Fancher and his fellow leaders who wished to take the Southern Trail, while it was Apostle Rich, acting on behalf of the benevolent and public-spirited governor, Brigham Young, who urged the Arkansas travelers to take the northern route. Time and again, according to the Apostle, he had warned the emigrants of the current Indian unrest in the southern part of the Territory, of the dangers they would be risking if they stubbornly persisted in their plans to go south, and had urged them most emphatically, but without success, to avoid the disaster that well might lie ahead.

Unfortunately for the good name of the Prophet and his associates, there were several people in the Fancher Train who were familiar with what really transpired that day at Great Salt Lake, and one of them, Malinda Cameron Scott, not only lived for a considerable time afterward, but ultimately proved herself the most important member of the party, for she was able to describe under oath what actually had occurred, following Apostle Rich's visit to their camp.

According to Mrs. Scott, the Fancher Party had arrived in the Mormon capital late in the afternoon, "on the 3rd day of August, 1857. We stopped," she said, "at Salt Lake one day [the 4th], and on the morning of the 5th of August, my father [William Cameron] came to our wagon and said, 'I think I am going to take the southern route.'"

But Mrs. Scott's husband was either a stubborn or a suspicious man—or perhaps both. He had come this far intending to take the Northern Trail to California, and his father-in-law's sudden change of plans did not impress him favorably. As Mrs. Scott testified, "My husband said, 'For what reason?' And my father said *that he had heard* there was good feed and plenty of water.

"And my husband said, 'I do not think I will take that route. I [still] will go by the *main* road.'"

And so, on the fifth of August, 1857, Malinda Cameron Scott, now eight or nine months pregnant, climbed awkwardly aboard the family wagon, and in company with her husband and three children, and some seven or eight additional emigrants in two or three other wagons, set out along the Northern Trail to California, while the great majority of the Fancher Party took the Southern Trail, so recently recommended by Apostle Rich, acting on behalf of the Prophet and the Church. The two parties separated, the wagons rolled slowly away, and that day was the last that Malinda Scott ever saw her father, her mother, or a dozen other near relations with whom she had safely traveled from Fort Smith, twelve hundred miles, to the capital of the Utah Territory.

Chapter 26

On the fifth of August, 1857, the Fancher Train left
the vicinity of Salt Lake City on the last leg of its taxing,
transcontinental journey. Before departing from the Mormon
capital, one of the emigrants, William Eaton, the midwestern
farmer who had joined the Fancher Party in Arkansas, wrote a
cheerful letter to his wife in Indiana, declaring that all was well
in the train and that he and his companions were leaving shortly
for the Pacific Coast.

Eaton apparently made no mention of any feelings of surprise
or uneasiness, but by the time the train started south from Salt
Lake City there must have been more than a few members of the
company who felt concern over the Saints' extraordinary conduct,
especially their refusal, against all previous custom, to sell food
to an emigrant party from their abundant stores. Because of this
action the train leaders, among them Captain Alexander
Fancher, William Cameron, "Uncle Jack" Baker, the Dunlap
brothers and Charles Mitchell, had been compelled to change
plans and to leave the public grazing lands by the Jordan River
far earlier than they had wished or intended. Still, with no
prospect of adding to their scant provisions while they remained
at the capital, there really had been no other choice but to move
out at once, in the hope that food could be purchased farther
along the trail. There was, however, an obvious drawback to this
plan—the animals in the train, after just a single day's rest,
would scarcely be in the best condition to travel three hundred
miles to the Rim of the Great Basin and then to cross the arid
desert to San Bernardino.

If several members of the company had felt suspicious or

resentful of the Mormons back in the capital, their numbers could only have increased as the train moved slowly south through the mountainous countryside. On every hand the emigrants were greeted with averted looks, sullen words and even outbursts of open hostility and anger, and in each community along the way they heard the same absurd story, parroted by a local Church officer or district militia captain, that the town or village had no extra food to sell, even though the crops in the nearby fields were standing tall and ripe and it was no secret among travelers on the road that the Saints' stocks of flour, bacon, vegetables, poultry, butter, cheese and eggs were not only large that year but far in excess of their requirements.

Mile after mile the wagons lurched and rocked along the rough, narrow trail, from one frontier settlement to another; for eight miles, past scattered houses and farms to Big Cottonwood Fort, then for another five to Little Cottonwood, built near a trout stream that was used by the inhabitants to irrigate an extensive tract of land; another short stretch of the trail and the train arrived at Lehi, a farming community of five hundred souls, where each year great quantities of potatoes and vegetables were raised, although on this occasion none were sold to the needy travelers from Arkansas. Then on to tiny Battle Creek, also called Pleasant Grove, a village set precariously on the side of a hill, and eight miles farther along the important city of Provo, situated by the banks of the Provo River, a body of water, reputedly the second largest in the Territory, teeming with trout and other edible fish. Here once again the members of the train sought to buy food or to trade some of their weary oxen for fresher animals, but again their efforts were unsuccessful, and they were turned away with what must have been, on their side, mounting uneasiness and anger.

While pausing a few hours at Provo, the train leaders were approached by a solitary Gentile traveler, twenty-year-old William Aden, a native of Tennessee. Aden already had been in Utah for a number of weeks that summer and had left Salt Lake City for California well in advance of the Fancher Party. An artist, he had proceeded along the trail, sketching as he went, and on reaching Provo had been hired to paint scenery for the city's dramatic association. The Fanchers and their companions were the first group of Gentiles to pass that way, and Aden asked whether there might not be room in the train for an additional hand? After considering the matter briefly, the train leaders said there surely was room enough, and soon Aden had taken his place among the emigrants, in all probability the last person to join the party on its journey south.

At first, after leaving Provo, the train passed through a number of small communities located relatively near one another— Springville, Spanish Fork and Payson—but then the frontier towns became more widely separated, and the land between them seemed to grow more barren and desolate. Twenty miles beyond Payson the travelers came to Salt Creek, or Nephi, a village noted mainly for the large amounts of plaster-of-Paris it produced, an item of great importance in the construction of public buildings throughout the Territory. Then along the trail again, some fifty miles to the village of Buttermilk Fort, and another ten to Fillmore City, which a few years earlier had served briefly as the capital of Utah and where now the red sandstone statehouse could still be seen, the most notable feature in an otherwise featureless town. Halting at each of these places, the increasingly harrowed travelers asked to buy food, but at each their requests were brusquely and sometimes angrily refused by the Elders in authority, although now and again an independent-minded Saint—or more often his kindhearted wife—slipped out to the train, and at the risk of physical punishment or perhaps even death, covertly offered to sell a dozen eggs or a few loaves of bread to the hungry emigrants.

Finally, at Corn Creek, eight or ten miles south of Fillmore, and almost halfway to Mountain Meadows, the travelers' luck temporarily changed. At Corn Creek there was an Indian Farm, one of several under the supervision of Indian Agent Garland Hurt, by then the only Federal officer who still remained in the Utah Territory. Agent Hurt was not present on that mid-August day, but evidently his humane influence was felt, for the Pah-Vant Indians proved friendly and, after a mutually satisfactory discussion, sold the Fancher Train thirty bushels of corn—all that they had to spare. Not long afterward, the Saints would disseminate a particularly sordid lie, claiming that it had been these same Corn Creek Indians who had followed the Fancher Train a hundred and fifty miles to the Meadows and there had ambushed the half-starved party—a party that, in reality, only the Pah-Vant Indians of Corn Creek had elected to befriend.

While the families in the Fancher Train paused for a day or so at Corn Creek before resuming their journey, an interesting

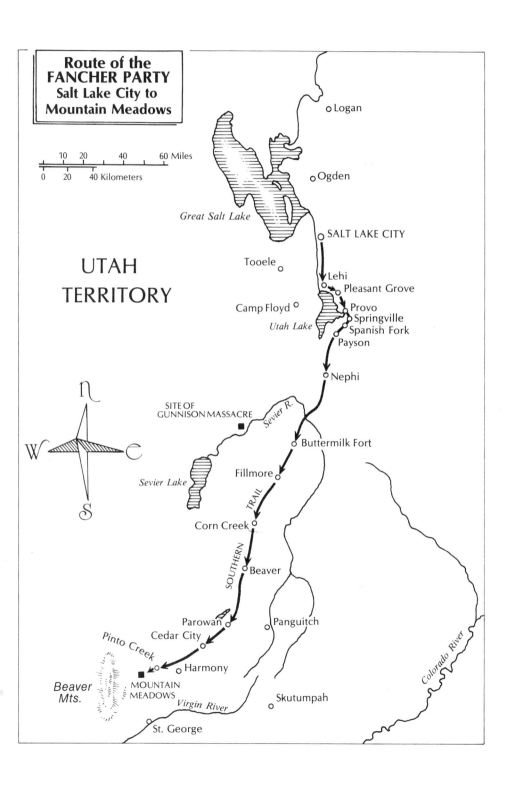

Route of the FANCHER PARTY Salt Lake City to Mountain Meadows

10 20   40   60 Miles

0   20   40 Kilometers

Logan

Great Salt Lake

Ogden

SALT LAKE CITY

UTAH TERRITORY

Tooele

Lehi

Pleasant Grove

Camp Floyd

Provo

Springville

Utah Lake

Spanish Fork

Payson

Nephi

SITE OF GUNNISON MASSACRE

Sevier R.

Buttermilk Fort

Sevier Lake

Fillmore

TRAIL

Corn Creek

SOUTHERN

Beaver

Parowan

Panguitch

Pinto Creek

Cedar City

Beaver Mts.

Harmony

MOUNTAIN MEADOWS

Virgin River

Skutumpah

Colorado River

St. George

variety of other travelers might have been seen, riding north and south along the Southern Trail. Some, like the Fanchers, were Gentile emigrants making their way as best they could to California, either as individual passengers in a Mormon party or as members of their own company. One spectacular band of riders were Pah-Ute Indian chiefs, from the Santa Clara and Virgin rivers. Accompanying their overall leader, Tutsegabit, and under the guidance of missionary Jacob Hamblin, they now were heading north to Salt Lake City for an important conference with Brigham Young. And one horseman on the trail was the Apostle George A. Smith, busily engaged in making a public tour of the southern settlements, while at the same time arranging certain important private matters.

Among the Gentile travelers riding south a few days behind the Fancher Party were three men who soon were to provide the outside world with its first reliable news of Mountain Meadows. One was John L. Ginn, a journalist and printer from Georgia. Earlier that year in Missouri he had signed on as a civilian employee in one of the army's cattle trains. Reaching Utah in early August, Ginn had discovered that the Mormons meant to prevent all Federal soldiers and their supplies from continuing to Salt Lake City. Having no desire to spend the winter in a snowbound mountain bivouac, he had left the train and deliberately allowed himself to be captured by Mormon guerrillas. Eventually riding to Salt Lake City with one of his captors, the Danite gunman William Hickman, Ginn, after a brief, eye-opening stay in the capital, had obtained his release from custody and was now proceeding south with a strong Mormon party, the Huntington and Clark Company, bound with the mail for San Bernardino.

The other two Gentile travelers were George Powers, from Little Rock, Arkansas, and P. M. Warn from Genesee, New York. For safety's sake each decided at different times to become passengers in the Matthews and Tanner Train, a Mormon company, Powers after journeying beyond Corn Creek with his own small party of Gentiles, and Warn several weeks earlier, before the company's departure from Salt Lake City. By joining the train both men were placed in an ideal position to observe conditions in the southern part of the Territory, and Warn especially was able to draw a number of shrewd inferences from what he noted while passing along the trail. In his published account, Warn stated that "on his journey through the southern settlements . . . he at various places heard . . . threats of vengeance against them [the Fancher Party], for their boisterousness and abuse of Mormons and Mormonism . . . and these threats seemed to be made with the intention of preparing the mind to expect a calamity, and also, when a calamity occurred, [that] it should appear to fall upon the transgressors, as a matter of retribution."

Obviously it seemed curious to Mr. Warn, as it did to other Gentile observers, that the Fancher Party, on finding itself in the hands of a fanatical enemy, should have gone out of its way to antagonize the enemy further when common sense would have dictated that all means be employed to placate the frenzied people who controlled the trail and the rest of the countryside. And it was even more curious that in settlement after settlement the populace seemed to know beforehand a tragedy was destined to take place, although the victims had not yet reached the site of the crime, nor had the attackers yet gathered to assault them.

During the few hours when the Fancher Party was resting at Corn Creek near Garland Hurt's Indian Farm, its members were approached by a seemingly friendly and helpful Mormon missionary from the extreme south who gave his name as Jacob Hamblin. This Mormon Elder, so cordial when compared with other recently encountered Saints, was traveling north accompanied by one of his assistant missionaries, a young man named Thales Haskell, and a half-dozen Indian chiefs from some of the more remote reaches of the Territory.

Afterward in his laconic and guarded diary, Hamblin mentioned his trip north. "I started for Salt Lake City," he wrote, "in company with Thales Haskell and Tutsegabit, [who] had felt anxious for a long time to visit Brigham Young." Hamblin's next words revealed that early in the journey a significant conference had been held, for he wrote in his diary: "We fell into company with George A. Smith," and doubtlessly it was then that Hamblin had received his instructions to ride ahead, meet the Fancher Party and advise the travelers from Arkansas to rest their animals at Mountain Meadows, before they set out to cross the "90-Mile Desert" to California.

After departing from Apostle Smith, Hamblin and his companions had resumed their trip north and soon reached the Indian Farm. "We encamped at Corn Creek, on our way up," Hamblin wrote, "near a company of Emigrants from Arkansas, on the——"

But here, just as the narrative promised to become most revealing, it came to a tantalizing close, thanks to the destruction of the
diary's next pages—the sort of destruction that so often seemed to
occur whenever a personal journal was commandeered and depos-
ited in the archives of the Church.

Ultimately, though, this effort at concealment proved unsuccessful, for two years later Hamblin was obliged to testify about
his activities just prior to the affair at Mountain Meadows, and
during the examination he unwittingly disclosed a good deal
more about himself and his associates than either he or the
Church hierarchy could have desired. The interrogation took
place at the scene of the ambush, and Brevet Major James H.
Carleton, the United States Army officer who questioned Hamblin, wrote down the exact words the Mormon Elder used.

"About the middle of August, 1857," Hamblin told Carleton, "I
started on a visit to Salt Lake City. At Corn Creek, eight miles
south of Fillmore City, I encamped with a train of emigrants, who
said they were mostly from Arkansas. . . . This information I got
in conversation with one of the men of the train. The people
seemed to be ordinary frontier 'homespun' people, as a general
thing. . . . Several of the men asked me about the condition of the
road and the disposition of the Indians, and where there would be
a good place to recruit their stock."

Then Jacob Hamblin indicated the words he had spoken to
tighten the last cords of the net around the Fancher Party. "I
asked them," he said, "how many men they had. They said they
had between forty and fifty, 'that would do to tie to.' I told them I
considered if they would keep a good lookout that the Indians did
not steal their animals, half the number would be safe, and that
the Mountain Meadows was the best point to recruit their
animals, before entering upon the desert. I recommended this
spring, and the grazing about here, four miles south of my house,
as the place where they should stop."

Finally, unable to resist further elaboration, and never dream-
ing that one day a middle-aged woman, daughter of two of the
ambush victims, and sister and aunt of countless others, would be
able to testify to his deception, Hamblin told the officer, "The
most of these men seemed to have families with them . . . and,
being Southern people, had preferred to take the southern route."

While Jacob Hamblin was making certain that the Fancher

Party would spend at least a week or two at Mountain Meadows before entering the desert, Apostle George A. Smith was continuing his whirlwind tour of the southern settlements. Earlier in the month, on his way south, he had paused at Buttermilk Fort, Fillmore City, Corn Creek and Beaver, before riding on to Parowan, almost the last sizable town a southbound traveler encountered along that remote part of the trail. At Parowan, Apostle Smith had been able to combine pleasure with business, paying a conjugal visit to one of his wives who was a resident of the place, and also conferring with Colonel William H. Dame, the thirty-five-year-old commanding officer of the Iron County Militia. Then the Apostle, accompanied by Dame and a few carefully chosen Parowan Elders, had proceeded still farther south, to Cedar City, about thirty-five miles east of Mountain Meadows. Here a meeting was held with the community's leading citizens, including Philip Klingensmith, George Higbee, and Major Isaac C. Haight, the bishop of Iron County and the chief religious and political officer in that section of the Territory.

Among other matters discussed at Cedar City was the rumored approach of six hundred United States soldiers, said to be advancing on Parowan directly from the east, presumably along the Old Spanish Trail, and the equally improbable incursion of a "mob" of California civilians, reported to be on the march from the opposite direction. Should either rumor prove true, Bishop Haight purportedly assured the Apostle, he and the other young men of the district would take swift and vengeful action against the invaders, without waiting for direct orders from the Prophet in Salt Lake City. It was this alleged, off-the-cuff remark that the Church and its apologists afterward seized upon, in an effort to persuade a sceptical Gentile world that Haight, Dame and Indian Farmer John D. Lee had indeed acted entirely on their own initiative in the discreditable Mountain Meadows affair, and that as a consequence, it was demonstrably certain Brigham Young had known nothing about Captain Fancher and his party until after the ambush was over.

Yet doubtlessly the truth was that Apostle Smith, Brigham Young's personal representative, discussed far more than improbable invasion rumors with Haight, Dame and the other assembled Elders, and that among the principal topics examined by the conspirators, at that late August meeting, was the most effective way to despoil the emigrant parties then known to be en

route south to Parowan and Cedar City, with particular attention
being given to the plans already made for Mountain Meadows
and the exceptionally wealthy Fancher Train.

At last, when these discussions were finished, and with the
leaders of Iron County fully apprised of the Prophet's wishes and
intentions, the conclave broke up, Dame and his contingent
returning north to Parowan, Haight and his fellow Elders remaining in Cedar City and Apostle Smith setting off alone for the
nearby village of Harmony, a few miles to the southwest. At
Harmony, John D. Lee had his principal residence, and it was
here that Rachel Lee, sixth of his eighteen or nineteen wives,
noted in her diary on the seventeenth of August that the Apostle
George A. Smith had come to their village and delivered "a
discourse on the spirit that actuated the United States towards
this people," an envenomed sermon that seemed even to so
unwavering a Saint as Rachel Lee to have been "full of hostility
and virulence."

At this point in his travels, Apostle Smith still had two
assignments to fulfill: he had to meet with the remaining
Pah-Ute chiefs and solicit their further loyalty and cooperation,
and he had to prepare Lee for the leading role he had been
selected to play at Mountain Meadows. Deciding that both tasks
could be undertaken together, the Apostle asked Lee for his
assistance and then set out with him in one of Lee's wagons to
visit the Pah-Utes.

For a long time afterward nothing at all was known about their
tour of the area. Many years later, however, when Lee finally
realized he had been betrayed by the Church and that life was
drawing to an end, he wrote his confessions, including a description of the days he had spent in the extreme south during late
August 1857 with his old friend and Church superior, the Apostle
George A. Smith.

Only the unwary, of course, would accept Lee's entire account
at face value, for when death draws close even the most hardened
criminal may feel an overpowering need to deny his guilt or to
place his misdeeds in the best possible light. And by the end of his
life, John D. Lee was especially eager to shift the blame for his
crimes onto the shoulders of others, not simply to vindicate his
own conduct but because he knew that if he failed to regain at
least some measure of respectability, his name and reputation
would condemn his descendants to a future of acute shame and
suffering. And so, in defense of his past acts, Lee fell back on the

same curious farrago of excuses which the Church first had contrived for itself and its guilty officers two decades before—that at the time of the Mountain Meadows Massacre, martial law had been declared, the Territory had been under arms and in this warlike atmosphere, Apostle Smith had been acting not as a Church Elder but as a high-ranking military commander. Moreover, Lee contended, an invasion by United States troops and California "mobocrats" had been momentarily expected in the southern settlements, and fearful of what lay ahead for themselves and their families, a number of Saints had indeed behaved unwisely, but only as any fearful men all too probably would have behaved under similar circumstances. As for himself, Lee insisted, he was to be forgiven for whatever excessive zeal he might have displayed, on the ground that he merely had been following orders—the military orders of his superior officers.

Distorted, contradictory and self-serving though much of it was, Lee's account did offer a unique outline—and confirmation—of what had occurred when he and Apostle Smith left Harmony for the Santa Clara River. "In the latter part of August, 1857," Lee said, "about ten days before the company of Captain Fancher . . . arrived [at Mountain Meadows] . . . General George A. Smith called on me . . . and wished me to take him round by Fort Clara. . . . He said, 'I have been sent down by the old Boss, Brigham Young, to instruct the brethren of the different settlements not to sell any of their grain to our enemies . . . for the enemy is coming to attempt our destruction. . . . But . . . God is on our side and will fight our battles for us, and deliver our enemies into our hands. Brigham Young has received revelations giving him the right and power to call down the curse of God on all our enemies who attempt to invade our Territory."

According to Lee's account, he then drove Apostle Smith by horse and carriage to two or three remote settlements before stopping at the Santa Clara, where a large number of Pah-Ute Indians had assembled. Lee's description of the meeting can be accepted as reasonably accurate, since the Apostle's seditious address clearly had been composed by Brigham Young and did little to compromise Lee himself. "Their chiefs," Lee recalled, "asked me where I was going, and who I had with me. I told them that he was a big captain.

"'Is he a 'Mericat captain?'

"'No,' I said. 'He is a Mormon.'"

Lee then began to translate Brigham Young's message to the

Indians. "The General told me," Lee said, "to tell the Indians that the Americans were their enemies and the enemies of the Mormons, too. That he wanted the Indians to remain the fast friends of the Mormons, for the Mormons were all friends to the Indians. That the Americans had a large army just east of the Mountains, and intended to [invade] Utah and kill all the Mormons and Indians in the Utah Territory. That the Indians must keep ready for war against all of the Americans . . . and obey what the Mormons told them to do. That this was the will of the Great Spirit. That if the Indians were true to the Mormons and would help them against their enemies, then the Mormons would always keep them from want and sickness, and give them guns and ammunition to hunt and kill game with, and would also help the Indians against their enemies when they went to war."

And Lee concluded his recollection of the meeting by adding, with unconscious significance, "This talk pleased the Indians, and they agreed to all that I asked them to do."

After these negotiations had been concluded, Lee and Apostle Smith turned north again and for a time traveled along in silence. Then the Apostle, who had been "in a deep study," raised the complex and absorbing question of how best to deal with the Fancher Train. Lee's version of what was said, while highly fanciful, was also oddly revealing; for the ideas themselves mirrored perfectly the thinking of Brigham Young at the time and no doubt were used in the southern settlements by Apostle Smith, Lee, Haight, Dame and a few others when discussing the Fancher Train with Saints who were not privy to the Church's confidential plans.

As Lee remembered it, "Apostle Smith said, 'Suppose an emigrant train should come along through this southern country, making threats against our people, and bragging of the part they took in helping to kill our Prophets, what do you think the brethren would do with them? Would they permit them to go their way, or would the brethren pitch into them and give them a good drubbing?'"

Here were two separate matters to be considered—the formulation of an excuse to explain a future massacre, if such an excuse should prove useful, and the method by which a militia detachment of ordinary Saints could be stirred up sufficiently so that they would complete the task of despoiling the Fancher Party if Lee and the Indians found themselves unable to complete the task alone.

Lee's version of his own response was equally revealing. "I reflected a few minutes," he admitted in his confession, "and then said, 'You know the brethren are now under the influence of the late reformation, and are still red-hot for the gospel. The brethren believe the Government wishes to destroy them. I really believe that any train that may come through here will be attacked, and probably all destroyed. I am sure they would be wiped out if they had been making threats against our people."

It was not long, Lee declared, before the Apostle replied, "Brother Lee, I am satisfied that the brethren are under the full influence of the reformation, and I believe they will do just as you say they will, with the wicked emigrants that come through the country making threats and abusing our people.'"

And so, having agreed that such stories about the conduct of the Fancher Party would satisfactorily explain its ultimate fate, and could be used to arouse the local populace to attack the train if that were necessary, Lee's version of the scene came to an end. No doubt the actual conversation between the two men had been much more direct and pragmatic, Lee and Smith having openly discussed their plans for both the attack itself at Mountain Meadows and also for the disposal of whatever loot might be secured by the attacking forces.

Finally, in his confessions, while still attempting to absolve himself of blame, Lee came to admit what he and his fellow conspirators had known from the start—that under the pretext of resistance to Federal control the Church planned to rob and murder all Gentile parties passing along the Southern Trail and that the orders to do so came from Salt Lake City and the Prophet himself. "General Smith did not say one word to me, or intimate to me," Lee insisted, "that he wished *any emigrants* to pass in safety through the Territory. But he led me to believe . . . that he did want, and expected every emigrant to be killed that undertook to pass through the Territory, while we were at war with the Government. I thought that it was his *mission* to prepare the people for the bloody work.

"I have always believed, since that day, that General George A. Smith was then visiting southern Utah to prepare the people for the work of exterminating Captain Fancher's train of emigrants, and I now believe that he was sent for that purpose by the direct command of Brigham Young.

"I acted through the whole matter in a way I considered it my religious duty to act, and if what I did was a crime, it was the crime of the Mormon Church, and not a crime for which I felt individually responsible."

This was Lee's credo and excuse at the close of his life, and no doubt it was his credo and excuse twenty years earlier, at the end of August 1857, when he prepared to take command of the Mormons' Indian allies and to lead them into action against the enemy. Within a few days the drama would begin to unfold at Mountain Meadows, and then the expulsion from Nauvoo, the Haun's Mill Massacre and the murder of Joseph and Hyrum Smith in a Carthage jail would finally be avenged, and he himself, John Doyle Lee, as the agent of that vengeance, would know the joy of bringing down the Bloody Wrath of God on the hated Gentiles.

Chapter 27

MUCH OF WHAT TOOK PLACE in southern Utah during the last days of the Fancher Train was never fully disclosed during later times. Months afterward a few guiltless eyewitnesses were indeed found and questioned, but no one in authority thought it worthwhile to examine them thoroughly and then to record their testimony, while among the guilty there naturally enough was an orgy of lying and concealment, as each criminal sought to restore his own reputation—or to save his own neck—by placing the entire blame for the affair on one or more of his fellow conspirators. Still, it was not especially difficult to trace the course of the train itself, as it slowly drove the last 120 or 130 miles to The Meadows, and then to follow, in reasonably close detail, the climax of one of the most calculated, pitiless and shameful mass-murders ever perpetrated in the violent history of America's violent frontier.

The date is uncertain, but most probably on the twenty-fifth or twenty-sixth of August, the Fancher Party left Corn Creek and, with Jacob Hamblin's advice fresh in mind, set off southward toward Mountain Meadows, at the Rim of.the Great Basin. At Beaver, fifty miles south of Corn Creek, the weary, half-famished emigrants once again attempted to purchase food for themselves and hay for their livestock, but without success. Having no other recourse, they soon resumed their journey and arrived about forty-eight hours later at the walled city of Parowan, twenty-five or thirty miles farther along the trail.

By this time, Colonel William Dame had returned home to militia headquarters from his meeting at Cedar City with Apostle George A. Smith and Major Isaac Haight. Learning of the

Fancher Train's approach, Dame promptly gave orders that the gates were to be shut and the Arkansas emigrants kept from entering the town. There were two reasons for these orders. If the gates were left open and the party allowed to enter and spend time freely within the walls, the travelers soon would observe the unusual military preparations then being undertaken by the militia, and the sight of so much drilling and marching, and the abundance of firearms in public hands, might well alert them to the fact that they faced far more danger from the Mormons than they did from the Indians who inhabited the surrounding terri-tory. And if the Fanchers came into the settlement and were seen at close quarters, the ordinary Saints of Parowan would soon realize that here were no boisterous, dissolute, irreligious "mobo-crats," or drunken, blasphemous "Missouri wildcats," but sober, "homespun," God-fearing family people, much like themselves— with the result that the emigrants would be all too likely to win the sympathy of the very militiamen who soon might have to be used in an attack on the train.

Temporarily forced to leave the trail outside of Parowan, the Fancher Party turned right and circled the town along the western wall of the fort, before stopping to make camp on the bank of the neighboring stream. After pitching tents, the emi-grants asked to have their thirty pounds of Indian corn ground for a fee at the nearby gristmill, but once more their pleas for an act of simple kindness were refused by local Church authorities. At the same time, several less exalted residents of Parowan attempted to sell food to the train, in one instance the Samaritan being noticed immediately by an alert town Elder, who ran up to him, held a bowie knife to his throat and induced him to abandon his humanitarian efforts.

According to another account, the emigrants did, however, meet with limited success at Parowan, securing a small measure of wheat from one farmer and a few pounds of onions from a second. The latter, it was said, were offered to the Fancher Train by a Saint named Isaac Laney, who had been a loyal member of the Church for twenty years and who, during the old days back in the Midwest, had been severely wounded by shotgun blasts from a Missouri mob. Nevertheless, Laney took pity on the "Gentile oppressors" camped outside the walls of Parowan and sold them a modest quantity of onions—as it turned out, a foolhardy thing to do, for one day not long afterward, on orders from the local

Priesthood, he was attacked by several men armed with clubs, and, for his act of defiance, very nearly beaten to death.

From Parowan, the Fancher Party proceeded southwest along the trail, some eighteen or twenty miles to Cedar City. Here the emigrants were allowed to purchase fifty bushels of tithing wheat, and to grind it along with their Indian corn, at the local mill; but as one honest Mormon commentator noted afterward, there was little actual charity in this, since "the authorities that pretended to sell [the] wheat knew that they would have . . . most of it back in less than a week, [or] at least they knew that it would never leave the Territory."

Despite these minor acts of accommodation, the train, while resting at Cedar City, soon met with additional difficulties. According to the Mormon version—and there was no other—the emigrants were entirely at fault. Some of the party, the Saints asserted, were former residents of Missouri and boasted of having driven the Mormons from the state, while others shouted that they had been in Illinois a decade earlier and had assisted in the murders of Joseph and Hyrum Smith at Carthage, one egregious member of the train even claiming that he was the owner of the very pistol that had slain the Prophet outside the city jail. Some of the emigrants, it was said, in order to further insult the Saints, had nicknamed pairs of their oxen "Brigham" and "Heber" and now addressed the animals loudly and often by these offensive titles, laughing boisterously as they did so; allegedly the swaggering emigrants also snapped off the heads of numerous chickens with their long bullwhips and threatened to take as much food as they pleased when they passed through the last scattered and helpless Mormon hamlets that still lay ahead on their route. And when Bishop Haight and his fellow Elders attempted to arrest and fine the train leaders, because they had failed to obtain a safe-conduct pass from Brigham Young in Salt Lake City, the emigrants "swore like pirates, fired their pistols in the air" and defied the town authorities to detain them.

Certainly most of the accusations against the emigrants were transparently absurd, although no doubt, too, there was trouble that day at Cedar City, and in all likelihood the train leaders did resist—and resist vehemently—what they must have considered an arbitrary and obnoxious attempt to arrest them and force them to pay an unjust fine. Coming after so many weeks of calculated ill treatment, such high-handed behavior on the part of the Saints at Cedar City could only have infuriated the already much-abused emigrants, and it is difficult to see how an unbiased observer could have blamed them a great deal, had they, indeed, on this occasion, responded in anger. Moreover, whatever other considerations might have been true, one additional fact still was paramount: the members of the Fancher Train were United States citizens, passing legally through United States territory, and as a consequence, the Elders of Cedar City had no right to detain them, to demand a special pass or to fine them a sum of money because they failed to possess one—especially since, if one were to believe the Church's own records and depositions, Governor Brigham Young's "proclamation of martial law" had not yet even been issued and, indeed, was not to be issued for another two weeks.

But the reason why Stake President Haight and his fellow Elders chose to harass the Fancher Party, and perhaps provoke its members into violence, no longer was a mystery to anyone but the travelers themselves. The train was now doomed to extinction, and this was the Saints' last opportunity to blacken publicly their victims' reputation prior to the commencement of the ambush. And so no doubt there was a brief, spirited quarrel at Cedar City before the train managed to extricate itself from the toils of the local authorities, and quite possibly, too, several of the emigrants were restrained from attacking their tormentors only by the sobering, last-minute reflection that if they were to do so, they certainly would be endangering the safety of their own wives and children.

It was the beginning of September now, and the Fancher Train, its livestock all but exhausted, left Cedar City and once again began to drive slowly toward the southwest. Ahead lay the obscure village of Pinto Creek, and then Mountain Meadows itself, some thirty or thirty-five miles away; there, after four or five more days of travel, the weary emigrants finally would be able to rest and to restore their animals, in the green and pleasant valley that lay just to the south of Jacob Hamblin's summer ranch.

Although most of the countryside seemed utterly deserted, the Arkansas company, during its final days, never really was far removed from watchful eyes; a number of Mormon riders always were on the road, passing back and forth, and at every town and village along the way there were additional observers. Somewhere back along the trail, the emigrants already had passed at least one traveler who was particularly interested in their progress. This was the Apostle George A. Smith, riding briskly north to Salt Lake City, his tour of the southern settlements, and his secret mission for the Church, both having been concluded in a most satisfactory manner.

And then—almost certainly at some point between Cedar City and Pinto Creek—the Fancher Train was overtaken by a number of Jacob Hamblin's Pah-Ute Indian chiefs, although the missionary leader himself was not one of the party. As the Indians swept by the train, their sanguine thoughts can all too easily be imagined. No more than three or four days earlier, the band had been in Salt Lake City, where on the first of September its members had conferred privately with Brigham Young and Dimick B. Huntington. Whether this was the occasion on which the chiefs received a letter from Huntington, signed by the Prophet, with orders to kill the members of the Fancher Party is not certain, but there can scarcely be any doubt that such a letter eventually was placed in their hands, either at Salt Lake City or, more probably, in the south; nor can there be any doubt that the meeting in the capital was a success and a source of mutual satisfaction, it being agreed that from then on, all Gentile parties like the Fancher Train were to be fair game for the Pah-Utes and their Mormon collaborators. Departing immediately afterward from the city, the chiefs then had ridden south at top speed, and after passing the Arkansas emigrants near Mountain Meadows, were ready to take command of their warriors and to join John D. Lee for the grand assault on the unsuspecting company.

As for the wily Jacob Hamblin, he apparently had decided long since that this was no time to hasten back home to Mountain Meadows, knowing as he did what lay in store for the Fancher Train. And so, instead, he allowed the Pah-Ute chiefs to return south by themselves and rode from Salt Lake City to the town of Tooele, thirty or forty miles to the west, where he stayed with relatives for several days, establishing an unshakable alibi. During the same period, as a reward for good service, he was granted permission by Brigham Young to take a new bride, and this he did, receiving his endowments, and joyfully marrying young Priscilla Leavitt in the capital on the very day when, by a curious coincidence, the emigrants from Arkansas were being betrayed and slaughtered only a mile or two from his summer home.

On Friday, the fourth of September, an hour or so before sunset, the Fancher Party entered the narrow, five-mile-long valley called Mountain Meadows, at a point a few yards to the south of Jacob Hamblin's ranch house and its nearby spring. Descending a short distance along the opposite slope, the Fanchers and their companions quickly made camp and before it grew completely dark were ready to settle down for the night.

The next morning the emigrants moved on again and by midafternoon, having traveled two or three miles farther south, finally halted at a spot thirty or forty yards to the north of a second and larger spring, which welled up at the bottom of a shallow depression six or eight feet below the valley floor. Within a short time a more permanent camp had been made, water carried from the spring to the campsite, the party's horses, oxen and mules turned out to graze on the tall meadow grass, and by dusk a frugal but welcome dinner was in preparation.

Saturday night, huddled for warmth around their campfires, the emigrants must have felt a number of strong emotions, not the least being a sense of relief at the thought that now they were beyond the power of the strange, frenzied people they had encountered along the Southern Trail. It was true, of course, that serious difficulties still confronted them: their food was in short supply, their animals were all but played out, and a few miles to the southwest, beyond the low-lying Beaver Mountains, there stretched a barren and forbidding desert where water holes were sometimes fifty miles apart and where almost the sole inhabitants were roving Indian tribes, said to be on much better terms with the Latter-Day Saints than they were with Gentile travelers. Nevertheless, after just one day at The Meadows, these difficulties already seemed less formidable. Because of the lush pasturage, a week or so of grazing would restore the strength of the company's animals, and then, as a consequence, a speedier passage across the desert would more than compensate for whatever food the train had been forced to consume during its stay at The Meadows. As for the danger of an Indian attack, the train's leaders felt little concern, for forty or fifty sharpshooters were in their own ranks, and the Pah-Ute braves of southern Utah were known to have few if any firearms and to be the least aggressive and warlike Indians in the entire Territory. Truly, after only twenty-four hours in the cool, sunny air at Mountain Meadows, the leaders of the company must have found it easy to persuade themselves that their worst problems already were safely behind them.

The scene in camp on Sunday, September 6, was a familiar one, enacted countless times before, during the weeks when the Fancher Train had been making its slow, fifteen-hundred-mile journey from northwestern Arkansas to southwestern Utah. Now, as the sun rose and the outlines of the valley and its cluster of wagons gradually became visible, there were early chores to be done, ablutions to be made and breakfast to be prepared and eaten. Toward midmorning, after the day grew warmer, the company's spiritual leader, a Methodist minister, led his congregation through the weekly Sabbath service, held in the extra-large tent that the company faithfully had transported all the way from Fort Smith. With services over, the doctor who was traveling in the train could treat such patients as presented themselves and visit the one or two mothers-to-be, who were resting in their tents and wagons.

During the pleasant summer afternoon the emigrants found themselves free to take exercise, to spend an idle hour talking or to work at domestic tasks, as suited their individual needs and temperaments. Several of the younger men untethered their horses and rode them through the waving meadow grass, inspecting as they went the low hills that rose to the east and south of the campsite, the taller hill to the northeast, and the rock-strewn escarpment directly to the west, all of which overlooked the spring and the emigrant wagons sprawled in disarray nearby. Exactly who all the riders were that afternoon can only be surmised, but surely John H. Baker, "Uncle Jack" Baker's oldest son, was one of them, as were young Hampton and William Fancher, two of the captain's eight children. And surely, too, another rider that day was Tilghman Cameron, one of William and Martha Cameron's five sons, on his racing mare "One-eyed Blaze."

For the women in the company that tranquil summer afternoon, there was sewing, mending and the airing of clothes and bed linen; while for the thirty-five or forty children there were games to be played in the sunlit, sweet-smelling meadows, favorite stories to be heard when their mothers were willing to recount them and duties to be performed as well, such as caring for younger sisters and brothers, gathering brushwood for the campfires and carrying up water from the spring. For the older men in the party there were tools and equipment to be repaired and draft animals to be examined closely and doctored when necessary, because without a healthy pair or two of oxen or a team of mules, the desert that lay ahead might not be crossed swiftly enough and then a man and his family stood in danger of dying of thirst before reaching California. And for William Cameron—and quite possibly for a few other men in the train as well—the care of the family wagon was additionally important, since money acquired during a lifetime of toil had been concealed in that homely, familiar vehicle, and to be forced to abandon it while crossing the desert—unless one had the time to remove one's fortune and the strength left to carry it on one's back to California—would be nearly as great a tragedy as the loss of life itself.

Of all the emigrants in the valley that Sunday afternoon, none could have been more eager to observe the activities around him than William Aden, the twenty-year-old artist from Tennessee, who had joined the train only about three weeks earlier, at Provo. Here in the valley were any number of original subjects for his pens and brushes, and it would hardly be fanciful to suppose that as he watched the horsemen cantering through the tall grass, the children playing at their makeshift games and the men attending to the wheels and axles of their wagons, that the idea for numerous sketches began to crowd his mind and that before long he already had commenced to plan a series of pictures of the party and its campsite—studies of the surrounding hills and the rocky escarpment to the west, the spring below the valley floor, the wagons and the grazing oxen and mules, the cedars, the scrub pines and the other stunted trees and bushes, and on the horizon, the foothills of the Beaver Mountains.

By then it was evening at Mountain Meadows, and at last, as the campfires fell low again, Sunday, September 6, came to an end, and the settlers crept into their tents and wagons and fell asleep. Likely enough, from custom and simple prudence, a guard of some kind was posted during the night, but with no danger anticipated the watchers probably were few in number and not overly alert, and between dusk and daylight no member of the Fancher Company detected anything suspicious in the black silence of the surrounding hills.

Chapter 28

WHILE THE FANCHER PARTY had been riding toward the Rim of the Great Basin and then spending a calm and prayerful weekend at Mountain Meadows, the fanatical leaders of Iron County, eager to carry out the wishes of an even more fanatical Church hierarchy, had begun to assemble their widely dispersed Indian confederates and to complete other last-minute preparations prior to launching the long-awaited attack on the wealthy strangers from northwest Arkansas.

Toward the week's end, most probably either on Friday or Saturday, the fourth or fifth of September, John D. Lee was called to Cedar City from his home by Stake President—and militia major—Isaac Haight. Major Lee, for that, too, was his rank in the Iron County militia, did not ride openly to Haight's residence; instead he slipped furtively into town and met Haight at a corner of the main square. By then it was dark, and the two conspirators, having no wish to attract attention, took some blankets and sought out the most private place they could think of, a temporarily abandoned iron works on the outskirts of the community, where they prepared to spend the night together, completing plans for the destruction of the Fancher Train.

Although Lee's version of the meeting was biased and self-serving, it still was both unique and important. Among other things, it disclosed the justifications that he and his fellow criminals already were preparing for themselves, even before the commission of their crimes; moreover, it disclosed as well the explanations which they, the civil and ecclesiastical leaders of Iron County, already had begun to use to persuade their ingenuous followers that the Fancher Train deserved to be destroyed, that it was God's will that this should come to pass and that under conditions of "invasion" and "war," the Saints had every right to "defend" themselves and their homes from such wicked and dangerous enemies as the emigrants from Arkansas.

According to Lee's account, when he first arrived in Cedar City on that cool September evening, he had no idea whatever why he had been asked there to confer with his fellow Church Elder. The claim, of course, was simple nonsense, because Lee, as a member of the Mormon hierarchy's inner circle, already knew all about the ambush and exactly the role that the Prophet expected him to play. Nor was this Lee's sole misstatement of fact, for among other things, he apparently had forgotten that just a week or two earlier—by his own admission—he and Apostle Smith, while on their visit to the Pah-Ute Indians, had discussed, and even "invented," many of the very charges against the Fancher Party, which supposedly Haight now revealed to him for the first time.

"After we got to the iron works," Lee said, "Haight told me all about the train of emigrants. He said (and I then believed every word that he spoke, for I believed it was an impossible thing for one so high in the Priesthood as he was, to be guilty of falsehood) that the emigrants were a rough and abusive set of men. That they had, while traveling through Utah, been very abusive to all the Mormons they met. That they had insulted, outraged and ravished many of the Mormon women. That the abuses heaped upon the people by the emigrants during the trip from Provo to Cedar City, had been constant and shameful; that they had burned fences and destroyed growing crops; that at many points on the road they had poisoned the water, so that all the people and stock that drank of the water became sick, and many had died from the effects of the poison."

And according to Lee's confession, the Stake leader had yet other accusations to level against the evil Gentiles who had just passed through Cedar City a day or two before. Members of the train had boasted, Haight said, "of having friends in Utah who would hang Brigham Young by the neck until he was dead." The Fanchers then had bragged "that General Johnston was coming with his army from the East, and that they [the Fanchers] were going to return from California with soldiers, as soon as possible, and would then desolate the land, and kill every damn Mormon man, woman and child they could find in Utah.

"Haight said," Lee continued. "that unless something was done to prevent it, the emigrants would carry out their threats to rob every one of the out-lying settlements in the South, and that the whole Mormon people were liable to be butchered by the troops the emigrants would bring back with them from California. I was then told that the Council had held a meeting . . . to consider the matter, and that it was decided by the authorities to arm the Indians, give them provisions and ammunition, and send them after the emigrants, and have the Indians give them a good *brush*, and if they killed part or all of them, so much the better."

Still insisting that only now, for the first time, had he even learned of the proposed ambush, Lee claimed to have asked his fellow conspirator, in all innocence, "Brother Haight, who is your authority for acting this way?" And according to Lee, Haight had replied, "It is the *will of all in authority.* The emigrants have no pass from anyone to go through the country, and they are liable to be killed as common enemies, for the country is at war now."

And then—at long last—Lee's story of his secret meeting with Haight began to deal realistically with the way things had been. "We lay there," he said, "and talked much of the night, and during that time Haight gave me very full instructions what to do, and how to proceed in the whole affair. He said he had consulted with Colonel Dame, and everyone agreed to let the Indians use up the whole train if they could. Haight then said, 'I expect you to carry out your orders,'" which was no problem for Lee, since he believed, as he himself confessed, "that my superiors in the Church were the mouthpieces of Heaven, and that it was an act of godliness for me to obey any and all orders given by them to me, without my asking any questions."

Lee's instructions were plain enough, and actually he had been awaiting them ever since he had conferred with Apostle Smith some ten days or two weeks earlier. "My orders," he said, "were to go home to Harmony and see Carl Shirts [Shurtz] my son-in-law, an Indian interpreter, and send him to the Indians in the South." After that, Shurtz would hasten down to the Santa Clara and Virgin rivers and bring back the Indians from there, while Lee himself was to collect as many other braves as possible from those tribes living in the vicinity of Cedar City and Harmony. Nor were these the only warriors to be assembled. In addition, as Lee explained, "It was agreed that Haight would send Nephi Johnson, another Indian interpreter, to *stir up* all the other Indians he could find, in order to have a large enough force of Indians to give the emigrants a good *hush.*"

Then Lee went on to add these words, which left no doubt that

he and every other member of the conspiracy understood exactly
what Brigham Young's design had been from the very start. "It
was then intended that the Indians should kill the emigrants, and
make it an *Indian massacre*. . . . No whites were to be known in
the matter. It was all to be done [ostensibly] by the Indians, so
that it could be laid to them, if any questions were ever asked
about it. . . . [Haight and I] agreed upon the whole thing, how
each one should act, and then we left the iron works, and went to
Haight's house and got breakfast."

After tucking away some food, apparently with a good appetite,
the two conspirators prepared to part. "Haight said to me," Lee
recalled, " 'Go, Brother Lee, and see that the instructions of those
in authority are obeyed, and as you are faithful in this, so shall
your reward be in the Kingdom of God, for God will bless those
who willingly will obey counsel.' " And Lee concluded by saying,
"I then believed that he [Haight] acted by direct command of
William H. Dame, and others even higher in authority than
Colonel Dame. One reason for [my] thinking so was from a talk I
had only a few days before, with Apostle George A. Smith, [who]
had just seen Haight, and talked with him, [because] I knew that
George A. Smith never talked of things that Brigham Young had
not talked over with him beforehand."

And so on Sunday, September 6, while John D. Lee and the
handful of Saints under his command were secretly leading some
three hundred Indian braves toward Mountain Meadows, the
Church Elders of Cedar City were delivering their weekly anti-
Gentile sermons, at the same time preparing to hasten into the
field with their militia, in the event that Brigham Young's
original plan should fail and it prove necessary for the Mormons
themselves to complete the task of murdering a hundred and
forty or fifty innocent human beings.

Isaac Haight, in his capacity of religious leader and President
of the local Stake of Zion, offered his audience the sort of
bloodthirsty harangue that most of the southern Saints by now
were all too eager to hear. Haight said that the Fancher Train
was made up of a villainous mob of Godless Missourians, and
cried out for vengeance against them, recalling as he did a
number of events in the history of the Church which had taken
place two decades earlier. The Missourians, Haight told his
followers, "drove us out to starve. When we pled for mercy,

Haun's Mill was our answer, and when we asked for bread, they gave us a stone."

On went the familiar roll call of Mormon persecutions and Gentile injustices. "We left the confines of civilization," he declared, "and came far into the wilderness, where we could worship God according to the dictates of our own conscience, without annoyance to our neighbors. But the Gentiles will not leave us alone. They have followed us and hounded us. They come among us asking to trade with them, and in the name of humanity to feed them. All of these things we have done, and now they are sending an army to exterminate us! So far as I'm concerned, I have been driven from my home for the last time. I am prepared to feed to the Gentiles the same bread they fed to us. God being my helper, I will give the last ounce of my strength, and if need be, my last drop of blood, in defense of Zion!"

After this spirited church service had been concluded, a meeting of the local High Council was convoked, with Haight once again taking charge of the proceedings. Great anger was expressed by the Council against the Fancher Train and a public resolution passed unanimously for its destruction; the decision also was made that if necessary the town militia should be sent to The Meadows to destroy the train, Haight and his fellow Elders, including Bishop Philip Klingensmith, no doubt bearing in mind another important, though unspoken fact—that when the train had been destroyed there would be considerable plunder to claim for the Church, and John D. Lee and his handful of "white Indians" surely would need considerable assistance in herding off the victims' livestock, driving away their carriages and wagons and taking possession of their other valuables, while at the same time preventing the Indians from securing more than a minor share of the booty.

Perhaps during the meeting that Sunday at Cedar City, one or two Elders did protest against the appalling decisions taken by the High Council, but the Mormon legend that a young dispatch rider named James Haslam, soon after the end of the meeting, was sent off to Salt Lake City to seek Brigham Young's advice whether or not such decisions were justified, deserves little or no credence. Rather, two other, much less palatable, facts doubtlessly were true: first, that Haslam was indeed dispatched to the capital but only about two days later, with a far different set of queries to place before the Prophet; and second, that at the end of

Sunday's High Council meeting in Cedar City, the great majority of Saints were athirst to see the Fancher Party destroyed, believed it was God's will, and God's justice, that the cattle and other wealth of the train should be taken by force and "consecrated to the True Church," and that among the more violent followers of the Prophet, there was a willingness, bordering on enthusiasm, to proceed at once to The Meadows and there to commence the long-anticipated, and too-long delayed, shedding of Gentile blood.

Chapter 29

L ATE S UNDAY NIGHT, September 6, or during the early hours of Monday morning, September 7, John D. Lee and his three or four white assistants put aside their ordinary clothing, daubed their bodies with red paint, decorated themselves with feathers or whatever other items of native costume they considered necessary to complete their disguise and then led an army of three or four hundred Indian braves silently along the trail to Mountain Meadows, there to surround the sunken spring and the emigrants' camp prior to attacking the unsuspecting Fancher Train.

Under cover of darkness the Indians' main camp was established a mile or two south of the spring, just off the main trail that led to the desert, where it could serve as an observation post and roadblock, preventing the emigrants from escaping in large numbers toward California. Other strategic positions closer to the emigrants' camp also were occupied that night; they included the low, bare hills a hundred or a hundred and fifty yards to the east of the camp, a considerably taller and well-protected hill, almost the same distance to the north, and a long ridge, or escarpment, topped by a number of large, broken rocks, which lay a hundred or two hundred yards to the west and northwest. As a result, the guns and arrows of the attackers now looked down on the campsite from several directions and commanded the vital spring, thirty-five or forty yards from the emigrants' wagons.

Once these positions had been secured, the next step in the ambush plan called for running off the emigrants' livestock, and this the Indians undertook to do during the last hours of darkness. Unlike the score or so of horses which were tethered near the wagons, the emigrants' cows, mules and oxen were grazing freely in the valley, most of them out of sight of the camp, beyond the ridge to the west, in a wider and separate portion of The Meadows; here the Indians, who were adept at such clandestine activities, had no difficulty in approaching the animals, herding them together and then driving them off to a corral several miles distant, accomplishing the feat without causing the slightest suspicion or alarm in the sleeping camp.

The Fanchers, the Bakers, the Dunlaps and all the other family groups and individuals in the train arose once more at dawn and, after rebuilding their campfires, began to heat and drink their morning coffee and to eat the rough breakfast fare that served them daily on the trail. Gradually the sunlight grew stronger in the east, a few of the women took up their early chores, some of the younger children began to play among the wagons, while around the campfires a number of the men stood idly talking and finishing their last mugfuls of coffee, their figures plainly outlined against the eastern sky. It was a typically peaceful emigrant scene, until suddenly the stillness was shattered by a succession of Indian war whoops and a sharp outburst of arrows and gunfire; a few of the shots came from the low, exposed hills to the east, but Lee and the other Mormons, as well as a majority of the Indians, had chosen places of concealment along the ridge to the west, and even along the edge of the spring itself, so that most of the firing came from these positions.

The effect of the first barrage was devastating, and for a minute or two the wildest sort of confusion and panic filled the camp. Six or seven of the man lay dead, most of them sprawled near the campfires, while fifteen or sixteen others had been seriously wounded, at least three of them lying in such a welter of blood that it was evident they were beyond help. At this critical moment, if the Mormons and their several hundred Indian allies had rushed from cover and launched a mass attack on the disorganized emigrants, the ambush doubtlessly would have ended swiftly and it would have been said, forever afterward, that the affair at Mountain Meadows had been nothing more than an unusually large-scale but commonplace Indian attack on yet another party of unwary travelers. But the numerous braves whom John D. Lee had at his disposal were, at best, a sorry set of warriors, ill disciplined and poorly armed. All of them—those from the vicinity of Cedar City and Harmony who had come to The Meadows under their two chiefs, Moquetas and "Big Bill";

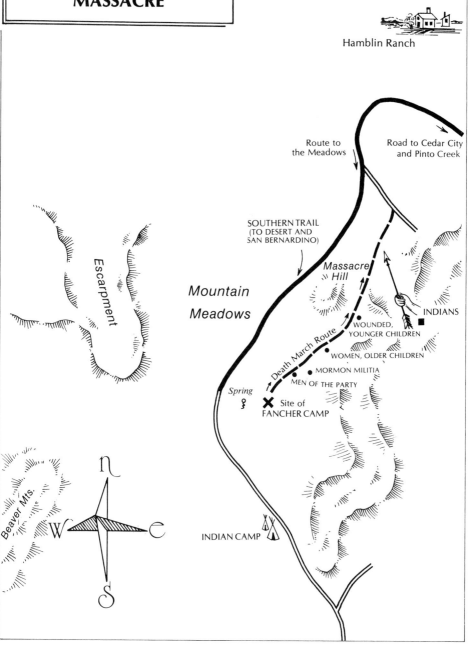

Site of
MOUNTAIN MEADOWS
MASSACRE

Hamblin Ranch

Route to
the Meadows

Road to Cedar City
and Pinto Creek

SOUTHERN TRAIL
(TO DESERT AND
SAN BERNARDINO)

Massacre
Hill

Mountain

Meadows

Escarpment

INDIANS

WOUNDED,
YOUNGER CHILDREN

WOMEN, OLDER CHILDREN

MORMON MILITIA

MEN OF THE PARTY

Death March Route

Spring

✗ Site of
FANCHER CAMP

Beaver Mts.

N

W   E

S

INDIAN CAMP

those from the Santa Clara under Chief Jackson and his brother; and still others from the south under Tutsegabit—shared at least two characteristics in common: they had little stomach for fighting except against a weak or defenseless enemy, and no taste whatever for assaulting a position whose defenders might strike back effectively—and so no charge was launched against the emigrant camp, and the chance to annihilate the Fancher Train swiftly and in absolute secrecy was irretrievably lost.

The many veteran frontiersmen among the emigrants, although taken completely by surprise, quickly regained a measure of their composure and, acting almost instinctively, began to organize a bristling and vigorous defense. First ordering the party's women and children to seek shelter behind and within the wagons, the emigrants seized their rifles and soon were throwing out a curtain of answering fire so accurate and deadly that within minutes the attacking force was compelled to retreat from its more exposed positions closest to the camp, taking cover principally behind the rocky outcroppings that crowned the long ridge to the west, and the similar protection afforded by the tall hill to the north.

Having driven the enemy back a considerable distance, the emigrants immediately began to convert their open campsite into a more secure and defensible position. Losing no time, they dragged their wagons together into a compact circle, with the wagons' tongues pointed toward the circle's center, thus forming the traditionally shaped corral, so often used by western parties when besieged by attacking Indians. With this done, the emigrants dug holes beneath each set of wagon wheels, and then, one by one, lowered their wagons into the earth, until a circular barricade had been formed, beneath which the enemy's bullets and arrows could not penetrate. Then the emigrants dug a protective trench, or pit, within the corral, about four feet deep and twenty feet long, to shelter the more seriously wounded, the women and the children. Finally, around the perimeter of their little fortress, they dug a second, circular ditch, and heaped up an earthen barricade in front of it, to provide the party's marksmen with secure positions from which to answer the sporadic shots that continued to be aimed at their camp from the hill to the north and the ridge that lay to the west.

By now it was late Monday, only a few hours after the ambush had been sprung, and already a stalemate had developed between besiegers and besieged. To the emigrants, the situation must have seemed grim and even terrifying, but at the same time far from hopeless, for as yet they had no inkling whatever that the Mormons were the real instigators of the ambush. Not realizing this, the leaders of the train undoubtedly made a number of false assumptions that would have been valid under ordinary circumstances—that they had suffered nothing more unusual than an exceptionally strong Indian attack and that the sound of gunfire had been heard and recognized by those Saints living at Jacob Hamblin's summer ranch house; that as a consequence, news of the train's peril already had been carried to Pinto Creek, and perhaps even as far as Cedar City; and that in the name of common humanity their fellow Christians in those communities soon would assemble a military force and dispatch it as quickly as possible to Mountain Meadows.

Assuming that relief either was on the way or would be shortly, the leaders of the train no doubt believed that they had only to hold out for a day or two longer and the worst would be over, and so, when they turned to examine their tactical problems, they must have been reassured to find that in every respect save one they were well equipped to fight off their assailants. Clearly favoring them in their defense was the fortress itself, which the party's surviving marksmen could easily man and hold secure and from which they could exact a terrible price if the Indians, having missed their earliest and only real chance to do so successfully should now prove foolhardy enough to leave their places of concealment and attempt a direct assault across the open meadowland. Also favorable to the defenders was the evident fact that many of the braves had arrived at their rendezvous too lightly armed, probably bearing no other weapons than tomahawks, bows and arrows and knives, and that those braves who did possess firearms, except when employing them at extremely close range, as they had been able to do briefly during the first attack, actually were very poor marksmen. Clearly, too, most of the Indians had been intimidated by the emigrants' superior rifles and their great efficiency in using them, for since the initial onslaught the braves in the surrounding hills had shown no disposition to expose themselves to the emigrants' fire.

On the other hand, one extremely grave problem already threatened the besieged. Two days before, the members of the Fancher Party had reached an unfortunate decision, electing not to camp directly beside the sunken spring because of the marshy

ground surrounding it, and subsequently, when the Indian attack
had come, they had been unable to move their wagons far enough
to enclose the spring within their hastily constructed corral. This
meant that their only source of water now lay thirty-five or forty
yards beyond the camp perimeter, across open ground—a fact
their assailants were well aware of, for every attempt to reach
the spring during the past eight or ten hours had drawn such
sharp fire from the nearby escarpment that no one in the party
had succeeded in reaching the spring, and as a result, even by late
Monday, drinking water had begun to be in ominously short
supply within the emigrants' camp.

Meanwhile, among the besiegers, there were difficulties, too.
Before the ambush, the Indians had been promised an easy time
of things. They had been assured by the Prophet himself in Salt
Lake City, and by his confidential agents in the south, particularly Apostle George A. Smith, John D. Lee and Jacob Hamblin, that
an attack on the Fancher Train, and on other Gentile parties
following in its wake, could be accomplished quickly and pain-
lessly, for the God of the Latter-Day Saints was all-powerful, and
would protect the chiefs and their braves against "'Mericat"
bullets, guaranteeing that casualties would be few and that
afterward there would be much agreeable looting.

Unhappily, these fine assurances had not proved true. During
the initial attack, the Fancher Party's answering fire had been
distressingly accurate: several braves had been killed, a greater
number wounded and what was worst of all, two of the Indians'
war-chiefs had had their knee-joints shattered by rifle balls and
were likely to die within a day or two from the effect of their
wounds. This was not, the remaining chiefs informed Major Lee,
what they had been promised, and if the Saints did not now send
quickly for additional men to help finish off the besieged party,
they and their braves well might decide to depart from the
battlefield, pausing on their way home to express their sense of
grievance by attacking one or two outlying Mormon settlements
that lay so conveniently along their route.

Whatever the specific threats and quarrels might have been,
within a few hours after the first assault, John D. Lee had sent off
several messages to Isaac Haight at Cedar City, describing the
situation and asking for reinforcements, possibly leaving The
Meadows temporarily himself to discuss the matter with Haight
face to face. The result was that by late Monday or early Tuesday,
Lee, Haight and even Colonel William Dame in distant Parowan

all were acquainted with the unanticipated difficulties that suddenly confronted them; they realized that the Prophet's plan for an "Indian massacre" had badly misfired; that the Fancher Party, despite heavy initial casualties, now occupied an entrenched and almost impregnable position from which the surviving defenders could only be dislodged, if at all, at a cost neither the Indians nor the Saints themselves would be able or willing to bear; and that the three or four hundred braves present at Mountain Meadows were capable of doing little more than maintaining the siege and preventing the members of the Fancher Train from moving off in a body. Therefore, a large force of Mormon militia was needed promptly at The Meadows, both to quell the Indians' discontent and to serve as part of an alternative plan for dealing with the ambushed but still defiant train. And so, by late Monday or early Tuesday, the Mormon leaders of Iron County were assembling reinforcements and preparing to send them to The Meadows, at the same time taking such other measures as the greatly altered and no longer promising situation now required.

Chapter 30

On Tuesday, September 8, while a number of Mormon messengers shuttled between The Meadows and Cedar City, and between Cedar City and Parowan, the original stalemate continued at the ambush site, neither the embattled emigrants nor the red or white Indians who had encircled them being able to gain any discernible advantage. Before long a few armed Mormon reinforcements arrived at the scene and reported to Lee, their appearance no doubt calming the Indians and stilling their more pressing complaints. For the remainder of the day the newcomers spent their time in a casual and entertaining fashion, first stripping themselves and staining their skins with a layer or two of paint and afterward slipping to the top of the tall hill between Jacob Hamblin's ranch house and the emigrants' fort—afterward known as Massacre Hill—from where they could look down on the surrounded Gentiles and pepper them with an occasional shot. Eventually growing weary of this diversion, the white besiegers took turns retiring from the hill and once out of sight of the camp, dined at leisure, and then, to while away more time, pitched a game or two of horseshoes in a neighboring field, before returning to their posts and firing down again at the besieged camp.

On the emigrants' side there was limited activity, too, as the travelers from Arkansas waited patiently for a Mormon force that they still supposed would arrive shortly and help in raising the siege. While waiting, the defenders tried to improve their position further, deepening the ditch where the women and children crouched, at the same time saving precious ammunition by refusing to answer most of the desultory shots that rang out from the surrounding hills. Now and again, as they had on Sundays, some of the more venturesome men in the party made a tentative sortie in the direction of the spring, but each time they did they were greeted by such a stream of arrows and bullets that nearly all their efforts were turned back, and on this day, too, little if any water was obtained by the thirsty families inside the fort. Nor had any substantial amount been collected from the spring during the previous night, for the risking of encountering a strong Indian party was so great that the men of the company were reluctant to leave the security of the fort once darkness fell.

Elsewhere on Tuesday, while the stalemate continued at The Meadows itself, the Mormon high command was far from idle. Lee, Haight, Dame and other local leaders, after exhorting their militia units to prepare for a march to the ambush site and for any subsequent action that might be required there, sent several scouts—or Danites—around The Meadows toward the southwest, to take up positions twenty or thirty miles farther along the trail, the duty of these assassins being to prevent any member of the train from escaping across the desert to California with news of the ambush and a plea for assistance.

Meanwhile, from Cedar City, the Mormon high command sent off another rider in the opposite direction, his destination the capital of the Territory and his mission—forever afterward—the subject of conjecture and controversy. The rider was James Haslam, and he set out for Salt Lake City on late Monday or early Tuesday with an important communication for the Prophet—that much undoubtedly was true. But what queries and information the communication contained was a matter of much less certainty. According to Mormon accounts, young Haslam's mission had been ordered by two or three disaffected but nameless Elders in Iron County, who had questioned the decision already taken to exterminate the Fancher Party and who felt that it was desirable to obtain Brigham Young's written approval before the slaughter should begin. Additionally, the fact that Haslam, despite his desperate haste, probably did not return with the Prophet's reply in time to affect the events at The Meadows, greatly heartened Church apologists, apparently reinforcing their naive belief that this circumstance alone exonerated Young and the Church hierarchy and proved that they were in no way responsible for the atrocious acts committed by Lee and more than fifty other Mormons at the ambush site.

Yet nothing about Haslam's ride, save his speed and probable tardiness in returning, ever was confirmed in later times. The written message he carried unquestionably did reach Salt Lake City, but its contents remained a mystery to all but Brigham Young and his close associates, and two decades later, when asked by United States authorities to produce a copy of the communication, Young blandly announced that—like so many other significant documents—it, too, had disappeared from the Church archives. And so an observer might reasonably have concluded that the communication had indeed been damaging to Young's claim of innocence and that on Haslam's ride to the capital, the youthful Saint had carried a far different communication from that suggested by the Mormons themselves.

In all likelihood, the letter first described the current situation in Iron County and informed the Prophet that his plan for a speedy Indian massacre had gone sadly awry. Everything in the south was running behind schedule, and other measures certainly had to be taken—and quickly—to dispose of the Fancher Train. However, this would not be easy, and it still would leave other vexing problems unresolved. For example, what were they to do with the younger children in the train? Church doctrine made it clear that all children under seven or eight, Mormon and Gentile alike, were innocent beings, and to kill those in the train, along with their parents, would be to "shed innocent blood," one of the gravest sins a Saint could commit. So were the children still to be spared, at the risk of having some of them bear witness at a later date to what they had heard and seen?

And then there was the question of what was to be done with the other Gentiles who now were crowding into Iron County, some at Parowan, and some even closer to The Meadows? At least one large train of Gentiles was well advanced toward the ambush site, and a number of smaller parties, and several individual Gentiles who were traveling in Mormon trains, were scattered along the Southern Trail. Should these possible witnesses be killed, too, or should they be allowed to pass on to California, perhaps after making a detour around The Meadows, with the possibility that they would be able to present firsthand accounts of the ambush on reaching the Pacific Coast?

Whether such questions were included in the message Haslam carried with him was never determined, but this much was certain: these questions were very much in the minds of the Iron County Elders at the beginning of the second week of September,

and it was likely that Haight, Dame, Lee, Higbee and Klingensmith attempted to consult the Prophet about them before their
own rapidly mounting sense of urgency—and their intimate
knowledge of the Prophet's private wishes and often-repeated
public sentiments—finally drove them to decide most of these
matters for themselves.

Wednesday, September the ninth, brought no relief to the embattled members of the Fancher Train. Hour after hour the sun
rose higher in a blazing summer sky, but still no Mormon force
appeared on the surrounding hills to raise the siege, and one or
two fresh sorties in the direction of the sunken spring were
driven back by renewed outbursts of arrows and bullets.

By day's end, the lack of water in camp had grown so acute that
the emigrant leaders decided to discuss what measures might be
taken to relieve their plight. Not wishing to think ill of the
Mormons—for perhaps there was a good reason why they had
failed to appear—the idea was put forward that their fellow
Christians still might be counted upon to provide help if they
knew that help was needed, and so it was proposed that after
dark, one or two scouts should attempt to pass through the ring of
surrounding Indians, ride back to Cedar City and alert the
Mormons there to the desperate situation that existed at The
Meadows.

Two volunteers stepped forward, one of them the artist William
Aden, the other a man whose name no subsequent investigator
ever discovered. Aden explained that if he could reach Cedar City
his chances of obtaining help would be especially favorable,
because, several years earlier, back home in Tennessee, his
father had saved the life of a Mormon Bishop, and recently, along
the Southern Trail, Aden himself had met the Bishop and had
received his personal thanks. Once the Mormons at Cedar City
had been apprised of this, Aden believed, their good will and
assistance would surely be forthcoming.

After it grew dark, Aden and his companion saddled their
horses, led them silently from the fort and then, walking cautiously toward the lightly guarded row of hills to the east,
managed to slip past the enemy, finally reaching the trail a mile
or so from the ambush site.

Once safely beyond The Meadows, Aden and his companion
mounted their horses and rode swiftly to the northeast, toward
Cedar City. Some fifteen miles later, they drew up at a place

called Richards' or Leachy Springs to water their horses. They were now about halfway to their destination, but unhappily, they were not the only travelers to reach the springs that night. Some accounts say that three Mormons from Cedar City—William C. Stewart, Joel White and Benjamin Arthur—already were there. Other accounts say that the main body of militia from Cedar City had camped at the springs earlier in the evening, some thirty-eight men in all, led by Major John Higbee, a Bishop in the Church at Cedar City and First Counselor to Isaac Haight, and Higbee's lieutenants, Bishop Philip Klingensmith, Samuel McMurdy and William Stewart, the latter also a High Priest and member of the Cedar City Council.

All accounts agree that it was Stewart who challenged Aden and asked him why he was traveling along the road. Aden described the situation at The Meadows and explained what he and his companion were sure they could accomplish once they had reached the Mormon authorities at Cedar City. All accounts further agree that Stewart then raised his rifle and shot Aden in the back, killing him almost instantly. Some say that Aden's companion, though wounded, succeeded in escaping from the springs, and after riding to the southwest, managed to re-enter the emigrants' camp, where he informed the party of what had taken place. Other accounts say that Aden's companion did indeed escape from the springs, but that he was caught by the Indians while attempting to infiltrate their lines again and was butchered not far from the emigrants' corral. This was probably the case, for had the leaders of the Fancher Party learned of Aden's murder, there was little likelihood that they ever would have trusted the Mormons afterward and placed their fortunes in such bloody hands.

In the meantime, only fifty miles away at Parowan, and only a few hours before William Aden was murdered at Richards' Springs, a more fortunate Gentile traveler, George Powers, traveling in the comparative safety of the Matthews and Tanner Train, had first learned of the troubled situation at Mountain Meadows and later reported what he had heard and observed, especially while he had been in the presence of Colonel William Dame, the Commanding Officer of the Iron County Militia. "During the afternoon," Powers recalled, "an express arrived from the Indians, stating that one of their warriors had run up and looked into the corral, and he supposed that 'only five or six of the emigrants were killed yet.' These were the words of the expressman. The same night, four men were sent out from Parowan to go and learn what was the fate of the train, and, as they pretended, to save, if possible, some of its members."

Powers, understandably enough, had been extremely curious about the emigrant train, which was reported to be surrounded at Mountain Meadows, and asked Colonel Dame for more information. The young colonel's words were of special significance, because his only superiors were in Salt Lake City and the only person he would "accept counsel" from was either Brigham Young himself or else a member of the Church hierarchy, like one of the Apostles, who had been specifically authorized to speak on the Prophet's behalf. "Mr. Dame informed me," Powers wrote, "that the attack on the train [had] commenced on Monday. . . . I asked him if he could not raise a company and go out and relieve the besieged train? He replied that he could go out and take them away to safety, but he dared not—he dared not disobey counsel."

Chapter 31

To the beleaguered members of the Fancher Train, Thursday, the tenth of September, was a day of despair. By then the train's leaders no longer were able to deceive themselves, or to deny the obvious—that their situation had grown all but hopeless. The Mormons, for whatever reasons, were not going to come to their aid, and there was no one else within hundreds of miles who could lend them assistance. At best the members of the party had but a short time left before the failure of their ammunition, or overwhelming thirst, drove them from their fortress and compelled them to attempt a flight *en masse* through the Indians' lines toward Cedar City, or in the opposite direction toward the desert, and in either case they were equally certain to meet an appalling death.

That day, in their growing desperation, the emigrants made an effort to find water within the corral itself, by digging a pit, five or six feet across and several feet deep, near the protective ditch they had dug earlier for the party's wounded and the women and children. No water, however, was discovered there, and before many hours had passed the attempt was abandoned.

It was then decided that after darkness came, the train's three ablest scouts, one of them John H. Baker, "Uncle Jack" Baker's oldest son, would slip out of camp, head toward the desert, and if possible, carry to California and the outside world a list of the names of the men, women and children of the party and their fate. It was a certainty that such a mission, even if successful, would take at least a week or more, and this meant that before any rescuers could appear, the last members of the train would long since have perished. But it would also mean that the true story of the ambush would be made known and that possibly one day measures could be taken to bring the guilty Indians—and any allies they might have had—before the bar of justice. And so, when night fell on Thursday evening, young Baker and two companions—one of them perhaps a son of Captain Fancher, another perhaps Tilghman Cameron on "One-eyed Blaze"—edged their way out of the corral, eluded the watchers along the western ridge and those at the nearby Indian camp and rode off toward the Beaver Mountains, their destination southern California, several hundred miles across the desert.

On Thursday evening, at almost the same time that Baker and his two companions were leaving the corral and riding toward the southwest, the last of the Mormon reinforcements were assembling at The Meadows and establishing a camp behind Massacre Hill, not far from Jacob Hamblin's summer ranch house, and just out of sight of the emigrants' fort, a mile or so away.

The only detailed description of the events that followed was written by John D. Lee, in his confessions. There, as always, were the endless protestations of his own innocence, but these, of course, could safely be disregarded, in the light of his past record and character.

The main militia party, Lee wrote, did not reach The Meadows until early Thursday evening. It was made up of about forty Saints, most of them from Cedar City. All were well armed, and they had had the foresight to bring with them two or three wagons, suitable for transporting either children who were too young to walk very far or the clothing and other personal possessions of a hundred or so well-to-do travelers. The remainder of the Mormon militia force, consisting of some fifteen or twenty men, had arrived earlier from Parowan, Harmony and a number of additional communities in the area.

The main party included most of Cedar City's leading officials, both ecclesiastical and civil. "I can remember the following," Lee wrote, "as a portion of the men who came to take part in the work of death which was so soon to follow: John M. Higbee, major and commander of the Iron [County] militia, and also First Counselor to Isaac C. Haight; Philip Klingensmith, Bishop of Cedar City; Charles Hopkins of the City Council of Cedar City; Ira Allen of the High Council; Robert Wiley of the High Council; Richard Harrison of Pinto, also a member of the High Council; Samuel McMurdy, one of the Counselors of Klingensmith . . . Daniel

McFarland, a son-in-law of Isaac C. Haight, and acting adjutant under Major Higbee . . . Nephi Johnson, with a number of Indians under his command . . . William Bateman, who afterward carried the flag of truce to the emigrant camp . . . and some others whose names I cannot remember. I know that our total force was fifty-four whites and over three hundred Indians."

After all the Saints had gathered at The Meadows, an announcement was made explaining the exact purpose of their mission. "Major Higbee," Lee said, "reported as follows: 'It is the orders of the President, that all of the emigrants be *put out of the way*. President Haight has counseled with Colonel Dame, or has had orders from him . . . none who are old enough to talk are to be spared.'"

Higbee's disclosure could hardly have come as a surprise to most of the assembled militia, since only four days earlier, at Cedar City, a resolution calling for the destruction of the Fancher Train had been passed unanimously at a public meeting there—a meeting attended by many of the same armed men who now were encamped near Jacob Hamblin's summer ranch house. A day or two after the meeting, these same thirty-five or forty militiamen had been summoned from their homes and ordered to march to The Meadows, and surely at that time they had understood the reason for their departure and had been in agreement that the members of the Fancher Train had been justly marked down for death.

Yet after only a scant hour or two at the ambush scene, a number of militiamen already had begun to experience stirrings of doubt and uneasiness. Prior to that evening at The Meadows, every man in the company had been subjected, during a period of many months and even years, to a ceaseless barrage of propaganda; he had listened, Sunday after Sunday, to hate-filled sermons that dwelled on the countless wrongs the Church had endured in Missouri and Illinois, and that called for punishment of the Gentile enemy; angry sermons, which promised that one day soon, revenge finally would be gained for the murder of Joseph and Hyrum Smith, a glorious day when there would be much cutting of Gentile throats and spilling of Gentile blood, as the first step was taken in purifying a sinful world and preparing for the establishment, in every corner of the Earth, of the new Kingdom of God.

But now—in the still darkness of The Meadows, under the first familiar evening stars—such inflammatory rhetoric suddenly seemed less persuasive and even a touch "unreal." For the men in the company, there were a number of new and disturbing thoughts to be faced, including the fact that the time for discourse and sermon was past, while the time for action was swiftly approaching, and that they themselves, most of them plain farmers who never had committed a single act of violence in their lives and who were not hardened Danites like some of their leaders, were being ordered to participate in a singular kind of "military operation"—an operation in which, at least some of them began to suspect, no God-fearing, decent militiamen, in the Territory of Utah or anywhere else, would be proud to take part. No doubt an hour or two earlier, at dusk, some of them had climbed Massacre Hill for a glimpse of the enemy camp, and the experience had been an unsettling one; for although their Church superiors had repeatedly declared that the Fancher Train was merely a part of the United States Army, then advancing into the Territory to destroy the Saints and their leaders, it was no easy matter for honest men to gaze down from Massacre Hill and believe they were observing a military force when their own eyes beheld the familiar prairie wagons of ordinary "homespun" country people like themselves, most of the men probably with wives and children much like their own.

Stirred by the thought that this was the "enemy army" they were supposed to destroy, at least a handful of the militiamen now began to voice serious objections, which later Lee, in his confessions, claimed had been exclusively his. It was he himself, Lee said, who stood up before the entire company and declared that it would be the height of sinfulness to kill the women and children in the train, but for this courageous act his only reward was a stern rebuke from his "military superior," Major John Higbee. "'Brother Lee,'" Higbee said to the company, "'is afraid of shedding innocent blood. Why, brethren, there is not a drop of innocent blood in that entire camp of Gentile outlaws; they are a set of cut-throats, robbers and assassins; they are a part of the people who drove the Saints from Missouri and who aided to shed [sic] the blood of our Prophets Joseph and Hyrum, and it is our orders from all in authority, to get the emigrants from their stronghold, and help the Indians kill them.'"

After further protests—again, according to Lee, raised solely by himself—he was overruled and told to be silent. "I was interrupted," he declared, "by Higbee, Klingensmith and Hopkins, who said it was the orders of President Isaac Haight to us, and that Haight had his orders from Colonel Dame and the authorities at Parowan, and that *all* in authority were of one mind, and that [Higbee and his lieutenants] had been sent by the Council at Cedar City to The Meadows, to counsel and direct the way and manner that the company of emigrants should be disposed of."

According to Lee's account, he and the other Saints then knelt in a prayer circle and prayed, invoking the Spirit of God to indicate to them how they were to act in the matter. "After the prayer," Lee continued, "Higbee said, 'Here are the orders,' and handed me a paper from Haight. It was in substance that it was the orders of Haight to *decoy* the emigrants from their positions, and kill all of them who [were old enough] to talk. This order was in writing. Higbee handed it to me and I read it, and then I dropped it to the ground, saying, 'I cannot do this!'" A dramatic moment indeed, but doubtlessly one that did not occur as described, although it surely represented one of Lee's more imaginative flights of fancy.

Whether or not Higbee actually carried such a written order from Haight to The Meadows never was determined afterward, and essentially it was a matter of little consequence; all that anyone could say was that the "final solution" for exterminating the Fancher Party might have originated in Salt Lake City many days earlier as one of a number of alternative schemes for completing the destruction of the doomed train; that the plan might have suggested itself as a necessary expedient, to Haight and Dame, only a day or two before and they then had immediately sent it to The Meadows; or that the plan had germinated in the mind of Lee himself, for now he had been on the scene more than a hundred hours and knew better than anyone else that the fortress was almost unassailable and that treachery alone would serve, where a frontal assault would probably fail.

But according to Major Lee—and perhaps truthfully—the scheme had been devised by those who held a much higher rank than he in the Mormon militia. "The words *decoy* and *exterminate*," Lee said, "were used in the message or order, and these orders came to us as the orders from the Council at Cedar City, and as the orders of our military superiors, that we were bound to obey. The order was signed by Haight, as commander of the troops at Cedar City. Haight told me the next day . . . that he had got his orders from Colonel Dame."

Still, some of the militiamen continued that night to express their misgivings, and so there were further prayers, before John Higbee, having received divine inspiration, finally rose from his knees and declared, "'I have the evidence of God's approval of our mission. It is God's will that we carry out our instructions to the letter.'"

In his efforts to excuse himself from blame, Lee now allowed his imagination to rise to unprecedented heights. According to his account, he wrung his hands and said, "'My God! this is more than I can do! I must, and do refuse to take part in this matter!'"

Then, supposedly, the wily Higbee began to play on Lee's naive religious beliefs, in an attempt to persuade the old Danite to carry out his decisive role in the massacre. "'I am ordered by President Haight to inform you,'" he purportedly told Lee, "'that you shall receive a Crown of Celestial Glory for your faithfulness, and your eternal joy shall be complete.' I was much shaken by this offer," Lee recalled, "for I had full faith in the power of the Priesthood to bestow such rewards and blessings. But I [also] was anxious to save the people. I then proposed that we give the Indians all of the stock of the emigrants except sufficient [sic] to haul their wagons, and let them go. To this proposition all of the leading men objected. No man there raised his voice or hand to favor the saving of life, except myself."

Continuing his description of the night's activities, Lee wrote: "The meeting was then addressed by someone in authority. I do not remember who it was. [Quite possibly, of course, the orator was Lee himself.] He spoke in about this language: 'Brethren, we have been sent here to perform a duty. It is a duty we owe to God, and to our Church and people. The orders of those in authority are that all the emigrants *must* die. Our leaders speak with inspired tongues, and their orders come from the God of Heaven. We have no right to question what they have commanded us to do; it is our duty to obey. . . . We must kill them all, and our orders are to get them out by treachery, if no other thing can be done to get them into our power.'"

By now the long night was almost over, and with the last reluctant holdout having yielded either to persuasion or intimidation, it was time to discuss in detail the scheme for deceiving the members of the Fancher Party and leading them on to destruction, and also to assign the roles that the various squads and individuals would play in the coming drama. A little after daylight the militiamen stacked their arms and ate breakfast; afterward, Major Lee and Major Higbee called upon their Indian confederates and explained the positions which they and the Mormons would occupy on The Meadows and the work that each contingent would be expected to perform. Next Lee stripped off the last of his Indian costume, washed away all traces of red paint and donned his ordinary civilian clothing; then, accompanied by William Bateman, bearing a white flag of truce, he descended Massacre Hill, and after meeting two of the train leaders at the bottom of The Meadows, was allowed to enter the emigrants' corral to begin negotiations.

Chapter 32

Employing his most artful and persuasive manner, John D. Lee set out step by step, early that Friday morning, to gain the trust and confidence of the travelers from Arkansas, in order to betray them and deliver them over to their waiting assassins. At first he described in an earnest voice the ostensible reason for the ambush. Their train, he explained, had been attacked because earlier Gentile trains, passing through that section of the Territory, had injured the local Indians and aroused their anger, and it then had been the Fancher Party's undeserved misfortune to arrive at The Meadows just as tribal rage had reached its peak.

Having learned of the ambush, Lee continued, and of the desperate plight of the surrounded train, he and a number of hastily recruited Saints had raced with all possible speed to The Meadows and now had succeeded in calming the Indians to some degree, although many of the more belligerent braves still were in such a high state of excitement that they scarcely could be controlled, even by as skilled an Indian interpreter as he was himself. However, Lee said, he *had* managed to persuade the chiefs to agree to a truce, and had won their solemn pledge not to renew their attacks, or to otherwise harm the emigrants, if the members of the train, on their part, would agree to lay down their arms and place themselves in Mormon custody. A few of the Indians, Lee said, already had left The Meadows, on his assurance that the train members certainly would be willing to do this, but to avoid any trouble with the several hundred braves who remained in the neighborhood, and to placate their feelings, it would be necessary for the emigrants not merely to give up their rifles and ammunition to their Mormon protectors but also to participate in some sort of "surrender ceremony," a charade really, which would greatly impress the childlike Indians and lessen their anger against "the 'Mericats."

If the emigrants agreed, Lee suggested, the ceremony could be carried out in this way: first the corral would be opened and the men would place their weapons in one of the two wagons brought by the Mormons to The Meadows; next, the youngest children would be placed there, too; the sick and wounded members of the party would be helped into the second wagon; and then the departure from the corral, and the journey to Cedar City, would begin. At the head of the column would come the two wagons, followed by the women and older children, walking in single file, and finally, as the Indians had insisted, the unarmed men would march out of the fortress and bring up the column's rear; each man would be accompanied and safeguarded by at least one armed Saint, the entire "performance" designed to convince those braves still lingering near The Meadows that the 'Mericats had indeed carried out the agreement and had "surrendered" to the Mormons, as the various chiefs, without exception, had demanded. Lee then assured the leaders of the train that if all this was done, he and the other Saints would protect the entire party from the Indians, lead everyone back to Cedar City unharmed, and once there, the travelers would receive the protection of the Church and civil authorities until such time as the Indians could be further pacified and an opportunity presented itself to send the travelers safely on their way to California.

Afterward no fully satisfactory explanation ever was offered to explain why the emigrants agreed to Lee's terms, turned over their ammunition and arms to the Mormons and placed their lives, and the lives of their wives and children, in the hands of the very men who had treated them with so much violent abuse at Cedar City scarcely a week before. Surely such experienced pioneers as Alexander Fancher and "Uncle Jack" Baker were anything but absolute fools—and therefore they must have realized only too well the dire risks they were taking when they agreed to Lee's scheme.

Yet in the last analysis, what other choice did the emigrants really have? At best, even if the Indians had departed from The Meadows that same day and troubled them no further, they still would have been unable to cross the desert, having lost almost all their cattle in the ambush, and so they would have been compelled to return to Cedar City and there throw themselves on the mercy of the same men who now stood at The Meadows, proclaiming themselves the emigrants' friends and protectors. If, instead, they had decided to turn down Lee's offer, their prospects would have been even worse—because certainly most of the Indians would have remained at the The Meadows to continue the siege, and in only another day or two, thirst would have driven the emigrants out of their camp, and all would have perished in a savage massacre.

Finally, despite darkest misgivings, the leaders of the train no doubt were able to persuade themselves that they had at least one strong reason for supposing that matters still might turn out well. For when everything was said and done the Latter-Day Saints, like themselves, were practicing Christians, and surely no people who loved the ideals of the gentle Nazarene, whatever particular sect they might adhere to, could so forget or corrupt His teachings that they would betray their pledged honor and injure those they had sworn to protect.

And so, for all or perhaps merely for some of these various reasons, the members of the Fancher Party agreed to Mormon terms, and shortly after high noon, on a bright, clear summer's day, they opened their fortress and began to perform those actions that they hoped would permit every member of the company to leave The Meadows in safety. First the men took their rifles and ammunition and placed them in the wagon that Samuel McMurdy had driven up to the corral, and then, with words of reassurance, they lifted up the youngest children and placed them in the wagon, too. Next, the sick and wounded were carried aboard the second wagon, driven by Samuel Knight, and finally, with Major Lee walking between the two wagons, the head of the procession set out toward the north, in the direction of Massacre Hill.

Meanwhile, about two hundred yards away from the camp, the Mormon militia already had drawn up in a double file, one on each side of the narrow trail. A half-mile or so beyond these riflemen—but completely hidden from sight—were three hundred Indians, most of the braves having concealed themselves an hour or so earlier on the side of a hill to the east of the path, among stands of small cedars and low, scrub oaks.

The pair of wagons rolled north along the path and soon were followed from the corral by the women of the party and those girls and boys old enough to walk a considerable distance. A few of the women were carrying infants in their arms, the rest a handful of personal possessions, and according to at least one account, many of the women and children began to smile as they turned up the path and caught their first glimpse of the Mormon militiamen, whom they believed had come to save them from the Indians.

On reaching the double file of riflemen, neither the two wagons nor the band of women and children stopped, but all kept moving ahead, as had been arranged beforehand; then, some minutes later, and last of all, the men of the Fancher Party departed from the corral and marched up to the double rank of Saints. Here they halted, and the Mormons fell in around them, and if the testimony of more than one eyewitness can be credited, the men of the train gave a friendly shout, to signal their gratitude for what these men had undertaken to accomplish on their behalf. For a few minutes the Mormons and the men of the train held still, before moving off in turn, and this pause gave the wagons, and the band of women and older children, a chance to move out farther ahead of them, as Major Lee had previously said was to be done. Then the men of the train and their Mormon guards also moved off along the path toward Massacre Hill, a troop of five or six Mormon horsemen following behind, at the rear of the column.

Slowly the two creaking wagons inched past the hidden Indians and continued along the path. Then, a few minutes later, the women and older children reached a position on the path directly below the Indians, and Major Higbee, who had been observing the procession from a nearby hill, raised his hand and shouted the prearranged words: "Do your duty!"

Within seconds, the slaughter of the Gentile enemy had begun. The men of the company were the first to die. At the back of the column the Mormon militia caught Major Higbee's signal, each man spun about, raised his rifle, and shot the emigrant beside him from point-blank range. The initial barrage killed or mortally wounded all but three or four of the emigrants. The others, who were only slightly wounded, managed to burst past their assailants and run a short distance away, but the horsemen at the rear of the column quickly fanned out and rode them down, clubbed each fleeing man to the ground with the butt of their guns, and then, after jumping from their mounts, leaped upon each of their bloody victims and cut his throat with their knives.

At the same time, toward the center of the column, the Indians sprang from hiding, and with a hideous outcry, rushed down upon the terrified women and older children. This part of the slaughter took a few minutes longer to complete, for the Indians were armed chiefly with knives and tomahawks, rather than with firearms, and so, of course, the pace of their work was necessarily slower. It was, by all accounts, a grisly scene, some of the women and children falling to their knees and begging for their lives, others shrieking loudly as they attempted to flee through the tall meadow grass. Without exception, though, they were cut down, some by tomahawks crashing into their skulls, others by knives driven into their hearts and bowels. The few women who had been carrying small infants in their arms did not escape, at least one of the infants being killed along with his mother, and a second infant being seriously wounded, her arm almost torn off, either by a rifle ball or by the slashing stroke of a tomahawk.

At the front of the procession, the two wagons had halted at Major Higbee's signal, and now it was up to Lee, McMurdy and Knight to kill all the sick and wounded. According to Lee's account of the next few minutes, he alone refrained from doing so. "McMurdy and Knight got out of their wagons," Lee wrote afterward. "Each one had a rifle. McMurdy went up to Knight's wagon, where the sick and wounded were, and raising his rifle to his shoulder said, *'O Lord, my God, receive their spirits. It is for Thy Kingdom that I do this!'* He then shot a man who was lying on another man's breast; the ball killed both men."

Although numerous witnesses testified that Lee murdered several of the wounded, and a number of other men, woman and older girls as well, in his confession, Lee, not surprisingly, denied all such acts. His explanation for his failure to take part in the killing undoubtedly represents the most implausible excuse ever offered by any of the conspirators to a doubting Gentile world. "I also went up to the wagon," he said, "intending to do my part in the killing. I drew my pistol and cocked it, but somehow it went off prematurely, and I shot McMurdy across the thigh, my pistol ball cutting his buckskin pants. McMurdy turned to me and said, 'Brother Lee, keep cool, you are excited. You came very near killing me. Keep cool, there is no reason for being excited.'

"Knight then shot a man with his rifle; he shot the man in the head. Knight also brained a boy that was about fourteen years old. The boy came rushing up to our wagons, and Knight struck him on the head with the butt end of his gun and crushed his skull. By this time many Indians had reached our wagons, and all

of the sick and wounded were killed almost immediately. . . . I
fully intended to do my part of the killing, but by the time I got
over the excitement of the coming so near [sic] killing McMurdy,
the whole of the killing was done. There is no truth to the
statement of Nephi Johnson where he says I cut a man's throat."

The rest of Lee's account painted a vivid, and generally
accurate, picture of what next occurred at The Meadows. "After
all the parties were dead," Lee said, "I ordered Knight to drive
[off] to one side, and throw out the dead bodies. He did so, and
threw them out of his wagon at a place about a hundred yards
from the road, and then came back to where I was standing. I
then ordered Knight and McMurdy to take the [youngest]
children . . . and drive on to Hamblin's ranch. . . . After the
wagons with the children, had started for Hamblin's ranch, I
turned and walked back to where the brethren were. . . . While
going back to the brethren, I passed the bodies of several women.
In one place I saw six or seven bodies near each other. . . . I
walked along the line where the emigrants had been killed, and
saw many bodies . . . on the field, near where the women lay. I
saw ten [older] children; they had been killed close to each other;
they were from ten to sixteen years of age. The bodies of the
women and children were scattered along the ground for quite a
distance, before I came to where the men were killed.

"I did not know," Lee said, "how many were killed, but I
thought that there were some fifteen women, ten children, and
about forty men killed, but the statements of others that I have
since talked with about that day on the Mountain Meadows, and
the ten who died in the corral and young Aden killed by Stewart
at Richards' Spring, would make the total number one hundred
and twenty-one.

"When I reached the place where the dead men lay," Lee
continued, "I was told how the orders had been obeyed. Major
Higbee said, 'The boys have acted admirably, they took good aim,
and all of the damned Gentiles but two or three fell at the *first
fire*.' He said that three or four got away some distance, but the
men on horses soon overtook them and cut their throats. Higbee
said the Indians did their part of the work well, that it did not
take over a minute to finish up when they got fairly started."

By early Friday afternoon, the victims of the massacre lay
scattered across the meadowland, and it was time to commence
the task of stripping the dead of their clothing and other
valuables. Although he denied any part in it, Lee unquestionably

directed the ghoulish proceedings. Then, he went on to say: "After the dead were searched . . . the brethren were called up, and Higbee and Klingensmith, as well as myself, made speeches, and *ordered* the people to keep the matter a secret from the *entire* world. Not to tell their wives, or their most intimate friends, and we pledged ourselves to keep everything relating to the affair a secret during life. We also took the most binding oaths to stand by each other, and to always insist that the massacre was committed by Indians alone. This was the advice of Brigham Young . . . as I will show hereafter.

"The men," Lee concluded, "were mostly ordered to camp there on the field for that night, but Higbee and Klingensmith went with me to Hamblin's ranch, where we got something to eat, and stayed there all night. I was nearly dead for rest and sleep; in fact I had rested but little since the Saturday night before. I took my saddle-blanket and spread it on the ground soon after I had eaten my supper, and lay down on the saddle-blanket, using my saddle for a pillow, and slept soundly until the next morning."

Three members of the ambushed train were still alive in addition to the eighteen young children Lee had brought back to Jacob Hamblin's ranch house in the two wagons. The three, however, were not destined to survive their fellow travelers for many hours. Soon after leaving the emigrants' corral on Thursday night, John H. Baker and his two companions had been observed heading toward the west, and they were immediately followed by a Mormon party under Indian missionary Ira Hatch. On Friday or Saturday night, their pursuers found the trio sleeping by their campfire and shot all three. Baker, wounded in the wrist, managed to escape temporarily, but his two companions were killed. A day or so later, near the Muddy River, Baker met two other Mormons, who were returning to Salt Lake City from San Bernardino. By this time Baker was feverish from his wound and allowed himself to be convinced that he had no chance to cross the desert in his weakened condition. He turned back east with the two Mormons, and Hatch's party found him soon afterward. Hatch killed Baker himself and then confiscated all the papers he had been carrying, including the emigrants' report of the ambush and the list of the members of the train who had been present at Mountain Meadows.

With young Baker's death, the Saints had completed their plan to annihilate the party of emigrants from Arkansas. Meanwhile, at The Meadows, on Friday night, the eleventh of September, all was still, the bloody and butchered corpses of more than a hundred and twenty men, women and children as mute as the hills themselves. Their fate was the logical result of lawlessness, carried to its inevitable extremity by those who believed that other human beings were of no consequence, and that their own higher laws—called in their religion the Laws of God—justified robbery, murder or any other crime, if these things were done to strengthen God's Kingdom, under the direction of the Prophet of the Lord.

Chapter 33

During the stormy years that followed the Massacre at Mountain Meadows, Brigham Young's policy never deviated from its original course—to deny any responsibility for, or involvement in, the crime, while doing his utmost to save his fellow conspirators from trial and punishment. At first the Church attempted to ignore the ambush, as though it had not occurred, but within a few weeks damaging accounts had appeared in the California newspapers, and this fiction no longer could be maintained. It then became Mormon practice to blame the tragedy on the travelers' conduct and to insist, despite overwhelming evidence to the contrary, that no white men had ben involved in the matter and that the massacre had been an exclusively Indian affair. Eventually, two decades later, the sick, aging and hard-pressed Mormon leader finally decided to sacrifice a single Saint for the good of the many and chose as scapegoat John D. Lee.

It was a grossly cynical and shabby way to reward years of loyalty and devotion, however misguided they might have been, but fortunately, for Lee himself, the day of his betrayal still lay far in the future, on that warm, sunny morning in September 1857, when he joined Isaac Haight, William Dame, Philip Klingensmith and other local Church leaders at the scene of the massacre. There they examined the corpse-strewn field, took possession of the victims' property, including their cattle, wagons, clothing and personal effects, and then began to make arrangements for distributing among various Mormon families in the area the eighteen surviving Gentile children Lee had brought to Jacob Hamblin's ranch house the previous afternoon.

In later times it often was said that the bodies of the murdered victims had remained unburied, and seemingly this would have been consistent with the Saints' efforts to pass of the affair as an Indian massacre. Lee, in his confessions, though, insisted that such had not been the case. "We went along the field," he said, "and passed by where the brethren were at work covering up the bodies. They piled the dead bodies up in heaps, in little gullies, and threw dirt over them. The bodies were only lightly covered, for the ground was hard, and the brethren did not have sufficient tools to dig with. I suppose it is true that the first rain washed the bodies all out again, but I never went back to examine whether it did or not." Why Lee claimed that the ground at the Meadows was hard, when at least a considerable area was extremely marshy, he was never asked to explain.

"After the dead were covered up," he continued, ". . . the brethren were called together, and a council was held at the emigrant camp. All the leading men made speeches; Colonel Dame, President Haight, John M. Higbee, Hopkins and myself. The speeches were—Thanks to God for delivering our enemies into our hands; next, thanking the brethren for their zeal in God's cause; and then the necessity of always saying the Indians did it alone, and that the Mormons had nothing to do with it.

"The most of the speeches, however, were in the shape of exhortations and commands to keep the whole matter secret from everyone but Brigham Young. . . . The brethren then all took a most solemn oath, binding themselves under the most dreadful and awful penalties, to keep [the affair] secret from every human being, as long as they should live. No man was to know the facts. The brethren were sworn not to talk of it among themselves, and each one swore to help kill all who proved traitors to the Church or the people. . . . It was then agreed that Brigham Young should be informed of the whole matter. . . . It was also voted to turn all the property over to Klingensmith, as Bishop of the Church at Cedar City, and he was to take care of the property for the benefit of the Church, until Brigham Young was notified, and should give further orders what to do with it."

It was Lee's contention that Haight and Dame quarreled bitterly at The Meadows that morning over who had been directly responsible for ordering the massacre. But if such a quarrel did indeed break out, it must have been settled quickly, to judge from the account of George Powers, a Gentile emigrant, who witnessed the conduct of the Saints as they returned home from the ambush scene. Powers at the time was traveling along the trail to California in the Mormon Matthews and Tanner Train. "On Saturday," he wrote, "at twelve o'clock, we left Cedar City. About the middle of the afternoon we met four men, who [had been] sent out the previous night, returning in a wagon. Matthews and Tanner held a council with them, apart, and when they left, Matthews told me the entire [Fancher] Train had been cut off, and, as it was still dangerous to travel the road, they had concluded it was better to pass the spot at night. We continued on . . . and about dusk met Mr. Dame . . . and three other white men, coming from the scene of the slaughter, in company with a band of some twenty Indian warriors. One of the men in company with Mr. Dame was Mr. Haight, President of Cedar City. Mr. Dame said they had been out to see to the burying of the dead . . . but from what I heard, I believe the bodies were left lying naked upon the ground. . . .

"These Indians," Powers concluded, "had a two-horse wagon filled with something I could not see, as blankets were carefully spread over the top. The wagon was driven by a white man, and beside him there were two or three Indians! Many of [the Indians] had shawls, and bundles of women's clothes were tied to their saddles. . . . The hindmost Indians were driving several head of the emigrants' cattle. Mr. Dame and Mr. Haight, and their men, seemed to be on the best of terms with the Indians, and they were all in high spirits, as if they were mutually pleased with the accomplishment of some desired object."

Within a few days of the massacre, the Pah-Utes had been given their modest share of the loot, and the rest of the emigrants' possessions either had been distributed among the murderers themselves or had been placed in official custody, some of the more portable items, including the victims' bloody clothing, having been stacked away for future sale in the Church's tithing office at Cedar City. However, the gold hidden in William Cameron's wagon had not yet been discovered—nor was its ultimate fate ever disclosed.

Relieved for the moment from other responsibilities, John D. Lee now was at liberty to report to the Prophet, and before the end of September he had ridden north to the capital and made his way into Brigham Young's private office. "I went over the whole affair," Lee said afterward, "and gave him as full a statement as it was possible for me to give. I described everything about it. . . . I told him, 'Brother McMurdy, Brother Knight and myself killed the wounded men in the wagons. . . .' " Then, Lee said, "I gave him the names of every man that had been present at the massacre. I told him who killed various ones. In fact I gave him *all the information there was to give.*"

This much, no doubt, was substantially true, for Lee trusted his religious mentor implicitly. On the other hand, much of what Young said in response could not fully reflect his real thoughts or feelings, for by long custom the Prophet was extremely cautious in all his dealings and surely had no intention, either then or later, of being completely candid with any subordinate on such a dangerous subject as the extermination of the Fancher Train.

Despite his calmness of manner, Young's first words revealed that he was greatly upset by Lee's disclosures, not because so many people had been murdered at The Meadows but because the scheme had gone so far awry and that with at least fifty or sixty Saints having been directly involved, it now would be extremely difficult to pass the affair off as an Indian massacre, and worse still, almost impossible to prevent one of the participants, sooner or later, from revealing the truth to the outside world.

"When I had finished talking about the matter," Lee recalled, "[Young] said, 'This is the most unfortunate affair that ever befell the Church. I am afraid of treachery among the brethren who were there. If anyone tells this thing so that it will become public, it will work us great injury. I want you to understand now, that you are *never* to tell this again, not even to Heber C. Kimball. *It must* be kept a secret among ourselves.' "

Then Young's practical mind turned in a new direction, and he said to Lee, " 'When you get home, I want you to sit down and write a long letter, and give me an account of the affair, charging it to the Indians. You sign the letter as Farmer to the Indians, and direct it to me as Indian Agent. I can then make use of the letter to keep off all damaging and troublesome enquiries. . . . ' "

Clearly, there were a number of other vital matters on which the Prophet had to decide without delay, the most important, from Lee's point of view, being the question of what he was to say to the brethren on his return south and how he and the other southern leaders were to answer whatever criticism might be raised against them. But when Lee introduced the subject, Young had no ready reply, and his next words must have sounded distressingly evasive. According to Lee, the Prophet said, " 'If only the men had been killed, I would not have cared so much; but the killing of the women and children is the sin of it. I suppose the men were a hard set, but it is hard to kill women and children for the sins of the men. This whole thing stands before me like a horrid vision. I must have time to reflect on it.'"

Such pious remarks, however, were of no use or comfort to Lee, especially since he must have recognized that the Prophet already was attempting to shift the entire blame for the massacre onto a few of his loyal subordinates, like Haight, Dame, Klingensmith and himself. And so when Young then instructed Lee "'to withdraw and call the next day, and he would give me an answer,'" Lee decided to speak out—as much as anyone dared to speak out against the Prophet—and to remind him that, as both of them knew, the orders for the massacre had emanated from Salt Lake City, that the Apostle George A. Smith had carried to the southern settlements Young's plan for exterminating the Fancher Party and that from the beginning the entire scheme had been known to the Prophet and had had his full approval. "I said to him" Lee wrote, "'President Young, the people all felt, and I know that I believed I was obeying *orders*, and acting for the good of the Church, in strict conformity with the oaths we have all taken to avenge the blood of the Prophet. You must either sustain the people for what they have done, or you must release us from the oaths and obligations we have taken.'"

This was an unpleasant dilemma for the Prophet, and according to Lee's account, "The only reply he made was, 'Go now, and come [back] in the morning, and I will give you an answer.'" By the next day, though, when Lee returned, Young had found a satisfactory solution to the problem. "The Prophet," Lee observed, "seemed quite cheerful. 'I have made that matter a subject of prayer,' he said. '*I went right to God with it*, and asked Him to take the horrid vision from my sight, *if it was a righteous thing* that my people had done in killing those people at The Mountain Meadows. God answered me, and *at once the vision was removed*. I have evidence from God that He has overruled it all for good, and the action was a righteous one and well intended.'"

Here was exactly what Lee had sought—and what he was to say after his return south—that God Himself, through his anointed Prophet, had given a sign that the massacre had been a necessary and worthy step in establishing His Kingdom, and that any criticism against Haight, Dame or himself not only was unjustified but certainly did not have the approval of Brigham Young or the sanction of the Church. Then the Prophet went on to elaborate the answer that Lee was to give on his return. "'The brethren,'" he instructed Lee, "'acted from pure motives. The only trouble is they acted a little *prematurely;* they were a *little* ahead of time. *I sustain you* and all the brethren for what they did. . . .'"

And Lee concluded by saying: "I was again cautioned and commanded to keep the whole thing a sacred secret and again told to write the report as Indian Farmer, laying the blame on the Indians."

Two months later, obeying the Prophet's instructions, Lee wrote the required letter and sent it to Brigham Young in Salt Lake City. "My last report," the letter began, "under date of May 11th . . . showed a friendly relation between [the Indians] and the whites, which doubtless would have continued to increase, had not the white men been the first aggressor, as was the case with Captain Fancher's company of emigrants. . . . [At] Corn Creek, fifteen miles south of Fillmore . . . the company poisoned the meat of an ox, which they gave to the Pah Vant Indians to eat, causing four of them to die immediately, besides poisoning a number more. The company also poisoned the water where they encamped, killing the cattle of the [Mormon] settlers. This . . . policy, planned in wickedness by this company, raised the *ire* of the Indians, which soon spread to the southern tribes, firing them up with revenge, till blood was in their path. . . . Captain Fancher and company fell victim to their *wrath*, near Mountain Meadows; their cattle and horses were shot down in every direction, their wagons and property mostly committed to the flames."

At the end of the letter, Lee added a list of what he said had been his official expenditures, and those of other Mormons in the area, "all of the items [being] completely false," he confessed long afterward. "I put the expense account of $2,220, just . . . to help Brigham Young to get something from the Government. It was the way his Indian Farmers all did. I never gave the Indians one of the articles named in the letter. Not one of the men mentioned ever furnished such articles to the Indians, but I did it this way for safety. Brigham Young never spent a dollar on the Indians in Utah, while he was Indian Agent."

There remained one further act of cynicism, to complete the Mountain Meadows affair. This involved the submission to the Federal Government of a voucher for $3,527.43, for goods of various kinds, which Levi Stewart, a Mormon, claimed to have "furnished to sundry bands of Indians, near Mountain Meadows . . . on Superintendent [Young's] orders."

An examination of Stewart's voucher makes it clear that most, if not all the goods listed, such as work pants, shirts, handkerchiefs and other clothing had belonged to the massacre victims and that many of these items had been given to the Indians at Mountain Meadows as their share of the booty. The Indians had included "Tutsegabit and his band, Chief Walker and his band, and Chief Moquetas and his band." Stewart's claim required the support of two trustworthy witnesses, and so John D. Lee and Dimick B. Huntington swore to its validity. "We certify on honor," they attested, "that we were present and saw the articles mentioned in this voucher distributed to the [above named] Indians." And Brigham Young, as governor and superintendent of Indian Affairs, added, "I certify on honor that the above accounts are correct and just, and that I have actually paid the amount thereof."

In effect, not satisfied with having robbed and murdered more than a hundred and twenty innocent men, women and children, Young and his associates then attempted to profit further from their crime by falsely claiming that they had "purchased for" and "given to" the Indians at Mountain Meadows what actually had been the victims' own possessions.

Chapter 34

BRIGHAM YOUNG LIVED for two decades after the Mountain Meadows Massacre, and although deposed as governor in 1857, during all but the last two or three years of his life he succeeded in defying the laws, the will and the immense power of the United States, remaining in effect the unrepentant and despotic ruler of a private kingdom that he and a small band of Mormon pioneers had carved out of the nation's vast western empire. By controlling the local courts in Utah through his numerous and obedient followers, and by preventing the Federal courts from functioning within the Territory, Young was able to protect himself and his fellow conspirators from prosecution; in addition, through such control he deprived Gentile critics of an opportunity to demonstrate legally the Church's connection with the massacre itself and with many earlier and later crimes. Only at the end of his life did the Prophet finally bow to superior force and then merely to grant his enemies a single, minor and far from satisfying victory. Before that day came, however, there were years of tension and turmoil, of endless combat with the Federal Government, and a series of exhilarating though impermanent triumphs over the hated Gentile officials arrayed against him.

Between 1857 and 1860, the Prophet faced some of his most perilous tests, and without the aid of the Church's impassioned friend and advocate from Philadelphia, Colonel Thomas Leiper Kane, it is probable that several prominent Mormons, including Young himself, would have ended in the defendant's dock, if not on the public scaffold. But Kane worked sedulously during these critical years and, through connivance and manipulation, helped the Prophet to avoid punishment for his crimes. Eventually, with

Kane's assistance, Brigham Young was able to occupy once more a position of power almost as great as he had enjoyed in former times, when he had possessed the title of governor, and there had been no effective Federal presence, and certainly no Federal troops, within the Territory.

Kane's zealous activities during those years took him from one end of the continent to the other. In early January 1858, having been appointed an "unofficial" emissary to the Latter-Day Saints by President Buchanan, Kane, calling himself "Dr. Osborne," traveled secretly by ship from New York to Panama, and then on to California. In San Bernardino he found that the Saints had just sold their land and homes in obedience to the Prophet's latest command—generally at ruinous prices—and now were about to return to the Great Basin, to strengthen and defend Zion against a Federal army encamped on her eastern borders. This "enemy" force, consisting of about 2,500 soldiers, had been ordered by President Buchanan to escort the new governor, Alfred Cumming, to Salt Lake City, and to help him and the Federal judges, marshals and attorneys restore public order in Utah. By the time Kane arrived at the capital the Federal soldiers still had not entered the Territory, the so-called Mormon War had been in progress for almost six months, and Brigham Young's flagrantly rebellious conduct had placed him and the rest of the hierarchy in danger of being prosecuted for treason.

Or at least, so it appeared. Having decided during the previous summer that in order to maintain his ascendancy over his followers he would have to make a serious show of defiance against the Federal Government, Brigham Young had declared martial law in September 1857 and then, in October, after fortifying the approaches to the capital, had launched elements of the Nauvoo Legion against the approaching army's supply trains; these had advanced recklessly toward South Pass ahead of the main body of troops and without any cavalry protection, the assumption having been made at headquarters that Mormon threats were mere bluster and that the trains would be as safe in Utah as back at Fort Leavenworth, Kansas. Within a short time, however, Mormon guerrillas, led by such expert plunderers as Porter Rockwell, Lot Huntington and Bill Hickman, had killed or run off hundreds of oxen, mules and horses, destroyed a considerable amount of forage in the area and appropriated or put to the torch thousands of pounds of food, along with dozens of wagons and other valuable equipment.

Arriving late on the scene because of bureaucratic inefficiency in Washington, Colonel Albert S. Johnston—soon to be appointed brigadier general—had coolly gathered together his troops and remaining supply trains, and on being informed by Brigham Young that he would not be allowed to purchase supplies at Salt Lake City or to approach the capital peacefully, had gone into winter quarters at Camp Scott, two or three miles south of Fort Bridger. After doing so, he answered the Prophet's protests and fulminations, as a number of junior officers had previously—stating that the Federal troops neither wished nor intended to interfere with the Mormons in their religious practices and that he and his men had every desire to avoid bloodshed, but that Young's ill-advised resistance to President Buchanan's orders would lead, the following spring, to the formation of a much larger army, the occupation of the Territory and, if necessary, to the forceful suppression of the Mormon rebellion. At the same time, Johnston assured the Prophet that his sole object as commander in chief of the expeditionary force was to see that the Federal authority was upheld and that the President's orders were obeyed.

Such was the state of affairs in February 1858 when President Buchanan's emissary, the mysterious "Dr. Osborne," arrived at the Mormon capital and took matters deftly in hand. Kane already had the solution to many of Brigham Young's difficulties, as he no doubt was able to inform the Prophet during the private meeting they held immediately after Kane's arrival—a meeting that dealt in matters so secret that not even Heber C. Kimball was allowed to attend. First, and most important, Kane again could point out to Young—as he had the previous summer—that the new governor, Alfred Cumming, was Kane's own handpicked candidate, a naive, idealistic and pliant man, of much affability and little discernment, whom they could easily influence and lead in any direction they pleased. As a consequence, when Cumming assumed the governorship, Young's power would in no way be threatened or diminished, and ultimately, through Cumming's good offices, and through the use of other carefully selected intermediaries, peace could be arranged with the Federal Government on terms highly favorable to the Church.

That this was so, Kane pointed out, could hardly be disputed, for conditions back in Washington had changed radically during the past few months, and now, on every side, there were numerous signs favorable to the Mormon cause. To begin with, President Buchanan had lost most of his initial zeal for the "Utah War." A number of major political considerations lay behind this change; for one thing, there had been a severe financial panic during the summer and autumn, and Congress and much of the country had suddenly found the Utah Expedition far too costly. Also there had been scandals over the purchase of army supplies, and some of the President's political enemies already were gleefully calling the expedition "Buchanan's Blunder." Truthfully, the nation as a whole had little interest in Utah at present, its concern being focused almost exclusively on the troubles in Kansas and the related slavery question. Realizing all this, Colonel Kane, before leaving Washington, had worked diligently with John M. Bernhisel, the Mormon delegate to Congress, to persuade President Buchanan that a full-scale war could be avoided and peace arranged on mutually satisfactory terms between the Saints and the Government, and after that, he and Bernhisel had suggested that the President send two commissioners to Utah with a reasonable offer of reconcilation.

Colonel Kane, having placed these facts before the Prophet, and having received his approval, soon left Salt Lake City and proceeded to Camp Scott, where he quarreled with General Johnston—no doubt deliberately—flattered the new governor and succeeded in greatly increasing the hostility already latent between the two officials, each jealous of his own prerogatives and authority. Then, having gained Cumming's assent, Kane returned to Salt Lake City and completed arrangements for receiving the governor there, and not long afterward, Cumming arrived to confer with the Prophet, accompanied not by General Johnston and the Army but instead by a Mormon escort provided by Brigham Young.

During the months that followed, Governor Cumming often was grossly deceived, for he was a trusting gentleman and assumed that men like Young and Kane were as honorable as he was himself. For Cumming's benefit, and for its general effect on the rest of the nation, the Prophet and Kane soon embarked on the next step in their plan: to present the Saints in the dramatic and touching role of martyrs-to-their-religion, and it was not long before the northern settlements and the capital had been evacuated, as Young for months past had been threatening to do. Now he announced again, as he departed from the capital, that his followers would burn their houses and farms and "retreat into the wilderness," taking with them three years' supply of food, rather than have a Federal army encamped near any of their towns, their religion interfered with and Federal judges and other grasping Gentile officials holding office in the Territory and persecuting the Church. The Mormon exodus advanced as far south as Provo, most of the 25,000 refugees dressed in little better than rags, and Governor Cumming's heart was duly wrung at the sight, as Young and Kane had intended, so that when the two peace commissioners arrived a short time later, the governor was ready to fully support all Mormon demands.

In June 1858, Major Ben McCullough of Texas, and Senator-elect L. W. Powell of Kentucky, President Buchanan's special commissioners, arrived at Camp Scott from the East with the President's Peace Proclamation, signed two months earlier, in which Buchanan offered "a free and full pardon to all who will submit themselves to the just authority of the federal government." The commissioners had been enjoined to avoid making any treaties with the Mormons but were to "bring those misguided people to their senses" by convincing them of the uselessness of resistance; they were urged to talk with the Mormon leaders and advised to make full use of the obliging and resourceful Colonel Kane.

Commissioners McCullough and Powell proceeded to Salt Lake City and there found that Brigham Young was at Provo with his army of tattered and homeless refugees. A conference was arranged, and aided greatly by Governor Cumming and Colonel Kane, a peaceful settlement soon was reached, Brigham Young and all his followers receiving a complete pardon for their seditious and rebellious acts. Only then was the army permitted to enter the Valley of the Great Salt Lake and to march through the deserted capital, eventually moving on fifteen or twenty miles to the southwest, where General Johnston began to supervise the construction of a permanent post, Camp Floyd, to quarter his officers and men. On July 4, the Mormon refugees, obeying the Prophet's orders, streamed back from Provo and reoccupied their homes in the capital and the northern settlements, acknowledging that a new governor and other Federal officials were indeed in their midst but indicating by their actions that they still yielded obedience to no one but the Prophet of the Lord.

For Brigham Young the negotiations had ended in a dramatic and much-needed victory over the Gentiles, and yet, after he had lead the Saints back from Provo to the capital in triumph, his political position still remained anything but secure. It was true that the new governor was malleable and easily deceived and certainly could be used in a variety of ways against the enemies of the Church. Unhappily, though, nothing so agreeable could be said for most of the other important Federal officials now stationed in the Territory. Particularly distressing to the Prophet was General Johnston—a man equally unmoved by Mormon threats or flattery—and the three judges who had arrived with the general's army and who seemed intent on re-opening the Federal courts and then, quite possibly with the support of the general's troops, of challenging the right of the Church to run the Territory without interference.

As if such prospects were not grim enough, additional difficulties soon began to arise for Young and the hierarchy with the unwelcome appearance of the *Valley Tan*, the first Gentile newspaper ever to be published in Zion. From the start its founder, Kirk Anderson, formerly city editor of the *Missouri Republican*, proved the most irksome of gadflies. His specialty, it turned out, was the reporting of recent Mormon crimes and transgressions, and within a short time he managed to publish accounts of the Parrish-Potter Murders at Springville, committed a few months before the Mountain Meadows Massacre, the murder of the six-man Aiken Party for its $18,000 in gold, a crime committed on the Southern Trail shortly after the massacre, and finally, the destruction of the Fancher Train itself. As the paper pointed out, neither Brigham Young nor his successor, Governor Cumming, had inquired with any vigor into these matters, which, in the case of the Fancher Train, was especially shocking on two counts—that sixteen or seventeen of the children apparently had survived and still were in Indian hands, awaiting rescue from their captivity, and that scarcely a soul could be found in the rest of the country who believed the incredible Mormon assertions that the Fancher Train had been exterminated by an Indian band, angered over the poisoning of an ox or a spring, and that no white men had been involved in the affair.

With the encouragement of the *Valley Tan*, and also following orders received from the Government in Washington, a number of civil and military officers soon began to take an active concern in these notorious crimes, which had yet to be investigated impartially and which the Church's own newspaper, the *Deseret News*, had not even bothered to report. For the most part the investigators' attention was centered on the Mountain Meadows

Massacre, by reason of its size alone the most horrifying act of violence in the history of the troubled Territory and an event that had deeply shocked much of the nation when disclosed a year and a half earlier, by California newspapers and then by other newspapers throughout the country.

Now, at last, during the spring and summer of 1859, two military parties, one from California and the other from Camp Floyd in Utah, and two civilian parties, one under the newly appointed superintendent of Indian Affairs, young Jacob Forney, and one under Justice John M. Cradlebaugh, whose jurisdiction included all of Utah's "Dixie," each set out separately for the southern settlements, and before they were done, they had compiled a mass of previously undisclosed information, all of it leading to several common and dismaying conclusions. Their investigations indicated, among other things, that the Church itself, at the highest levels, had been involved in the affair; that the Indians had received a letter from Dimick Huntington, signed by Brigham Young, authorizing the massacre; that the Indians had received little of the booty; that most of the victims' bloody clothing, referred to facetiously in the southern settlements as "Spoils from the Siege at Sebastopol," had been stored for weeks in the tithing office at Cedar City, the stench of it still being all too easily discernible eighteen months afterward; that most of the victims' cattle had received Mormon brands, and had been sold for the benefit of the Church, along with the victims' jewelry and other valuables; that John D. Lee, Isaac Haight, William Dame and from four to five dozen other Saints had been immediately responsible for the crime; that the surviving children, contrary to the accounts of John D. Lee, Jacob Hamblin and other Church members, never had been in Indian hands but, instead, had lived since the day of the massacre with various Mormon families, including at least one family headed by their parents' murderer; and that several of the children were old enough to remember the massacre in detail and could testify against the criminals, and that one of them had said, "I wish I were a man, for then I know what I would do—I would shoot John D. Lee—I saw him shoot my mother."

Most damaging of all to the reputation of the Church—and most menacing to the safety of the Prophet and his fellow conspirators—was the work of Judge Cradlebaugh, who set out from Salt Lake City toward the south, in March 1859. At Provo the judge empaneled a grand jury of local citizens and, using

Federal soldiers to maintain order, assembled a small army of witnesses and had them present to the jury, over a two-week span, testimony concerning the Parrish-Potter and Aiken Party murders, several other murders and violent crimes and a considerable amount of testimony relating to the Mountain Meadows Massacre. After two weeks, however, Judge Cradlebaugh realized that his jurymen had received instructions from the capital to take no action and to return no indictments, and so he decided to dismiss the jury, after first delivering a speech unlike any previously heard in the Territory during the twelve years of Brigham Young's reign.

Speaking particularly of the Parrish-Potter affair, a case in which the evidence was strong and complete and which indicated clearly that the Church hierarchy had ordered the execution of several unsuspecting Apostates who had wished to emigrate to California, Judge Cradlebaugh told the jurymen: "Until I commenced the examination of the testimony in this case, I always supposed that I lived in a land of civil and religious liberty, in which we were secured by the Constitution of our country the right to remove at pleasure from one portion of our domain to another, and also that we enjoyed the privilege of 'worshipping God according to the dictates of our own conscience.' But I regret to say, so far as Utah is concerned, I have been mistaken in such a supposition. Men are murdered here. Coolly, deliberately, premeditatedly murdered—their murder is deliberated and determined upon by church council-meetings, and that, too, for no other reason than that they have apostatized from your Church, and were striving to leave the Territory. You are the tools, the dupes, the instruments of a tyrannical Church despotism. The heads of your Church order and direct you. You are taught to obey their orders, and commit these horrid murders. Deprived of your liberty, you have lost your manhood, and become the willing instruments of [evil] men. I say it will be my earnest effort, while with you, to knock off your ecclesiastical shackles and set you free."

Frustrated by the grand jury's inaction, and yet unwilling to accept defeat, Judge Cradlebaugh found that a small detatchment of United States soldiers was going south to the neighborhood of Cedar City and Mountain Meadows, and after deputizing several special assistants, he accompanied the soldiers to their destination and, in the southern settlements, gathered a wealth of fresh information about the fate of the Fancher Train. Taking temporary possession of an empty house in Cedar City, Judge Cradlebaugh announced to the inhabitants that he was ready to sit as an examining magistrate, if anyone cared to testify about the massacre. According to one of his deputies, William H. Rodgers, "As soon as it became known that Judge [Cradlebaugh] intended to hold a court, and that he would have troops to insure protection, and to serve writs if necessary, several persons visited him at his room, at late hours of the night, and informed him of different facts connected with the massacre. All those that called thus, stated that it would be at the risk of their lives if it became known that they had communicated anything to him, and they requested Judge Cradlebaugh, if he met them in public in the daytime, not to recognize them as persons he had seen before.

"One of the men who called thus on Judge Cradlebaugh, confessed that he [had] participated in the massacre, and gave an account of it . . . he also gave Judge Cradlebaugh the names of 25 or 30 other men living in the region, who [had] assisted in the massacre. He offered also to make the same statement in court and under oath, if protection was guaranteed him. He gave as the reason for divulging these facts, that they had tormented his mind and conscience since they [had] occurred, and he expressed a willingness to stand trial for his crime."

Within a short time Judge Cradlebaugh issued warrants for the arrest and trial of all the immediate principals in the massacre, but without exception—Lee, Haight, Dame and the others—were warned of the judge's action, slipped away from their homes and went into hiding in the surrounding hills. Still, the danger was acute that the judge's deputies would succeed in trapping one or two of the wanted men, and that with General Johnston's soldiers acting as a guard, the judge would be able to bring the murderers to trial, and by so doing, reveal to the outside world the full story of the Mountain Meadows Massacre.

At this point, when it was most desperately required by the Prophet and the Church, vital assistance once again was provided by Colonel Kane. An official message arrived from Washington, stating that it had been called to President Buchanan's attention that Judge Cradlebaugh had been employing Federal troops to guard his courtroom and to provide protection to prospective witnesses. It was the President's desire that the practice was to cease at once. Troops in General Johnston's command were to be put to these or similar uses only at the request of Governor Cumming—and now, General Johnston was informed by the governor, he was to withdraw his troops from Cedar City immediately and have them return to Camp Floyd, and in the future, his soldiers were not to be employed in support of the Federal courts. Deprived of all protection, Judge Cradlebaugh's witnesses no longer were willing to testify, and the judge soon abandoned his efforts to bring the murderers to justice. Often enough before, Colonel Kane had toiled on behalf of the Church, but never with results more gratifying to the Prophet or more disastrous to the frail cause of Truth.

Chapter 35

THE COLLAPSE of Judge Cradlebaugh's efforts and his eventual departure from the Territory greatly reduced the Prophet's immediate personal danger and marked the beginning of a final ten-year period during which he managed to rule over Zion with much the same authority as he had exercised before the outbreak of the Mormon War. Despite the presence of Gentile governors, judges, marshals and a small army of supporting troops, Young still was able to frustrate the enemies of the Church through a combination of physical intimidation, unscrupulous political tactics and a series of chance events that temporarily played into his hands.

It was the Prophet's good fortune that the Civil War began when it did, distracting the rest of the nation and leading President Abraham Lincoln to conclude that with the defiant South committed to Secession, a renewal of the insurrection in Utah would do little to help preserve the Union. Although in 1862 Lincoln signed into law an Act of Congress that made the practice of polygamy illegal in United States territories, his Administration showed no strong desire to implement the act or even to curb Brigham Young's chronic intransigence. "I will let the Mormons alone," Lincoln said, "if they will let me alone"—a remark that accurately reflected his calculated indifference to all but the nation's paramount problem.

Also fortunate for the Church was the fact that the Utah Territory—though now much reduced in size as new states were formed—still remained almost entirely isolated from the rest of the country. As a result, until the completion of America's first transcontinental railroad in 1869, there were so few Gentiles resident in Salt Lake City and the outlying settlements that Brigham Young could control every jury selected in either the Federal or territorial courts and, in effect, prevent any deserving Saint from suffering the penalties of the law.

Yet all the while, a small but persistent specter continued to haunt the aging Prophet and his Church. It was the specter of a single monstrous crime, perpetrated under circumstances that each year became more difficult to justify or explain, not merely to Gentile outsiders but to younger members of the Church itself, who had experienced neither the ancient conflicts in Missouri and Illinois nor the singular days of the Reformation and Blood Atonement. And so, as time passed, the Prophet and his fellow leaders struggled to disassociate themselves entirely from the Mountain Meadows Massacre, though never with a great deal of success. Eventually, to their discomfort, the massacre became the subject of a popular local ballad, sung to the strumming of a guitar or banjo; there were seven or eight versions, and in each, without exception, blame for the crime was placed on John D. Lee, while in several, the Prophet was blamed as well. One version ended in this way:

> By order of Old Brigham Young this deed was done, you see,
> And the captain of that wicked band was Captain John D. Lee.

And another version ended with these lines:

> By order of their President this bloody deed was done.
> He was the leader of the Mormon Church, his name is Brigham Young.

At first none of the massacre leaders suffered even the slightest inconvenience because of their participation in the crime, nor did they seem to have incurred the Church's displeasure for whatever they had done at The Meadows. Indeed, during the winter following the massacre, Lee, Haight and Dame served as members of the territorial legislature and the constitutional convention, and while in Salt Lake City, Lee received permission from Brigham Young to take a new bride, always an unmistakable sign of the Prophet's high favor. Gradually, though, with the passage of years, the known criminals were relieved of their civil and ecclesiastical offices and forced to retire from public life. Ultimately, it became necessary for many of them to move from Parowan and Cedar City to more distant and less pleasant communities, and in some cases to withdraw entirely from the

Territory, mostly into a remote corner of Nevada or Arizona, where no Utah marshal could arrest them nor Utah judge try them for their crimes.

Despite his retirement from public office, however, through most of the 1860's John D. Lee still remained on cordial terms with Brigham Young. In 1861, four years after the massacre, Young made one of his periodic trips to the southern settlements, and when he reached the small village of Washington, greeted Lee warmly and stayed with him as a guest. Nor did this by any means mark the end of their close and long-standing intimacy. All during the next six or eight years, Lee continued to receive personal assignments from the Prophet, which he carried out with undiminished pride and enthusiasm. In October 1867 he drove a flock of Brigham Young's goats from Harmony to Salt Lake City, was received in the friendliest fashion and spent several days living at the Prophet's mansion.

But in 1869, the year when the newly completed railroad first began to bring a large number of Gentile settlers into the Territory, Brigham Young suddenly altered his conduct, and when he visited the southern settlements, failed for the first time to invite Lee to join his train or to participate in any public ceremonies. Evidently the Prophet already was looking to the future and even then was considering the possibility of sacrificing his faithful follower, if that step ever should become necessary.

The next year Young twice returned to the south, talked with Lee privately and on each occasion "counseled" him, for safety's sake, to move farther away. After their second meeting, Lee reluctantly obeyed. Accompanied by several of his families he resettled in Skutumpah, a remote village to the southeast, in what was the beginning of an exodus that eventually would take him across the Arizona border. Lee scarcely had settled in his new quarters when he received word, in October 1870, that he had been excommunicated from the Church for the part he had played in the massacre—thirteen years before.

Journeying back from Skutumpah, Lee met Brigham Young in the town of St. George and protested the treatment he had been accorded. Later he described the meeting in his journal. "I asked [Brigham Young] how it was that I was held in fellowship thirteen years for an act committed [in 1857], and all of a sudden I must be cut off from the Church? If it was wrong now, it certainly was wrong then. He replied that they never had learned the particulars until lately."

At the end of the interview, Young seemingly relented, told Lee that "he had no feelings against [him]" and advised his adopted son to "go to Brother Erastus Snow and set a time for a new hearing." As a result, Lee enjoyed a cheerful Christmas, in the belief that his case would be heard again, and that this time he would be allowed to testify on his own behalf. But within a few days he received an unsigned note in Apostle Snow's handwriting. "If you consult your own safety and that [of] others at this time," the note said, "you will not press yourself, nor an investigation, on others at this time, lest you cause others to become accessories with you, and thereby force them to inform upon you, or to suffer. Our advice is, trust to no one. Make yourself scarce, and keep out of the way."

Clearly in 1871 Lee already was considered a liability to the Church and, although he did not recognize it himself, had become a leading candidate for the dubious role of scapegoat.

The difficulties of the Prophet and his close associates now began to multiply alarmingly. In 1871 a Federal grand jury was empaneled, and Young, Daniel H. Wells, formerly the commanding officer of the Nauvoo Legion, and several other prominent Saints were indicted under the nation's 1862 antipolygamy law, for "lewdness and improper cohabitation." The same grand jury—which included only seven Mormons among its twenty-three jurors and seventeen talesmen, or substitutes—also brought indictments for murder against Wells, William Kimball and Hosea Stout for the murder of one Richard Yates "during the 1857 war." In addition, the jury indicted Brigham Young, Porter Rockwell, Bill Hickman and two other lesser-known Saints for the murder of a member of the Aiken Party in 1857, all five of the accused then being admitted to bail.

Two adjournments in the polygamy case were granted the Prophet because of alleged "ill health." He then appeared in court during November 1871 and after his attorney had filed an appeal, was confined to his house, under legal detention, for several months. This vexing episode ended in 1872, when the United States Supreme Court considered his appeal and gave the Prophet his last great victory over the Gentiles. The court declared that in the absence of a suitable Federal statute to the contrary, all jury selection should be governed by territorial laws, thus leaving the process safely in Mormon hands and, at the same time, invalidating all the proceedings against Young and the other indicted Saints.

The court's decision left powerless the Federal officials in Utah, and after his release from detention, Brigham Young once again seemed free to conduct himself without restraint and, through his position as President of the Church, to rule his mountain domain in much the same style as he had before. But this time his triumph was extremely brief. Two years afterward, in June 1874, Congress, at the urging of President Ulysses S. Grant, passed the so-called Poland Bill, which established for all time Federal supremacy over the Territory and signaled the ultimate end of both polygamous marriage and unlicensed theocratic rule. Under the Poland Bill, the common law acquired full force in the Territory; United States attorneys were granted the power to prosecute all criminal cases; United States marshals alone could serve and execute writs and draw up jury lists in both civil and criminal cases. The new law also provided that in any prosecution for bigamy, adultery or polygamy, a juror could be removed if he practiced polygamy himself or if he believed that plural marriage was a worthy or desirable institution. The Poland Bill threatened jail for every member of the Church hierarchy and every other practicing polygamist in the Territory, and it also enabled Federal officers for the first time to arrest and try, with at least a modest chance of obtaining a conviction, those Saints who had committed violent and well-documented crimes.

Within a few weeks of the bill's passage, warrants were issued against the massacre leaders, and Sheriff William Stokes set out for the southern settlements to arrest as many of them as he could find. On previous occasions, whenever Federal officers had planned to visit the area, the Prophet always had managed to send word in advance and the officers had discovered on their arrival that the wanted men had mysteriously vanished from their homes. This time, however, John D. Lee either recklessly ignored the warning or else never received one. Returning from Arizona to visit those wives and children he had left behind, and to pick up much-needed supplies, he was surprised by Sheriff Stokes and several special deputies in the town of Panguitch, and after a futile attempt to hide in a wooden storage pen near his house, surrendered without a shot being fired. Lee and Stokes then departed for Beaver, where the sheriff placed Lee in jail.

None of the other massacre leaders were arrested at the time, although Haight, Higbee, Dame and the rest were named in subsequent murder indictments.

Lee's first trial was little better than a farce. The Church had decided to protect him for its own sake, and the Faithful in the area, including four Saints on the jury, had been alerted to the fact. As a result, most Mormons were unwilling to testify, the usual excuse being that they knew nothing whatever about the affair. Those from Parowan and Cedar City declared that they never had heard of the massacre; those from Harmony claimed that John D. Lee was a stranger whom they had never seen before. The principal witness for the prosecution—and an exceptionally strong one—was the Apostate Philip Klingensmith, who unhesitatingly placed Lee at the massacre scene although he would not swear that he actually had seen Lee kill any of the victims. Several other witnesses also testified against the defendant, and the weight of circumstantial evidence alone made it certain that Lee had been a leader in the affair, most probably had committed a number of the murders himself and was responsible for much of what had been done.

The line chosen by the defense caused universal dismay among the members of the hierarchy. Lee told the familiar and unconvincing tale of the victims' wicked conduct before the massacre, of the poisoned ox and drinking water, and of the Indians and Mormons who had died as a result of them. Worse still, he insisted that at the time of the massacre he only had been carrying out the orders of his military and ecclesiastical superiors, and he stated openly, for the rest of the world to hear, that responsibility for the crime rested with the Mormon Church because its leaders long had maintained that "the blood of the Prophets" should be avenged by the Saints as the highest duty they owed to God.

At this point, according to at least one account, the Prophet concluded that Lee had to be sacrificed but unhappily could find no opportunity of communicating his sudden change of plans to the Saints on the jury. The four dutifully held out for acquittal, while the eight Gentile jurors voted for a verdict of guilty. After two days it was realized that no decision could be reached, the jury was discharged, and a new trial was scheduled for the following year.

During the intervening months, Lee continued to ignore the warnings of his attorney, steadfastly refusing to believe that

Brigham Young would betray so loyal a servant for the sake of his own safety or the good of the Church. But in September 1876, when the second trial was held, it soon became evident that such was indeed the case. Obviously a complete understanding had been reached by Brigham Young and the prosecution, both sides agreeing that Lee was to be convicted and that he alone was to bear the stigma for the massacre, and that in return, neither the Church nor any Saints other than Lee were to be implicated by the court's proceedings.

At Lee's second trial, unlike the first, as the prosecution's opening remarks made amply clear, the Church's role in the massacre was not to be investigated or questioned. As a consequence, various members of the hierarchy now found it incumbent upon themselves—for the sake of Truth and Justice—to break their nineteen years' silence and to bear witness against the defendant. Damaging though perjured affidavits from Brigham Young and George A. Smith were placed in evidence and Daniel Wells of the Nauvoo Legion appeared in person to say that at the time of the massacre Lee had *not* been an officer in the militia and therefore his claim, that he had been following military orders, was false.

During the course of the second trial, a number of Mormon memories underwent a remarkable improvement. Such massacre participants as Nephi Johnson, Samuel Knight and Samuel McMurdy suddenly recalled a good deal about Lee's activities, including the essential fact that they had seen him kill one or more of the massacre victims. Jacob Hamblin, who previously had remembered nothing, now was allowed to relate a hearsay account of Lee's conduct at The Meadows and to describe how his old friend had thrown to the ground two attractive young women as they begged for mercy and then had taken out his bowie knife and cut their throats.

The testimony against Lee was overwhelming, and realizing at last that he had been betrayed, he broke down and wept. He was allowed to retire briefly to his cell, and after he returned, his attorneys offered no direct testimony on his behalf—all their first trial witnesses no longer remembering anything at all. The jury of twelve reliable Mormons—carefully selected and given their instructions at the outset of the trial—deliberated for an hour and then brought in a verdict of murder in the first degree. Judge Boreman informed Lee that he had the choice either of being shot, hanged or beheaded, and Lee said calmly, "I prefer to be shot."

Execution was set for the following spring. Lee could have escaped death by making a full confession, but though seriously tempted, he refused to do so. Instead, he compromised by writing a brief sketch of his life, in which he implicated the Prophet and other leading Saints in numerous crimes, although he could not bring himself to take the final step and reveal the full truth about Brigham Young's role in the Mountain Meadows Massacre. Such reluctance was not difficult to understand: to have condemned the Prophet as a calculating mass-murderer would have been to inflict on himself an intolerable injury, for if God's anointed spokesman was nothing better than a debased and vile criminal, then the Church was hopelessly defective and corrupt, the struggles of his own lifetime would have been meaningless and, worst of all, his belief in God, and in his own eternal happiness, would have been destroyed.

Yet at the very close of his life, Lee did bring himself to speak a portion of the truth. "I have been treacherously betrayed, and sacrificed in the most cowardly manner," he wrote, "by those who should have been my friends, and whose will I have diligently striven to make my pleasure for the last thirty years at least. In return for my faithfulness and fidelity to *him* and *his cause*, he has sacrificed me in a most shameful and cruel way."

On the morning of March 23, 1877, Lee was taken under armed guard to Mountain Meadows for his execution. The weather was chilly and he wore a hat, coat and muffler. Two decades had passed since the massacre, and during that time the narrow valley had undergone a great change. Doubtless Lee noted how little grass remained now and how constant overgrazing, and the terrible floods of 1861 and 1873, had caused widespread erosion. No doubt, too, Lee recalled an early and memorable visit that Brigham Young had paid to the scene of the massacre, when a rough, pyramidal stone monument still had stood near the site of the emigrants' fort, the monument having been erected two years before by United States soldiers. A cedar cross had stood atop the monument, and on it had been inscribed the words "Vengeance is mine, saith the Lord, I will repay." The Prophet had inspected the words and then had said exultantly, "Vengeance is mine, saith the Lord, and I have taken a little of it!" And within the hour

those Saints present had torn the monument to pieces and had
scattered the stones across the grass.

Patiently now, Lee sat on his wooden coffin and waited for the
photographer to set up a camera and then to take the official
pictures of the scene. Finally these preliminaries were over, and
the execution squad filed into position. Lee still remained calm as
he rose from the coffin and addressed those within hearing. "I am
ready to die," he said. "I trust in God. I have no fear. Death has no
terror. Having said this, I feel resigned. I ask the Lord my God, if
my labors are done, to receive my spirit."

He shook hands with those in attendance, removed his hat, coat
and muffler, and gave them to one of the men standing beside
him. After reminding the guards to aim for his heart, so that his
body would not be mutilated, he allowed a blindfold to be
fastened over his eyes but requested that his hands be left free.
At the signal, five shots rang out and Lee fell back into the open
coffin, making no cry or sound. His body was given to two of his
sons, taken in a wagon to Panguitch and buried there, with his
temple robes first placed inside the wooden coffin.

Brigham Young survived his faithful disciple by only six
months. After a painful illness, he died on August 29, 1877,
almost exactly twenty years from the day when John D. Lee had
sat in his office and revealed that their initial plans for the
Fancher Company had gone sadly awry. Brigham Young died as
he had lived, still vengeful and unrepentant, the builder of a
Church, the leading citizen of a vast, half-settled territory, the
possessor of property and other assets worth more than two
million dollars, and the architect of a cold-blooded crime, unique
even in a nation inured to violence.

With Lee's execution and the Prophet's death, interest in the
Mountain Meadows Massacre slowly began to subside. No other
participant was tried or punished, although at one time William
Dame was arrested and held in custody before being released on
bail. No explanation for the Government's failure to act against
Dame was made afterward, but there can be hardly any doubt
that it was part of the overall agreement arranged with the
Prophet before Lee's second trial. At that point, a third trial
would have embarrassed the Church acutely, especially since
Dame was all too ready to reveal the source of his orders, for
earlier he had threatened "to put the saddle on the right horse" if
ever he was forced to stand trial for his part in the crime.

In all, eighteen children survived the massacre, and of these, seventeen were found by Jacob Forney, the superintendent of Indian Affairs, who collected them from the Mormons, brought them north to Salt Lake City and eventually returned them to their relatives in Arkansas. The eighteenth child, however, was not so fortunate; she was Nancy Cameron, a cousin of Malinda Cameron Scott and, according to her aunt's testimony, remained in Mormon country for the rest of her life, surrounded by those who had murdered or abetted the murderers of some fifteen or twenty of her near relations, a prey to what dark thoughts and memories it would be no easy matter to say.

As for the site of the massacre, it was left unmarked for many years, until at last, in 1932, some local residents, in cooperation with the Utah Pioneer Trails and Landmarks Association, placed a small monument and a memorial plaque near the place where the members of the Fancher Party had made their last stand. In 1966, though, the land was purchased by the Mormon Church, and shortly afterward all road markers disappeared, so that for a time at least, visitors had no way of finding the monument. And so, apparently even today in Utah, there are those who still would make a virtue of concealment and who have no wish to face the implications of that now ancient but still unforgotten crime.

Perhaps, though, instead of attempting to conceal the massacre site, or instead of speaking vengeance, as both the Prophet Brigham Young and the United States Army officers once did when they came to The Meadows more than a hundred years ago, other words might better be placed on that desolate patch of ground, the words of a man whose philosophy was far different from that of Young and so many other empire builders.

"In the end, there is no way in which people can live together decently," the American author Morris Cohen once wrote, "unless each individual group realizes that the whole of truth and virtue is not exclusively in its possession. This is a hard lesson to learn, but without it there can be no humane civilization."

With such words placed in the narrow valley, perhaps the restless ghosts that still are said to haunt the massacre site finally would be exorcised, and the people of the Great Basin could fully accept, and make peace with, their own past.

APPENDIX

Those Traveling in the Fancher Train

Captain Alexander Fancher. Age 45
His wife, *Eliza Ingram Fancher.* Age 33.
Their children:
Hampton Fancher. Age 19.
William Fancher. Age 17.
Mary Fancher. Age 16.
Thomas Fancher. Age 14.
Martha G. Fancher. Age 11.
Sarah G. and Margaret F. Fancher. Twins. Age 8.
Christopher Carson Fancher. Age 5. Known as "Kit."

James M. Fancher. Age 25. Nephew of Captain Alexander Fancher.
The name and age of his presumed wife are unknown.
Robert Fancher. Age 19. Younger brother of James M. Fancher.
Triphena Fancher. Her name also was spelled "Trifina." Age 2 or 3.
    Almost certainly James Fancher's daughter.

Peter Huff. Age unknown.
His wife. Name and age unknown.
Sophronia Huff. Their youngest child. Age 2 or 3.
There were at least two other children in the family, one possibly named
    Ephraim W. Huff. Ages uncertain.

Captain John T. Baker. Age 52. Known to everyone else in the train as
    "Uncle Jack."
His wife, *Mary Baker.* Age 44.
Their children, all, or most, of whom were in the train:
John H. Baker. Age 23.
Sarah C. Baker. Age 21.
Abel Baker. Age 19.
Silas M. Baker. Age 17.

Mary J. Baker. Age 13.
Mariah E. Baker. Age 11.
Peter S. Baker. Age 8.

Abel Baker. Age 47. Brother of John T. Baker.
His wife, *Elizabeth Baker.* Age 43.
Their children, all, or most, of whom were in the train:
Ann Elisha Baker. Age 20.
Margaret Baker. Age 18.
Melissa Baker. Age 16.
Almeda Baker. Age 14.
David W. Baker. Age 12.
Alford T. Baker. Age 10.
Salinda Baker. Age 8.

George W. Baker. Age 27. Probably a nephew of John and Abel Baker.
His wife, *Minerva A. Baker.* Age 25.
They had one or more children, names and ages uncertain.

In addition, there were three other Baker children in the train:
Martha Elizabeth Baker. Called "Betsy." Age 4 or 5.
William Baker. Age about 3.
Sarah Jane Baker. About 1 year old.
Most probably they were the children of George and Minerva Baker.
   Possibly, though, they were the youngest children of "Uncle Jack" and
   Mary, or of Abel and Elizabeth Baker.

Melissa A. Beller. Age 14.
Her brother, *David W. Beller.* Age 12.
In special agent William Mitchell's report, these two children were listed
   in the train unaccompanied by an adult. This was an obvious error.
   Almost certainly they traveled with some older relatives, perhaps with
   the John or the Abel Bakers, who were from the same county. Census
   records suggest that Melissa and David Beller were orphaned several
   years before the departure of the Fancher Train.

Charles R. Mitchell. Age unknown.
His wife. Name and age unknown.
Their son, four or five, name unknown. This boy was the only grandson
   of special agent Mitchell.
Joel D. Mitchell. Age unknown. A younger brother of Charles R.
   Mitchell.
Lawson Mitchell. Age unknown. Youngest brother of Charles R. Mitch-
   ell.

John Prewitt. Age 20.
William Prewitt. Age 19.

Lawson McIntyre. Age unknown.

Jessee Dunlap. Age 39.
His wife, *Mary Dunlap.* Age 39.
They had at least six children in the train. Among them, the three
   youngest probably were:
Rebecca Dunlap. Called "Becky." Age 6.
Louisa Dunlap. Age 3.
Sarah Ann Dunlap. Age 1.

Lorenzo D. Dunlap. Age 42.
His wife, *Nancy Dunlap.* Age 42.
They had at least five children in the train. Among them, two of the
   youngest probably were:
Prudence Angelina Dunlap. Age about 6.
Georganna Dunlap. Also about 6.

William Wood. Age 34.
His wife, *Malinda Wood.* Age 33.
They had at least three children, probably more. The oldest were:
Thomas Benton Wood. Age 10.
Sylvester Wood. Age 9.
James Irvine Wood. Age 8.

Solomon R. Wood. Age 38.
His wife, *Martha Wood.* Age 39.
Their children:
James Wood. Age 18.
John H. Wood. Age 11.

Two other families named *Wood* were said to have been members of the
Fancher Train, but whether or not they actually left Arkansas is
unclear.

Richard Wilson. Age 27.

J. Milum Jones. Age 32.
His wife. Name and age unknown.
Their child, whose name may have been *Felix Jones.* Age unknown.

Cyntha Tackett. (Perhaps Cynthia.) The mother of at least seven
   children. Possibly a widow. Her husband, *Martin Tackett,* was not
   listed among the members of the train.
The children of Martin and Cyntha Tackett, all, or most, of whom were
   in the train:
William H. Tackett. Age 23.

Marian Tackett. Age 20.
Sabbyrd Tackett. Age 18.
Matilda Tackett. Age 16.
James M. Tackett. Age 14.
Jones M. Tackett. Age 12.
Also the Tackett's oldest child, *Pleasant Tackett.* Married. Age 25.
His wife. Name and age unknown.
Their elder child was *Milum Tackett.* Age 7.
A second child, *William Tackett.* Probably about 3 or 4 years old.

William Eaton. Age unknown. The first out-of-stater to join the train.
    Left a wife and young daughter back home in Indiana.

Silas Edwards. Age unknown. Possibly joined the train en route.

William Cameron. Age 45–55.
His wife, *Martha Cameron.* Age unknown.
Their five sons, ages unknown, all of whom were in the train:
Tilghman Cameron.
Ison Cameron.
Henry Cameron.
James Cameron.
Larkin Cameron.
An unmarried daughter, also named *Martha Cameron.* Age unknown.

William and Martha Cameron had two married daughters who joined
    the train along with their families. The first daughter was:
Mathilda Cameron Miller. Age unknown.
Her husband, *Joseph Miller.* Age unknown.
Their children:
William Miller. Probably about 8 or 9 years old.
Alfred Miller. 7 years old.
Eliza Miller. Probably about 4 or 5.
Joseph Miller Jr. About 1 or 2 years old.

William and Martha Cameron's other married daughter was:
Malinda Cameron Scott. Age 28.
Her husband, *Henry Dalton Scott.* Age unknown.
Their children probably were all less than ten years old. They were:
Joel Scott.
Martha Scott.
George Scott.
Malinda Cameron Scott's fourth child was born en route. Name un-
    known.
Malinda Cameron Scott had a young cousin in the train. She was:
Nancy Cameron. Age 11.

Richard Scott. Brother of Henry Dalton Scott and brother-in-law of Malinda Cameron Scott.
His wife. Name and age unknown.
Their children. Names and ages unknown.

Milum Rush. Age unknown. Traveled without his two small children, *Alfred and Martha Rush,* who remained behind in Arkansas. It is uncertain whether his wife also was in the train. Possibly she had predeceased him.

Allen Deskazo. Age unknown. In all likelihood the spelling of his name was incorrect.

William A. Aden. Age 20. Very probably the last traveler to join the Fancher Train.

Frank E. King. Joined the train in transit. Age probably 30 or less.
His wife. Name and age unknown.

A family named *Morton.*

A family named *Haydon,* or *Hayden.*

A family named *Hudson.*

A family named *Stevenson.*

A family named *Hamilton.*

A family named *Smith.*

A Methodist minister. Name and age unknown.

NOTES

Chapters 1 and 2

In general, information about the members of the Fancher Train is skimpy and often contradictory. Some unique material on the Fanchers themselves is contained in *The Fancher Family*, a privately printed genealogy compiled by William Hoyt Fancher in 1947, a copy of which is in the New York Public Library. Among other things, it gives the names of the eight children of Captain Alexander Fancher who were in the train, with their ages and places of birth. It also indicates which of them were killed at Mountain Meadows.

A major source of information on the Fancher Train is the report of Special Agent William Mitchell, written at Crooked Creek, Arkansas, dated 27 April 1860 and now in the National Archives. Unfortunately, Mitchell was not a trained investigator, and an indifferent and harassed Federal Government placed few resources at his command. The result is that his report contains a number of significant omissions. For example, it lists an "Alexander Fancher wife & 4 children," thus reducing by three the number of dead in that particular family. Another entry reads: "William Cameron wife & 5 children," when there actually were six children, at least one grandchild and probably one or more daughters-in-law traveling in William and Martha Cameron's three wagons.

The Mitchell report includes a list of the seventeen children who returned to Arkansas after the Mountain Meadows massacre. In a few instances, the investigator has mistaken their Christian names. Confusion over the identities of the surviving children first arose in Utah; some of the children were too young to know their own names, while others were in such a severe state of shock that either they were unable, or did not choose, to tell their captors who they were. In several cases the criminals, or others who received the children, renamed them to suit their own fancies, and in the case of the surviving Miller children, these erroneous Christian names are repeated in the Mitchell listing.

J. P. Dunn's early classic, *Massacres of the Mountains*, contains further information about the children who returned to Arkansas. A number of years after the tragedy, Dunn made direct inquiries and through correspondence and other means learned where most of the survivors were living and what their family arrangements were.

Other information on members of the Fancher Train may be found in the Arkansas state census of 1850, from which the Arkansas History Commission most helpfully forwarded all pertinent material.

No picture of the Fancher Train, or of the events at Mountain Meadows, would be complete without Major James Carleton's invaluable *Report* of 1859, on file in the National Archives. The fate of several of the children is described in the report, which also contains statements made about the train by several reliable witnesses.

While Major Carleton was pursuing his investigation, Captain James Lynch also was present on the scene. Two of his letters, or informal reports, are in the National Archives; they offer interesting material on some of the surviving children, including their names, approximate ages and general appearance.

In Josiah F. Gibbs's book, *The Mountain Meadows Massacre*, there is useful information on the Fancher Train and on some of the families and individuals, including William Eaton and William Aden, who decided to travel in it. Some of this material comes from a firsthand account of a survivor who left the Fancher Train in Salt Lake City.

Finally, there is the closely detailed testimony of Malinda Cameron Scott Thurston, also located in the National Archives. Mrs. Thurston's description of her own family and of her father, William Cameron, and his family group, gives us the best picture of the train itself and of some of the people who formed it. Her testimony, some of it in question-and-answer form, was given under direct examination during the course of her suit against the United States Government, and in the two petitions placed before Congress on her behalf.

Mrs. Thurston's statements about her father's gold are of considerable interest. Long after 1857, rumors persisted throughout the southern part of Utah that a quantity of gold had been carried in the Fancher Train, and some local stories put its value at $3,000 or $4,000 dollars. My own reading of Mrs. Thurston's testimony leads me to believe that her father probably was not the only householder in the train who had converted part of his wealth into silver and gold coins. In any case, the discovery of the Cameron family's cache very likely did not surprise the Mormons who had attacked the Fancher Train. The ambush of the Aiken Party during the same lawless period, and many earlier depredations, suggests a different conclusion: that the Mormons knew from experience how often well-to-do travelers carried substantial quantities of gold and silver coins concealed among their household possessions and in the wagons themselves.

Chapter Three

Page 16. "*At first the Smiths . . .*" [1]Valuable information concerning the early years of the Smith family may be found in two most useful books, Fawn M. Brodie's biography of Joseph Smith Jr., *No Man Knows My History*, and William Linn's *The Story of the Mormons*. Brodie's work is generally favorable to her subject; at the same time the author has been honest with herself and has included several damaging appendices, which have long made the biography an extremely difficult item to obtain in Salt Lake City.

Both books, in addition, contain a great deal of information on the early history of the Mormon Church. Linn sometimes slips on minor matters, such as unimportant dates and the omission of full names in his index, but for the most part his book is an exceptionally authoritative study of the entire subject of Mormonism during the first half-century of its existence.

A number of other useful works deal with the early years of the Mormon Church. They include *The Rocky Mountain Saints* by Thomas Stenhouse; his wife, Fanny Stenhouse's, "*Tell It All*"; John D. Lee's *Mormonism Unveiled*; William Swartzell's privately printed *Journal*; M. R. Werner's *Brigham Young*; and *The City of the Saints* by Richard Burton.

Page 17. "There can be no doubt . . . '*Joe was the most* ragged, lazy fellow . . .'" Linn, *The Story of the Mormons*, p. 13. The account first appeared in a letter that Hendrix sent to the St. Louis *Globe-Democrat* from San Jacinto, California, on February 2, 1897.

Page 18. "*The future Prophet . . .*" The story of the affair with farmer Stowel is fully treated in Brodie's *No Man Knows My History*, App. A.

Page 19. "*A decade later . . .*" Brodie, p. 39.

Page 19. "Joseph Smith Jr.'s publication in 1830 . . . *Both place and time were propitious for the founding of a new religion like Mormonism . . .*" In 1829 the English poet Robert Southey, while writing on Sir Thomas More, made an amazing prophecy about the prospects of religion in the United States. "America," Southey wrote, "is in more danger from religious fanaticism. The Government there not thinking it necessary to provide religious instruction for the people in any of the new States, the prevalence of superstition, and that, perhaps, in some wild and terrible shape, may be looked for as one likely consequence of this great and portentous omission. An Old Man of the Mountain might find dupes and followers as readily as the All-Friend Jemima; and the next Aaron Burr who seeks to carve a kingdom for himself out of the overgrown territories of the Union, may discern that fanaticism is the most effective weapon with which ambition can arm itself; that the way for both is prepared by that immorality which the want of religion naturally and necessarily induces, and that Camp Meetings may be very

---

[1]Roman matter indicates the opening words of the paragraph refered to; *italic matter* indicates the phrase within the paragraph. If the reference is to the first sentence of a paragraph, italic is used.

well directed to forward the designs of Military Prophets. Were there another Mohammed to arise, there is no other part of the world where he would find more scope or fairer opportunity than in that part of the Anglo-American Union into which the older States continually discharge the restless part of their population, leaving laws and Gospel to overtake it if they can, for in the march of modern colonization both are left behind." The passage from Southey is quoted in both Stenhouse's *The Rocky Mountain Saints*, and in Werner's *Brigham Young*.

Page 20. *"Some frontier religions . . ."* See Brodie, pp. 12–13.

Page 21. "Whether or not this was the case . . . *There was the puzzling problem of why the lost Bible had been written in 'reform Egyptian' hieroglyphics . . ."* Brodie, p. 175. *"These were Oliver Cowdery . . . David Whitmer . . . Martin Harris . . ."* See Linn, pp. 35 ff., 45, 83; also Brodie, Ch. 4.

Page 21. *"Among the most serious charges . . . were those of plagiarism . . ."* For details of the controversy that raged around Solomon Spaulding's *"The Manuscript Found,"* see Linn, pp. 55 ff., and Brodie, App. B.

Page 22. "About 1822 . . . *a whimsical rumor . . . launched to spoof his own family . . ."* Linn, pp. 24–25, quotes a long affidavit, first published by Eber D. Howe, editor of the *Painseville Telegraph*, made out and signed by Peter Ingersol, in 1833.

Page 22. "These charges of plagiarism were denied . . . *Smith's successor, Brigham Young . . ."* Linn quotes Young on p. 98. The quotation is from an address by Young, delivered at Nauvoo in October 1844.

Chapter Four

Page 24. *"At Kirtland, and later in Missouri . . ."* The organization of the early Mormon Church is well described in Richard Burton's *The City of the Saints*, pp. 445 ff., first published in 1860. Since Burton was in Salt Lake City and was tutored by Church officials, his information on such noncontroversial matters may be taken as correct. Burton's book has long been described as a journalistic classic, but the great Victorian orientalist and adventurer was at times extremely gullible. His remarks on the Mountain Meadows Massacre, a crime committed only a year or two earlier, were limited to three inconsequential sentences and part of a footnote, it being the redoubtable explorer's belief that no such massacre had occurred.

Page 27. "But whether or not . . . *only the Mormon Church, among several . . . sects, aroused such hostility . . ."* On this significant matter, see Linn, pp. 135–36.

Page 28. *"The Mormons freely expressed their views . . ."* For the quotation from Pratt, see Stenhouse, *The Rocky Mountain Saints*, pp. 4–5; and the quotation from Orson Pratt's *The Kingdom of God*, Stenhouse, p. 496. Both Stenhouse and his wife, Fanny, were loyal members of the Church for many years and did not become Apostates until long after the Mountain Meadows Massacre. Stenhouse held many responsible posts in the Church and was privy to all but its most closely guarded secrets. His wife's book, *Tell It All*, contains interesting material on domestic conditions in the Mormon community, his own book much information on Mormon crimes that always made it a work of consequence. It has long been out of print, though, and copies are extremely difficult to obtain.

Chapter Five

Page 31. "But the Prophet had a more enterprising project in mind . . . '*I will consecrate the riches of the Gentiles unto my people . . .*'" This and a number of other Revelations of Joseph Smith Jr. concerning the emigration to Missouri are discussed by Linn, pp. 163–65. They originally appeared in Smith's *Doctrines and Covenants*, first published in 1835. In later editions, some of the Revelations have been considerably altered.

Page 32. "*The remaining years in Kirtland . . .*" Brodie and Werner both have information on the United Order of Enoch and affairs in Kirtland. William Swartzell's early (1840) private journal, App. C, contains information on the Church's desire to obtain wealth through the "consecration" of property.

Page 32. "Understandably enough, the United Order of Enoch . . . *Undaunted, they formed . . . the Kirtland Safety Society Anti-Banking Company . . .*" Linn, pp. 148 ff., and Brodie, Ch. 14.

Page 34. "There were a number of other reasons . . . *In a period of local Indian uprisings . . .*" See among others, Werner, pp. 100–101.

Page 34. "*Violence began in Jackson County . . .*" Linn, pp. 169 ff.

Page 35. "*Governor Dunklin's initial sympathies . . .*" Brodie, p. 151.

Page 35. "During their abrupt . . . departure . . . *Although they soon received a friendly welcome . . .*" Linn, p. 185.

Chapter Six

Page 39. "*The Church in later years . . .*" For a brief and reasonable summary of the Church's policy toward the Danites, see Linn, p. 192.

Page 40. "*The founder of the Danites . . .*" Brodie, p. 216.

Page 40. "Several weeks before . . . *The message said in part . . .*" The Danite leader's words may be found in Brodie, p. 215. They originally appeared in the *History of the Church of Jesus Christ of Latter-Day Saints. Period I. History of Joseph Smith, the Prophet, by Himself,* Vol. III (1835) pp. 180–81.

Page 41. "*The principal speaker of the day . . .*" Linn, pp. 196–98.

Chapter Seven

Page 42. "*The Election Day fight* . . ." For particulars see Brodie, p. 225.

Page 42. "After the Prophet and his riders . . . '*I, Adam Black* . . .'" A copy of Adam Black's affidavit, sworn at Daviess County, Missouri, August 8, 1838, is contained in Swartzell, App. D, pp. 43–44. It appeared originally in the Missouri *Western Star.*

Page 43. "On both sides . . . '*Men of former quiet . . .*'" Linn, p. 202, quotes John Doyle Lee and several other Mormon sources. The Lee quotations in this section are from his confession, *Mormonism Unveiled.*

Page 44. "After the raid on Gallatin . . . '*If the people will let us alone . . .*'" Brodie, p. 230.

Page 44. "With these developments . . . '*The Mormons must be treated as enemies . . .*'" For the fairest judgment on Governor Boggs's "order of extermination" see Linn, pp. 205–6.

Page 45. "*Before the hearing . . .*" For General Wilson's letter, see Linn, p. 211; on the final expulsion of the Saints from Missouri, see Linn, pp. 211–18.

Chapter Eight

Page 48. "Early in 1839 . . . '*and it shall be called Nauvoo . . .*'" Werner, p. 109.

Pp. 48–49. "Before long . . . *it was said that Nauvoo was a den of thieves . . .*" There undoubtedly was considerable substance to the charge. See *A Mormon Chronicle, the Diaries of John D. Lee,* edited by Robert Cleland and Juanita Brooks, p. 330, fn. 80; and *Among the Mormons,* edited by William Mulder and A. Russell Mortensen, pp. 154–55.

Page 49. "*Not all these complaints . . .*" The quotation appears in Linn, p. 259, taken from Lee's *Mormonism Unveiled,* p. 111.

Page 49. "But not all the new Saints . . . *at least a third of the population was illiterate . . .*" Linn, p. 230. He draws on Charles Dickens' analysis of illiteracy in England and Wales, which appeared earlier in *Household Words.*

Page 50. "Unlike many of his disciples . . . '*Brethren and sisters, I got drunk last week and fell in the ditch . . .*'" Werner, p. 153. Both Werner and Brodie are in agreement concerning the Prophet's heavy drinkling and the public's knowledge of his conduct.

Page 51. "With the doctrine of Plural Marriage . . . *at Nauvoo . . . he married twenty-five or thirty times more . . .*" See Brodie, App. C., pp. 434–65. The author has assembled an immense amount of information on the Prophet's marriages, with names and dates.

Page 52. "But perhaps most harmful of all . . . *and by the time they left Nauvoo . . .*" For the number of wives of Young, Smith, etc., during the exodus from Nauvoo, see Juanita Brooks, *John D. Lee,* p. 95.

Chapter Nine

Page 55. *"The rights granted . . . were extraordinary . . ."* For an analysis of the Nauvoo charter and the circumstances surrounding its passage through the Illinois legislature, see both Linn and Thomas Stenhouse.

Page 58. *"From the beginning it was assumed . . ."* Linn, p. 245, contains material on Porter Rockwell, along with the quotation attributed to the Prophet urging the assassination of Boggs.

Page 58. "At the time . . . *One was . . . William Law . . ."* For Law's testimony see Brodie, p. 331. *"Still later . . ."* Rockwell's admission was made to General Patrick E. Connor at Fort Douglas. The general was employing Rockwell at the time. Rockwell's words were first reported by Dr. W. Wyl in his *Mormon Portraits*, published at Salt Lake City, 1886. The material is referred to in Charles Kelly and Wolfman Birney's *Holy Murder*, pp. 49–50.

Page 59. "Month after month a succession of feverish schemes . . . *a new clandestine organization . . ."* For a description of the Council of Fifty, see Brodie, pp. 356–57. Also Linn, p. 316, from Lee's *Mormonism Unveiled*, p. 173.

Page 60. *"Oregon and California, though . . ."* The Prophet's western schemes are detailed in Brodie, Ch. 25, particularly p. 360.

Chapter Ten

Page 61. *"By the time the Saints had spent five tumultuous years . . ."* Brodie, pp. 367–79, offers a useful summary of the last days of the Prophet in Nauvoo.

Page 62. *"But the quarrel continued . . ."* See Brodie, pp. 372 ff., for a description of Law and the other dissidents opposed to Smith.

Page 63. "Cornered and afraid . . . *he delivered a frenzied sermon . . ."* Brodie, p. 374, quotes the Prophet's address, which first was published in *"History of the Church . . ."* Vol. VI, pp. 408–12.

Page 63. *"The dissidents also attacked . . ."* For quotations from the *Expositor*, see Brodie, p. 375.

Page 66. *"The murder of the Prophet . . ."* The quotation is from the unpublished journal of Allan Stout, quoted by Brodie, p. 396. The journal is in the manuscript collection of the Utah State Historical Society.

Chapter Eleven

Page 68. "After Rigdon had finished, *Brigham Young arose in turn . . ."* For the August meeting and speeches, see Werner, pp. 190 ff.

Page 68. "A number of Gentiles . . . *a sermon delivered long afterward by . . . Orson Hyde . . ."* Werner, p. 190, quoting from the *Journal of Discourses*, Vol. XIII, p. 181.

Page 69. "A few hours later . . . '*I do not care who leads this Church . . .*'" Werner, p. 191, quoting from *The Rise and Fall of Nauvoo*, p. 330, by Brigham H. Roberts.

Page 70. *Finally the chief Apostle . . .*" The principal speech that Young made against Rigdon, as quoted in Linn, p. 317, should be of particular interest to any student of early Mormon affairs. Evidently, Rigdon had threatened to expose the polygamous activities of Young and his close associates, and Young reminded Rigdon that two could play at the same game. The question remains, however, what secrets Sidney Rigdon, on his side, feared to have exposed? Was it possible that Young was thinking of the Golden Bible and the recurrent suggestion that its discovery had been tainted with fraud?

Page 71. "Considerably more menacing . . . *James Strang . . .*" For material on Strang, see Linn, pp. 322, 326, and Werner, pp. 195–199.

Page 71. "*The last major schism . . .*" Linn, p. 322; same page, quotations from Lee, *Mormonism Unveiled*, pp. 155, 161.

Chapter Twelve

Page 75. "On their side the Saints . . . '*Elders who go to borrowing . . .*'" Linn, p. 331. The quotation is from *Times & Seasons*, Vol. V, p. 696.

Page 76. "But once the decision had been made . . . *One day . . . a particularly vicious incident took place . . .*" The Lt. Worrell affair is mentioned briefly in Linn, p. 336. Also see Kelly and Birney, *Holy Murder*, p. 75.

Page 76. "*Authorities never have been able to decide the exact date . . .*" See *1846, The Year of Decision*, by Bernard DeVoto for his analysis of Young's problems and plans during the months preceding the exodus to the Far West. In general, DeVoto is quite fair to Young and the Mormons.

Page 77. "Between California, Texas and Oregon . . . '*The bottoms are extensive; water excellent . . .*'" DeVoto, in n. 6, p. 502, quotes from Frémont's journal; certainly Brigham Young was familiar with Frémont's encouraging descriptions of the region. J. P. Dunn Jr. makes this assumption in his early classic, *Massacres of the Mountains*, p. 238.

Page 78. "There is ample evidence . . . *the apostate John Hyde later wrote . . .*" Linn, pp. 354–55 quotes from John Hyde Jr.'s *Mormonism, Its Leader and Designs* p. 97., describing the oath sworn in the new Temple. Also see Linn, p. 335, for additional testimony on the same subject.

Chapter Thirteen

Page 80. "*In February 1846 . . .*" The quotation from the Springfield, Illinois, *Journal* may be found in Linn, p. 344. See Linn, and Werner, p.

202, for discussions of the counterfeiting charges against the Mormons during the last months at Nauvoo.

Page 81. "*And so, during the early months of 1846 . . .*" There are, of course, many descriptions of the exodus from Nauvoo and the emigration of the Saints across Iowa. See DeVoto, pp. 96 ff., for details, as well as Werner, pp. 211–12.

Page 82. "'*Brigham sent me word . . .*'" For material on Hickman, see his book, *Brigham's Destroying Angel*, with "explanatory notes by J. H. Beadle"; also, for the incident at Winters Quarters, see Werner, p. 213.

Page 82. "*Thomas Kane was twenty-four . . .*" Reference to Kane may be found in DeVoto, pp. 242 ff.; Mortenson, p. 195; Linn, pp. 372–74; Stegner, *The Gathering of Zion*, pp. 22, 60, 79–80; and President Polk's *Diaries*, pp. 106–11.

Page 84. "*No doubt following Young's instructions . . .*" For the patrician Kane's comments on "border scum" and his delight in associating once again with "people of eastern American origin," see Stegner, p. 22.

Chapter Fourteen

Page 87. "*The proposal to raise a Mormon Battalion . . .*" A balanced appraisal of Brigham Young's policies and actions during the transitional period between Nauvoo and Salt Lake City may be found in DeVoto, pp. 244 ff. The excerpt from Hosea Stout's diary, "'*I confess that I was glad to learn of war . . .*'" is quoted by Stegner, p. 60.

Page 89. "Some thirty years later . . . '*I had one wife and child . . .*'" See Lee, *Mormonism Unveiled*, pp. 287–88.

Page 90. "'*Hyrum told me that the man I was ordered to attack was Howard Egan . . .*'" Several years later it was the same Howard Egan who accompanied Lee to Santa Fe when the latter obtained the Mormon Battalion's pay for Brigham Young and the Church.

Page 91. "In earlier days . . . *and Young who made Lee his second 'adopted son' . . .*" For the Doctrine of Adoption see, among others, Juanita Brooks, *John D. Lee*, p. 73.

Page 93. "Prior to 1847 . . . '*They remained in deadly fear of persecution . . .*'" DeVoto, p. 457.

Page 93. "*But some of the pioneers . . .*" William Clayton's *Journal*, quoted in Mulder and Mortensen, *Among the Mormons*, p. 226.

Chapter Fifteen

Page 97. "In October 1849 . . . *according to one reliable estimate . . .*" See Linn, especially p. 416.

Page 98. "Sometimes, in their . . . eagerness . . . *The Apostle John Taylor promised . . .*" Taylor's words were published while Brigham Young was still en route to the Utah Territory with the first company of pioneers. This was long before the way west had been made easier, as Taylor claimed already had been done. Indeed, Young's exact destination was still uncertain when Taylor began to urge European Saints to emigrate to the American West.

Page 98. "Sometimes in their . . . eagerness . . . "*The elevated valley* . . ." Linn, p. 413, from the *Millennial Star*, February 1, 1848.

Chapter Sixteen

Page 100. "The naming of Brigham Young . . . '*In his judgment*' . . ." The quotation is from the Introduction to Vol. XXV, *Millard Fillmore Papers*, Buffalo Historical Society.

Page 100. "'*You will recollect* . . .'" Quotations from the correspondence between President Fillmore and Colonel Kane may be found in Linn, pp. 459–60. The author quotes in part from the *Millennial Star*, Vol. XIII, pp. 341–44.

Page 102. "*The California petition* . . ." The report, *Fruits of Mormonism*, written by Nelson Slater and signed by almost 250 California emigrants early in 1851, describes conditions in the Great Basin and particularly the treatment of outsiders, during the early period 1847–51. A copy may be examined in the Rare Book Room of the New York Public Library.

Page 103. "The memorial shrewdly noted . . . '*It appears . . . from the history of Mormonism . . . that it has ever been its policy to bring down vengeance upon all who foresake it . . .*'" At first it is puzzling to note the severity with which the early Church attacked its so-called Apostates. Undeniably, the leaders of the Saints, particularly Brigham Young, were extremely hostile to all such dissenters. There were at least three main reasons for their attitude. First, an Apostate was likely to know at least some of the Church's less savory secrets, and it was only natural that the President and his counselors would have preferred to keep them concealed. And then, once an Apostate had reached Gentile territory and had talked freely, he would make future proselytizing there that much harder. Finally, each Apostate was a rebuke to the Saints, a walking advertisement that said quite plainly that as yet all was not perfect in Zion. For these and other reasons as well, many Apostates were dealt with harshly, as Nelson Slater and his fellow emigrants soon came to understand.

Chapter Seventeen

Page 106. "*During the late spring and early summer of 1851* . . ." Although the five United States officials who came to Utah in 1851 were the first to be assigned to serve in the territorial government, they were not the first Gentile officers to reach the Great Basin. Two years earlier, in 1849, Captain Howard Stansbury, a member of the United States

Topographical Engineers, had arrived in the valley with instructions from the Federal Government to make a survey of the region's lakes. During his assignment the captain experienced considerable difficulty with Brigham Young, as he made clear in the report of his actions which he later submitted to United States authorities. Stansbury found Young extremely suspicious of him; the Mormon leader believed the United States wished to deprive the Church of the land it claimed by right of occupation, and he considered Stansbury's survey a first step in carrying out the Government's design. Because of this, the captain went to great lengths to reassure Young that his suspicions were unfounded. Quotations from the captain's report are in Linn, p. 438. For the full report, see Exploration and Survey of the Great Salt Lake of Utah, by Capt. Howard Stansbury, incorporated in Senate Executive Document 3, Special Session, March 1851.

Page 106. "*Judge Brandebury was the earliest . . . to ride into Salt Lake City . . .*" Information concerning the treatment of the officials, their observations and conclusions, the letter of Judge Brocchus to his friend back East, and the statement which Secretary Harris made to Governor Young in response to the governor's demand for the disputed funds, all were included in the report submitted by the United States officers to President Fillmore at the end of 1851. The report subsequently was included in House of Representatives Executive Document 25, 32nd Congress, 1st Session, and became part of the National Archives. Document 25 also contained the inadequate response of Brigham Young and the Mormons, much of it self-serving and evasive.

Page 106. "Within a short time *it became known . . . that the Gentile officers were planning to leave . . .*" Judge Brocchus' letter to his eastern friend was published in a St. Louis newspaper soon after it left the Territory. Quite possibly, though, Brigham Young learned of the Federal officials' plans several days earlier; the charge often was made by non-Mormons that their mail was opened and read before it left Salt Lake City, and such a reading of the judge's letter would immediately have told the governor that Secretary Harris and the disputed money were about to leave the Territory.

For a description of the problem of the mails in Utah at that period, see National Archives, *The Utah Expedition, 1851–1858*, House of Representatives Executive Document 71, 35th Congress, 1st Session, p. 139. Here is reproduced Indian agent H. R. Holeman's letter, dated 29 March 1852, Salt Lake City, to the United States Commissioner of Indian Affairs. Wrote agent Holeman: "'The Gentiles,' as we are called, who do not belong to the Mormon Church, have no confidence in the management of the post office here; it is believed by many that there is an examination of all letters coming and going, in order that they [the Mormons] may ascertain what is said of them, and by whom it is said. This opinion is so strong that all communications touching their character or conduct, are either sent to [Fort] Bridger or [Fort] Laramie, there

This opinion is so strong that all communications touching their character or conduct, are either sent to [Fort] Bridger or [Fort] Laramie, there to be mailed. I send this communication by a friend to St. Joseph, Missouri, there to be mailed to the city of Washington."

Chapter Eighteen

Page 113. "'At the head of this formidable organization . . . *No man pretended to embark on any kind of business without his [Brigham Young's] permission . . .*" It should be noted that this observation, first made in 1851 by Judges Brandebury and Brocchus and Secretary Harris, was repeated, in nearly identical terms, by almost every competent observer who subsequently came to Utah and gained an understanding of the way the Territory was run. The point could scarcely be more significant, since at a later time Brigham Young would disclaim all prior knowledge of the plans for the Mountain Meadows Massacre, and would insist that John D. Lee, acting on his own authority, had been entirely responsible for the crime. Considering how complete Brigham Young's control was over his subjects, how detailed his knowledge of their every activity and how great their fear of earning his displeasure, it seems unthinkable that Lee would have dared to organize and carry out such an elaborate and important scheme without first consulting Young, who, according to so many witnesses, planned every venture, no matter how small, that was undertaken by members of the Church.

Chapter Nineteen

Page 118. "For Brigham Young and his closest associates . . . *sending missionaries to such exotic locations . . .*" Linn, p. 229.

Page 119. "Each of these veteran Saints . . . *whenever the President . . . was anxious to keep the matter from becoming public, he invariably called on Dimick Huntington . . .*" Among other things, Huntington eventually became an author, and his book, *Vocabulary of the Utah and Sho-Shoe-Ne or Snake Dialects, with Indian Legends and Traditions,* enjoyed at least a modest success, reaching a third edition, which appeared in 1872. The preface contained a brief sketch of Huntington's past life. It said in part, "The author D. B. Huntington was born on the 26th of May 1808; and came to the mountains in 1847 as a soldier of the Mormon Battalion, his family accompanying him through New Mexico to Salt Lake Valley, where he learned the Utah and Shoshone dialects in the employment of the United States Government during a period of twenty years as Indian interpreter. His long acquaintance with the Indians, their language, manners, customs, has given him a thorough knowledge of their traditions and legends; *and the influence which he has acquired among them* [my italics] has enabled him to render the government valuable service with them since the first settlement in Utah."

members of his survey party (see note, Chapter 21) the following statement made by Huntington on page 4 of his book, is of particular significance: "In 1849, when fifty of us were exploring the 'Dixie' Country, in the month of December, we met Arapene on his way from the mountains *on the Sevier River* [my italics] coming down to winter." Arapene was one of Chief Walker (Wah-ker)'s three brothers, and Walker was one of the two Pah-Vant chiefs most deeply implicated in the attack on Captain Gunnison's party; the crime occurred near Sevier Lake and the Sevier River in 1853, and Huntington's long and intimate acquaintance with the region, as well as his self-proclaimed friendship and influence with the Pah-Vant chiefs are worth considering, in any attempt to decide the question of Mormon responsibility for the Gunnison Massacre. Also see note, Chapter 34, with reference to Huntington, in Carleton's *Report*, p. 9.

Page 120. "By contrast, the Apostle Charles C. Rich . . . *his name always was associated with the ambitious enterprise at San Bernardino . . .*" The important Mormon colony at San Bernardino, California, was founded by Rich and Apostle Amasa Lyman in 1851. Interestingly enough, when the two made their first trip over the Old Spanish Trail to California, their guide was none other than Brigham Young's first adopted son, the well-known Danite leader Porter Rockwell. In their book, *Holy Murder*, Kelly and Birney have this to say of Rockwell's activities: "Few of the Saints were busier, few traveled more extensively than Porter Rockwell during the years when the California emigration was at its height. . . . The Danite chieftain . . . appears to have had a roving commission, supervising the activities of his fellows who preyed upon the emigrants. His territory, in general, was south of Salt Lake City. Cattle and horses were stolen and the thefts blamed upon the Indians. . . . Porter was . . . of tremendous value to his Prophet and his Church in dealing with the many apostates who, completely disillusioned as to Deseret . . . followed the southern route to California."

Page 122. "Among the Gentile officials . . . *It was Major Holeman who first disclosed . . .*" The private communications of Major Holeman and, Indian Agent Garland Hurt may be found in House of Representatives Executive Document 71, 35th Congress, 1st Session. *The Utah Expedition, 1851-1858*.

Pages 124-125. "In order to survive . . . *and when Lee returned with his booty of 'powder, lead, harnesses, tools . . .'*" See *A Mormon Chronicle*, edited, and with an introduction, by Juanita Brooks, p. xxii.

Page 125. "To make up the loss . . . *Young explained to one midwestern newspaper . . .*" The President's advice to Gentile travelers was contained in a letter which he sent to the St. Louis *Republican*, and which appeared in that paper on May 27, 1853.

Page 126. "*The following year Young published a warning . . .*" This notice, or manifesto, as it was called, was published in the July 13 issue of the *Deseret News*, and was reprinted on 8 September 1854, in the *New York Times*.

Chapter Twenty

Page 127. "At the same time that Brigham Young . . . *Apostasy was a recurrent problem among the Saints . . .*" During the early years in Utah few matters were of more concern to the hierarchy than the question of apostasy and of dissatisfied members wishing to leave the Church. Benjamin Ferris, for a time secretary of the Territory, discussed this subject in his book, *Utah and the Mormons*, pp. 322 ff. He wrote: "The leaders are very anxious to gain sufficient population to raise the Territory to the rank of a state; and on this, as well as on other grounds, throw every obstacle in the way of those who are disposed to leave them." Ferris assumed that his readers would readily understand why the Mormons were so eager to gain statehood—for once they had achieved this status, Brigham Young would have been assured of the governorship for life and the Church would have been free to rule an area almost one-fourth the size of the continental United States, with scarcely any outside interference from Washington.

Page 127. "Benjamin Ferris, a Gentile official . . . '*on Sunday, the 20th of March . . .*'" See Ferris, pp. 327–28.

Page 127. "*On the same day . . .*" Young's speech may be found in Linn, p. 436, and Ferris, pp. 328–330.

Page 128. "*In the face of such flagrant intimidation . . .*" For Ferris' account of the twenty-seventh of March, see pp. 332–33.

Page 129. "Not all Brigham Young's accusers . . . *the publication of a small book . . .*" Ettie Smith's narrative, *Fifteen Years Among the Mormons*, as "told to" Nelson W. Green, was published in 1857, the year of the Massacre at Mountain Meadows. On the twenty-seventh of August, "in answer to a communication from the State Department relating to affairs in Utah," Ettie Smith swore out an affidavit in Livingston County, New York, accusing Brigham Young and a number of other Mormons of various crimes, including murder. Less than three weeks later, the Mountain Meadows Massacre took place.

Accompanying Mrs. Smith's affidavit was a preface by Green, which said in part, "There is a simple truth, an agreement and consistency, upon which the mind intuitively fastens, and upon which it bases its convictions never found in the creations of the imagination. It is with confidence, therefore, that we refer to the internal evidence which this narrative itself affords of its own truth. . . . The circumstance that real names are given throughout the book, of persons who are still living and who will be likely to make themselves heard, if they have been misrepresented, should furnish another argument in favor of its reliability." It goes without saying that Mrs. Smith's charges, like so many other charges made against Young and the Church, went unanswered in the courts, and that the Prophet did not sue for libel or personal damages.

Page 131. "Mrs. Smith, two years after escaping . . . *that said robbery was committed by . . . Hiram Clawson . . .*" Part of the credibility of

Ettie Smith's narrative results from her casual, almost offhand use of real names. Hiram Clawson, for example, was a leading Saint, and his mother, Catherine Reese, widow of Zepheniah Clawson, was sealed to Brigham Young on 19 June 1855, at the age of 51. Hiram married two of Young's daughters, Alice, a daughter of Mary Ann Angell, and Emily, a daughter of Emily Partridge. See *The Lion of the Lord*, a biography of Brigham Young, by Stanley P. Hirshon, p. 208.

Page 131. *"At another point in her affidavit . . ."* A full description of the Wallace Bowman affair appears on pp. 252–77 in Smith.

Page 133. *"Mrs. Smith was not present as a witness . . ."* The circumstances surrounding the Hartley incident and the murder of Hartley are described in *Fifteen Years Among the Mormons*, pp. 308–11.

Page 134. *"A number of years later . . ."* For Bill Hickman's version of Jesse Hartley's murder, see his autobiography, *Brigham's Destroying Angel, Confession of Bill Hickman*, pp. 96–98.

Chapter Twenty-one

Page 137. *"From the very beginning suspicions were voiced . . ."* On page 109 of their study of the Danite leader Porter Rockwell, Kelly and Birney say this of the Gunnison Massacre: "Again and again Porter and the Danites have been accused of inspiring or participating in the massacre of the government surveying party, commanded by Captain J. W. Gunnison . . . on the lower Sevier River. . . . He and eight of his men were slaughtered as they sat at breakfast in their camp. The atrocity was charged to the Indians . . . but to this day gossip in Utah alleges that Rockwell and the Danites participated in the slaughter."

Page 137. *"The Church, according to Gunnison . . ."* The passage quoted is from the conclusion of Captain John W. Gunnison's book, *The Mormons or Latter-Day Saints in the Valley of the Great Salt Lake*, Philadelphia, 1852, p. 165. Gunnison's words, considering his fate a few years later, were ironic, indeed.

Page 138. *"The next year Washington decided . . ."* Contemporary newspapers, such as the *New York Times*, provide useful and reliable information on the Gunnison expedition and the massacre at Sevier Lake. Another valuable source of information is an address by Dr. Nolie Mumey, *John Williams Gunnison, Centenary of his Survey and Tragic Death*, delivered on 23 December 1953 at the Annual Meeting of the State Historical Society of Colorado, Denver, Colorado, reprinted in the *Colorado Magazine*.

Page 138. "Having received his orders . . . *he had to deal with Indian tribes 'even more hostile' . . .*" This significant remark made, by one of the party who survived, is quoted in the *New York Times*, Monday, Dec. 12, 1853.

Page 138. "Leaving Colorado . . . *two Mormon brothers named Potter . . .*" The question of the two Potter brothers, and the part they might have played in the Gunnison Massacre, has never been thoroughly studied by non-Mormon historians. Clearly enough, if the Potters' assignment was to lure Gunnison into a trap, then the killing of William Potter was a mistake, of which the surviving brother would have been well aware. Evidence that this was so exists in a most unlikely corner. Several years later, after the second Potter also was killed "by mistake" during the course of the so-called Potter-Parrish Murders, his widow's suspicions were cited in an article from Salt Lake City signed "Vigo," printed in the *New York Times* 20 May 1857. "Potter had a brother killed in the Gunnison massacre," the article said. "His wife says that ever since that event, the Mormons have been very suspicious and have been watching him continually, supposing that he knew more about the affair than was consistent with the safety of certain men, particularly if he should escape from the Territory." The second Potter brother did not escape, and the truth about the Gunnison Massacre—and a possible link to the Parrish Murders—still remains unproved.

Page 139. "At this point . . . *According to the story that Brigham Young told the eastern press . . .* " The Prophet' version was sent east to special delegate John M. Bernhisel in a letter, dated 30 November 1853, long extracts of which were published in the *New York Times* of February 24, 1854.

Page 139. "Such was the governor's story—*which differed . . . from the testimony of the survivors . . .*" See, for instance, Mumey, "John W. Gunnison," page 30, *Colorado Magazine:* "On the morning of October 25th a small detachment, which included Kern, Creutzfeldt, a group of enlisted personnel, and a Mormon guide, William Potter, accompanied Captain Gunnison on a reconnaissance of the region around the border of Lake Sevier. *They saw several flashes of signal fires made by the Indians during their journey, but were careful and alert.*" (My italics.) Compare this with the strong implication of Gunnison's carelessness in Young's letter to Delegate Bernhisel.

Page 140. "The aftermath of the Gunnison Massacre . . . *President Pierce ordered Colonel E. J. Steptoe . . .*" The Steptoe mission, from first to last, was a curious affair. It is quite certain that the colonel actually had two assignments, one publicly announced, the other covert and ambiguous. The first, of course, was to determine who had been responsible for the Gunnison Massacre and to bring the culprits to trial. The second was to succeed Brigham Young as territorial governor—Young's term of office being very nearly up—if the colonel, after a stay in the Mormon capital, decided that he could overcome his personal doubts and accept the appointment.

Within a short time after Steptoe's arrival, a story became current in the Territory that Young had caught wind of the secret arrangement between the colonel and the President and that to prevent Steptoe from accepting the governorship, had arranged an ingenious frame-up, involving the help of two winsome young Mormon ladies, one an actress procured especially for the occasion from the local repertory company; that the blackmail plot had worked to perfection and that Colonel Steptoe, rather than face an embarrassing scandal, agreed to turn down the governorship, and to endorse—as he cheerfully did—Young's reappointment to the office for a new, four-year term. However, another less titillating explanation probably came closer to the truth: that Steptoe had no wish to interrupt his own military career and that, lacking both the enthusiastic support of Congress and an adequate number of soldiers to rule the Territory effectively, he simply decided not to accept the post.

Page 141. "*Considering that he was a responsible public official . . .*" For a description of the legal aftermath to the Gunnison Massacre, the activities of Young, Dimick Huntington's jury tampering and the trial itself, see a comprehensive lead article in the *New York Times*, May 18, 1855.

Chapter Twenty-two

Page 146. "Afterward . . . *In a letter . . . Young had written . . .*" The 1855 letter, in which Brigham Young stated that the handcart scheme was an old plan of his and that henceforth future emigrants were going to "foot it" across twelve hundred miles of prairies and mountains, appeared in the *Millennial Star*, Vol. VII, p. 813, as cited in Linn, p. 418.

Page 146. "Young had crossed the prairies . . . '*Fifteen miles a day . . . will bring them through in 70 days . . .*'" On this crucial point, Young's arithmetic was rather cavalier—perhaps significantly so; for if the emigrants had traveled at a rate of fifteen miles a day, a journey of seventy days still would have left them at least a hundred and fifty miles from their destination, and presumably, out of food and other necessary supplies. Curiously enough, the next year some of the handcart companies did, indeed, run out of food—about a hundred and fifty miles from Salt Lake City.

Page 147. "And so it was . . . *A Gentile traveler . . .*" This description of two of the handcart companies appeared in an obscure Ohio newspaper, the *Huron Reflector*, and is cited by Linn, p. 422. An informative picture of the 1856 emigration, from a different point of view, was presented by John Chislett, a Mormon who traveled in one of the handcart companies. His account was extensively reported in Thomas Stenhouse's *The Rocky Mountain Saints*; Fanny Stenhouse, his wife, offered further material in her book, *Tell It All*.

Page 148. "The weather turned colder . . . *out of one company of 400 . . .*" There were various estimates of the casualty rate among the handcart companies. I have used figures gathered by Linn, p. 425.

Chapter Twenty-three

Page 149. "Although Brigham Young was responsible . . . *it was Jedediah Grant . . .*" The reference to the Mayor of Salt Lake City serving as Brigham Young's "sledge-hammer" may be found in Linn, p. 444, from an article in the *New York Times*, 21 Sept. 1857. Also see Stenhouse, *The Rocky Mountain Saints*, pp. 292–308, for information on Grant, and other aspects of the Reformation. As is generally the case with Stenhouse, however, care should be exercised in separating the unique and useful from the misleading and untrue—in this instance, the Apostate Stenhouse either was unaware, or chose to ignore, that the seeds of the Reformation and the Doctrine of Blood Atonement had existed long prior to Grant's activities in 1856—and, embarrassingly enough, while Stenhouse himself still was a member in good standing of the Church.

Page 150. "Whether a blackguard or not . . . *According to one eyewitness . . .*" See Thomas Stenhouse, p. 294.

Page 150. "By deliberate policy . . . '*Elders were sent . . .*'" Thomas Stenhouse, p. 295.

Page 150. "*A catechism was printed . . .*" Statement of the same observer. Thomas Stenhouse, p. 295.

Page 151. "Of all the incredible aspects . . . *implicitly endorsed by Christ himself in the Gospels . . .*" The truth of this, unhappily, is beyond cavil or dispute. For an indication of Young's belief, see Thomas Stenhouse, pp. 298–99, particularly the long quotation from one of Young's sermons, delivered in the Tabernacle, 8 February 1857, and later published in the *Journal of Discourses*, Vol. IV, pp. 219–20. On this occasion Young asked his listeners, "Will you love your brothers and sisters likewise when they have a sin that cannot be atoned for without shedding of their blood? Will you love that man and woman enough to shed their blood? That is what Jesus meant by 'Love thy neighbor as thyself.'"

Page 151. "Over the years . . . *John D. Lee . . . noted in his private journals . . .*" See Cleland and Brooks, editors, *A Mormon Chronicle*, Vol. I, p. 88, quoted in *The Lion of the Lord*, by Stanley Hirshon, p. 98. This was not by any means the sole reference in Lee's private journals to bloody executions or the cutting off of heads. See Hirshon's quote, p. 98, from *A Mormon Chronicle*, Vol. I, pp. 98–99.

Page 152. "As early as 1852 . . . *Gunnison wrote . . .*" The quotation is from *History of the Mormons*, p. 83. Cited in Linn, p. 445.

Page 152. "Quite independently . . . *Nelson Slater, in his early petition . . .*" The quotation is from *Fruits of Mormonism*, Nelson Slater; (see note, Chapter 16). "*And later in the same year, Judge Brocchus . . .*" (see note, Chapter 17).

Page 152. "*As early as March 1854 . . .*" For excerpts from Grant's sermon, see Thomas Stenhouse, pp. 304–5.

Page 153. "And finally . . . *Brigham Young took to the speaker's stand* . . ." Young's two speeches may be found in Thomas Stenhouse, pp. 304–5. See also p. 287, this work, for additional sermon on Blood Atonement.

Page 153. "And on the same day, *Jedediah Grant* . . ." Thomas Stenhouse, p. 305.

Pages 153–154. "Improbable as it may seem . . . *it involved a Danish emigrant, Rosmos Anderson* . . ." For the full account of the Rosmos Anderson incident, see John D. Lee, *Mormonism Unveiled*, pp. 280 ff. It should be noted that in later life Lee had good cause to hate Philip Klingensmith; the latter had participated with Lee in the Mountain Meadows Massacre and afterward confessed his own complicity, while seriously compromising Lee. Because of this, at the end of his life, Lee no doubt was all too happy to recount the story of Anderson and Klingensmith. Because of Lee's intimate knowledge of the case, the only question to be asked is whether Lee might not have been one of Klingensmith's assistants?

Page 154. "*The bishop and three of his helpers* . . ." Lee, *Mormonism Unveiled*, p. 283. The three were James Haslam, Daniel McFarland and John M. Higbee. All three were soon afterward involved in the Mountain Meadows Massacre.

Page 155. "During the course of the Reformation . . . *Warren Snow, the elderly Bishop of* . . . *Manti* . . ." Lee's account appears in *Mormonism Unveiled*, pp. 285 ff.

Page 156. "In Lee's account . . . '*Young* . . . *afterward did nothing against Snow*' . . ." Lee's assertion was no doubt correct; later the same year (see *Utah Expedition*, p. 210), while writing to an agent of the Indian department, Young said, "I would recommend that Bishop John L. Butler at Spanish Fork, Bishop Warren Snow, at Mante [sic], Bishop Lewis Brunson at Fillmore, and Bishop Farnsworth at Beaver, be requested by you to aid you in carrying out this instruction in their several localities." Still in charge after the atrocity, Snow remained the Bishop of Manti—and a man of merit, according to the Prophet's curious scale of values.

Page 157. "*No doubt adding* . . . *fuel to the Prophet's anger* . . ." An additional source of irritation was Brigham Young's loss of an exclusive mail contract, to provide service between the Great Plains and California, which Washington solemnly had pledged was to be his. Since the profits from such a concession promised to be enormous, Young immediately had formed a private company—with himself the major, if not the exclusive, stockholder—to undertake the work. Unfortunately, the plan was greeted by howls of protest in the East; the contract was revoked and awarded to a Gentile firm instead. But this affair had little or nothing to do with Young's political conduct, or the outbreak of hostilities with the United States, as some pro-Mormon writers have believed; for by the time the contract was canceled, on 10 June 1857, the new President, James Buchanan, long since had given orders for United States soldiers to march west to Utah. See Linn, p. 480.

Page 158. "'*Under this view of the subject . . .*'" Senator Douglas' speech appeared in the *New York Times*, 23 June 1857. Cited in Linn, pp. 476–77.

Page 159. "Among those . . . *were two Gentile justices . . . W. W. Drummond . . .*" No Federal official aroused more controversy than Drummond, and the consensus has always been that he was the worst of President Pierce's undistinguished appointees to the Utah Territory. Such a conclusion was initially fostered and greatly influenced by the writings of the Mormons themselves. The hatred between Drummond and the Church was spontaneous and mutual—of that, apparently, there could be no question. But many of Drummond's accusations were formidable and never really disproved; he concerned himself with the Gunnison Massacre and named those Mormons who, he said, had been involved—one of them the notorious Bill Hickman.

Several of Drummond's letters appeared in the eastern press in 1857. Among the most remarkable was one dated May 4th, which was printed in the *New York Times* on May 20. The letter dealt with some of Drummond's earlier charges and then went on to make a number of new ones. After accusing the Mormons of having murdered several Gentiles and Apostates, including Almon W. Babbitt, long a prominent Mormon, Drummond concluded with these words: "But, Sir, why is it that *all* the appointees under Fillmore and Pierce's administrations so nicely agree as to the disloyalty of the Mormons, and their open and secret rebellion to the laws and instructions of the country? Does not the universal language of all these men agree in this state of facts? . . . Tear up the graves of a Shaver, a Harris, and of Babbitt; call together all the judges, secretaries and Indian agents, who have not been under the baneful influence of Mormonism, and in one universal tongue will they reiterate the same state of stubborn facts which constitute now a record that will yet agitate this happy country from center to circumference."

Page 160. "For several months . . . '*The United States Courts . . .*'" Surveyor General David H. Burr's letter to Hon. Thomas H. Hendricks, Commissioner of the General Land Office, is included in *The Utah Expedition, 1851–1858*, House of Representatives Document 71, 35th Congress, 1st Session, pp. 118–20.

Page 160. "The same threats . . . *three men were killed at Springville . . .*" The Potter-Parrish affair is the one referred to here by Burr. Details of it soon appeared in the East; in its edition for 20 May 1857, the *New York Times* carried a long, significant story from Salt Lake City, signed "Vigo"; it included, among other features of life in the Territory, a reasonably full account of the Parrish murders and mentioned as well the provocative remark of Potter's widow, that during the past four years her now deceased husband had lived most uneasily under the wary eye of the Church, following his brother's death at Sevier Lake in 1853, and his own involvement, too, in the unsolved Gunnison Massacre.

For the attacks on Stiles and Burr, see the *New York Times*, May 18, 1857. In this account, the violent conduct of the Danite James Ferguson was considerably at odds with Thomas Stenhouse's description. For according to Stenhouse, Ferguson "was by instinct a gentleman," a remark made, perhaps for reasons of personal friendship, for surely there could have been no other.

Chapter Twenty-four

Page 162. "*But this year travelers of a different sort . . .*" The military units that participated in the "Mormon War" of 1857–58, with their orders, names of commanding officers, etc., are to be found in the *Utah Expedition, 1851–1858*, House of Representatives Executive Document 71, 35th Congress, 1st Session. Much unique and valuable background information—official correspondence, private letters of Indian agents, etc., covering the years 1851–58, are included in this comprehensive report, submitted by the executive branch to Congress.

For the activities of one young California-bound adventurer who served as a civilian teamster during the summer of 1857, see "A Trip Across the Plains," by William Clark, published in the *Iowa Journal of History and Politics*, April 1922, pp. 163–223.

A simple explanation of President Buchanan's conduct at the beginning of 1857 may be found in his *First Inaugural Address*, later incorporated into the *Work of James Buchanan*, Vol. X, pp. 152–54. Also cited in Werner's *Brigham Young*, p. 383. Extracted from the full address, the following is worthy of close consideration, for it shows, despite various "subtle" and misguided interpretations to the contrary, that there was an obvious and imperative need for a military presence in the Utah Territory: "His [Brigham Young's] power has been therefore absolute over both church and State. The people of Utah, almost exclusively, belong to this church, and believing with a fanatical spirit that he is governor of the Territory by divine appointment, they obey his commands as if they were direct revelations from Heaven. If, therefore, he chooses that his government shall come into collision with the government of the United States, the members of the Mormon church will yield implicit obedience to his will. Unfortunately, existing facts leave but little doubt that such is his determination. Without entering upon a minute history of occurrences, it is sufficient to say that all the officers of the United States, judicial and executive, with the single exception of two Indian agents, have found it necessary for their personal safety to withdraw from the Territory, and there no longer remains any government in Utah but the despotism of Brigham Young."

Some writers, such as Werner, have blamed the Mormon War on the devious anti-northern activities of Buchanan's Secretary of War, the southerner John B. Floyd. For their part, the Mormons, declaring themselves innocent of any responsibility blamed the war on the machinations of Judge W. W. Drummond and other Federal officers who had fled the Territory. But a simpler explanation was the true one—that after ten years of crime and tyranny, the time had come when the United States Government either had to exercise authority over a rebellious minority or else become a laughing stock to its own citizens—this Buchanan understood, and so the expedition was dispatched, with a new governor to replace Brigham Young.

Page 163. "Among the hundreds . . . of parties . . . *an army doctor en route to rejoin his unit . . .*" Dr. Brewer's testimony, collected in 1858 by Captain (Brevet Major) James Henry Carleton, is included in the vital Government summary usually referred to as *Major Carleton's Report*, House of Representatives Document 605, 57th Congress, 1st Session. The report contains invaluable material collected a year after the Mountain Meadows Massacre; its contents, so damaging to the reputation of the early Mormon hierarchy, have been ignored almost without exception by those members of the Church of Latter-Day Saints who have elected to "explain" the massacre.

Page 163. "On the other hand, *a number of . . . explorers . . . wrote voluminously . . .*" For reasons of personal taste, I have quoted directly in this section only from Francis Parkman's *The Oregon Trail*; it was my belief that his descriptions most nearly mirrored what the Fancher Party saw on its way to the Utah Territory. I did, however, find useful information and descriptions in each of the following: Richard Burton's classic travel book, *The City of the Saints*; William Clark's "A Trip Across the Plains"; John L. Ginn's untitled narrative, the most valuable part of which covers the period 1857–58; A copy of Ginn's rare account may be found in the Yale University Library; a second copy is reported to be in Salt Lake City in private hands; and a third copy, which at one time purportedly was in the Auerbach Collection, I was able to obtain several years ago. For this and later chapters, I also studied descriptions that appeared in a number of mid-nineteenth-century newspapers, among them the *Deseret News*, the *St. Louis Republican*, the *New York Times*, the *New York Tribune*, the *New York Herald* and that extremely informative early paper the *Daily Alta California*.

Page 164. "A few years before . . . '*During the whole trip . . .*'" The quotation is from Parkman, *The Oregon Trail*, pp. 59–60.

Page 164. "*Because of their early departure . . .*" For information about the presence of buffalo on the Platte, their time of arrival, etc., see *The Buffalo*, Francis Haines, Ch. 16, especially pp. 143–47. The same chapter is useful for information on the plains Indians, their attitude toward property, and their difficulties with passing travelers.

Page 164. "While the Fancher Train . . . '*The sun beat down . . .*'" This description is from Parkman, pp. 43–44.

Page 168. "Because of its size and the vigilance . . . *according to Ginn's account* . . ." pp. 2–3, typescript mms., by John L. Ginn.

Page 168. "For the children especially . . . *Parkman described* . . ." Parkman, pp. 274 ff.

Pages 170-171. "Unlike a majority . . . *the old-time rhetoric* . . ." Examples of such Mormon boasting are not difficult to find. For example, in mid-September 1857, Young indulged in the familiar exercise, with these words: "They say that their army is legal; and I say that such a statement is as false as hell, and that they are as rotten as an old pumpkin that has been frozen seven times, and then melted in the harvest sun. Come on with your thousands of illegally ordered troops, and I will promise you, in the name of Israel's God, that you shall melt away as the snow before a July sun . . ." See Stenhouse, *The Rocky Mountain Saints,* p. 360. Quoted from *Journal of Discourses,* Vol. V, p. 230. Also cited by Werner, p. 387.

Page 171. "*From the speakers' stand* . . ." Again, there is no difficulty finding examples of the insults and libels hurled by Young, Kimball and other Mormon notables against the United States and its various leaders. The following is a fair sample from Kimball, who referred to the senior senator from Illinois as "that nasty fop Douglas . . . that little nasty snot-nose: you cannot call him anything half so mean as he is . . ." Werner, p. 385. Or this, from Kimball's speech, Sunday afternoon, 5 July 1857, in the Bowery at Salt Lake City, as published not long afterward in the *Deseret News,* attacking the United States government: "Sending a man here with 2,500 troops!—they have no design in God Almighty's world only to raise a rookery with this people . . . and when they come here, the first dab will be to take br. Brigham Young and Heber C. Kimball and others, and they will slay us, that is their design, and if we will not yield to their meanness, they will say we have mutinized [sic] against the President of the United States, and then they will put us under martial law and massacre this people. . . ." See also the *New York Times,* September 14, in which was reprinted a long sermon by Brigham Young, which originally had appeared in the *Deseret News,* August 12; also sermons delivered on the tenth of July and second of August in the Bowery. Of the latter the *Times* said judiciously, "The speeches of Brigham Young were even more violent than his newspaper diatribes." Indeed, it was common practice for the editor of the *Deseret News* to purge a good deal of Young's language, and that of Kimball and other speakers, before releasing their crude and often offensive screeds to the world at large.

Pages 172-173. "Throughout the spring . . . *Finally, on the twenty-fourth of July* . . ." Various commentators have been impressed by the long, hard ride of two Mormons, A. O. Smoot and Porter Rockwell, the pair supposedly bringing the first news to Brigham Young on the twenty-third of July, that a Federal Army was marching on Utah. The story is a dramatic one—but hardly convincing. Surely Young and his close associates knew long before the twenty-fourth of July that an occupation army was being assembled and that President Buchanan already had ordered its departure for the Great Basin; see particularly the July 5 address of Heber C. Kimball, in which the "2nd in Israel" spoke of the United States sending "an army of 2,500." Clearly the announcement on the twenty-fourth was staged for its dramatic effect, to impress the more ingenuous Saints in the audience.

Page 174. "On the twenty-fourth of July . . . *had been joined by . . . Frank E. King and his wife . . .*" For the material on King, his testimony and affidavit, see Gibbs, *The Mountain Meadows Massacre,* pp. 12–13, 48–49.

Page 174. "They arrived at . . . *William Clayton, had written these words . . .*" See note, Chapter 14.

Chapter Twenty-five

Page 175. "*Church apologists always have clung to a comforting absurdity . . .*" Few men have played a more decisive part in concealing the truth about the Mountain Meadows Massacre than the eminent nineteenth-century American historian Hubert H. Bancroft. His account of the massacre and its aftermath, which appears in *The History of the Pacific States,* Volume XXI, *Utah,* 1540–1886, pp. 543–71, has been accepted for almost a century without further question or study by later historians—an acceptance that inevitably has led to a complete distortion of the facts. Among other things, Bancroft said of the massacre (p. 544): ". . . it may as well be understood at the outset that this horrible crime, so often and so persistently charged upon the Mormon church and its leaders, was the crime of an individual, the crime of a fanatic of the worst stamp, one who was a member of the Mormon church, but of whose intentions the church knew nothing, and whose bloody acts the members of the church, high and low, regard with as much abhorrence as any out of the church. Indeed, the blow fell upon the brotherhood with threefold force and damage. There was the cruelty of it, which wrung their hearts; there was the odium attending its performance in their midst; and there was the strength it lent their enemies to further malign and molest them. The Mormons denounced the Mountain Meadows massacre, and every act connected therewith, as earnestly and as honestly as any in the outside world. This is abundantly proved, and may be accepted as historical fact." For these incredible assertions, Bancroft, most uncharacteristically, cites not a single authority or source.

Linn, p. viii, says of the historian's Mormon volume, "While Bancroft's work professes to be written from a secular standpoint, it is really a church production, the preparation of the text having been confided to Mormon hands. 'We furnished Mr. Bancroft with his material,' said a prominent Mormon church officer to me. 'Its plan is to give the Mormon view in the text, and to refer the reader for the other side to a mass of undigested notes.'" Indeed, Bancroft himself confirms the truth of Linn's statement, on page 330, footnote 30, which reads: "The material for the preceding chapters has been gathered mainly from a number of manuscripts furnished at intervals between 1880 and 1885. As I have already stated, to F. D. Richards [long an important member of the Church hierarchy] I am especially indebted for his unremitting efforts in supplying data for this volume."

Page 177. "*From the moment the train reached the vicinity . . .*" See Reva Stanley, *The Archer of Paradise*, pp. 309–10; also Bancroft, who writes of the Fancher Party (p. 545, fn. 5): "I find no mention of their arrival in the files of the *Deseret News*, although the names of passing emigrants were registered in that newspaper at a nominal charge; and when the party was a large one, its passage was usually noticed among the local items of news."

Page 177. "*Criminal conspirators . . .*" Several works were of particular help in reconstructing the events preceding the Mountain Meadows Massacre, as well as the massacre itself. Among them were several previously cited: Major Carleton's *Report*; Stenhouse, *The Rocky Mountain Saints*; Gibbs, *The Mountain Meadows Massacre*; and Lee, *Mormonism Unveiled*. Other sources included John Cradlebaugh's speech to the House of Representatives, 1863; Malinda Cameron Scott's testimony in the National Archives, and Forney's *Report* incorporated into Senate Executive Document 42, 1859, 36th Congress, 1st Session, pp. 74–80. Besides these, I have used eyewitness accounts that appeared chiefly in various issues of the *Daily Alta California* during October 1857, including the testimony of P. M. Warn and George Powers; also John L. Ginn's account, which was printed afterward in the Gentile newspaper the *Valley Tan*, during Kirk Anderson's editorship, in 1859. In addition, the work of a contemporary Mormon writer, Juanita Brooks, must be mentioned. Her book *The Mountain Meadows Massacre* has one overriding purpose—to prove beyond any doubt that John D. Lee was not solely responsible for the crime. This much she successfully demonstrates; but because of her other and contradictory aim—to defend the Church's reputation at any cost—her study should be, in general, treated with extreme caution.

Page 180. "It long had been the conviction . . . *a description of the lawless conditions . . .*" For an extensive report on conditions in the Utah Territory prior to the Mountain Meadows Massacre, and the story of Tobin and his party, see the *New York Times*, 20 May 1857.

Page 181. "Having determined the site . . . *and because Apostle Rich happened to be in the capital . . .*" It was Bancroft (p. 547) who assigned Rich his role in the plot: "Thus, when the Arkansas families arrived at Salt Lake City, they found the Mormons in no friendly mood, and at once concluded to break camp and move on. They had been advised by Elder Charles C. Rich to take the northern route along the Bear River, but decided to travel by way of southern Utah."

Page 183. "*The letter began . . .*" Young's letter to Hamblin may be found in Brooks, *The Mountain Meadows Massacre*, p. 34.

Page 186. "Unfortunately for the . . . Prophet . . . *According to Mrs. Scott . . .*" Her testimony is in the National Archives, Records of the Court of Claims Section, Department of Justice, Record Group 205.

Chapter Twenty-six

Page 189. "Mile after mile . . ." For a description of the towns and villages the Fancher Party passed through, I have drawn on an article in the *Daily Alta California*, May 29, 1858.

Page 189. "While pausing . . . *William Aden, a native of Tennessee . . .*" Gibbs, p. 12.

Page 192. "*The two other Gentile travelers . . .*" *Daily Alta California*, 27 October 1857.

Page 193. "*Afterward in his . . . diary . . .*" Quotations from Jacob Hamblin's diary may be found in Brooks, *The Mountain Meadows Massacre*, p. 40.

Page 194. "Ultimately, though . . . *Hamblin was obliged to testify . . .*" Carleton's *Report*, p. 2.

Page 195. "Among other matters . . . *the rumored approach of . . . United States soldiers . . .*" See Brooks, *The Mountain Meadows Massacre*," p. 36; and Lee, *Mormonism Unveiled*, p. 219.

Page 196. "At last, when these discussions . . . *Rachel Lee . . . noted in her diary . . .*" Brooks, *The Mountain Meadows Massacre*, p. 37.

Page 196. "For a long time afterward . . . *including . . . the days he had spent . . .*" For Lee and Smith in the south, see Lee, *Mormonism Unveiled*, pp. 211 ff.

Chapter Twenty-seven

Page 201. "*The date is uncertain . . .*" Both Gibbs, *The Mountain Meadows Massacre*, and Stenhouse, *The Rocky Mountain Saints*, contain important material about the passage of the Fancher Train from Corn Creek to The Meadows. Stenhouse utilizes an extensive report, written by "Argus," a resident of Utah and a Church member for many years, who investigated the circumstances of the massacre. The articles by "Argus" had been published previously in the Corinne *Utah Reporter*, in the form of an open letter to Brigham Young, urging the Prophet to bring the criminals to justice and to relieve innocent Church members of the opprobrium they still suffered for the crime. Brooks, *The Mountain Meadows Massacre*, p. 184, concludes that "Argus" was a man named C. W. Wandell; she reports that Philip Klingensmith, before making his formal confession, talked with a "Charley" Wandell.

Page 205. "As for the wily Jacob Hamblin . . ." Hamblin's visit to Tooele is described in Brooks, *The Mountain Meadows Massacre*, p. 42.

Chapter Twenty-eight

Page 210. "*After we got to the iron works . . .*'" See Lee, *Mormonism Unveiled*, pp. 218 ff., for this quotation and for Lee's and Haight's subsequent quotations.

Page 212. "*Isaac Haight . . .*" For Haight's words, see Brooks, *The Mountain Meadows Massacre*, p. 52.

Chapter Twenty-nine

Page 215. "*Late Sunday night*" For the siege at Mountain Meadows and the massacre itself, my principal sources included the following: Major Carleton's *Report*; Dunn, *Massacres of the Mountains*; Lee, *Mormonism Unveiled*; Stenhouse, *The Rocky Mountain Saints*; the issues of two newspapers, the *Daily Alta California* and the *Valley Tan*; and with the reservations already noted, Brooks, *The Mountain Meadows Massacre*. Also, with equal reservations, the testimony given by numerous perjured Mormon witnesses at Lee's first and second trials.

It should be mentioned that John D. Lee, in his version of the massacre, stated that the Indians first attacked the Fancher Train during his absence and that only later had he been summoned to the scene. This would mean that he had no share in the earliest killings and, because he denied killing anyone at the massacre itself, that he had not been responsible for the death of even a single victim. Needless to say, this possibility was believed neither by the court nor by Lee's contemporaries, either within or outside the Church.

Chapter Thirty

Page 222. "*On Tuesday . . . to while away more time . . .*" Carleton's *Report*, p. 6. This was the testimony of Albert Hamblin, the young Indian adopted by Jacob Hamblin. Albert told Major Carleton, "Three men came down from Cedar City. . . . [They] stayed about the house awhile pitching horseshoe quoits while the fighting was on, then they afterwards went back to Cedar City."

Page 224. "And then . . . *what was to be done with the other Gentiles . . .*" In his account of his journey to California, John L. Ginn mentions at least one fellow Gentile who did not choose to join a Mormon company for safety. After having reached California safely, Ginn remarks, he never saw or heard of his fellow traveler again.

Page 225. "*After it grew dark . . .*" Accounts of Aden's attempt to reach Cedar City may be found both in Gibbs and Dunn: the story of his murder long was current in the Utah Territory; in some versions Aden had two companions rather than one.

Page 226. "In the meantime . . . '*During the afternoon,*' Powers recalled . . ." Powers' account, in its entirety, appeared in the *Daily*

Alta California, 27 October 1857. In her book, *The Mountain Meadows Massacre,* p. 114, Brooks gives a significantly shorter version. Absent is this vital part of Powers' account: "I asked him [Colonel William Dame] if he could not raise a company and go out and relieve the besieged train? He replied that he could go out and take them away to safety, but he dared not—*he dared not disobey counsel.*" (My italics.)

Chapter Thirty-one

Page 229. "*On Thursday evening . . .*" The account of the night's activities is taken principally from Lee, *Mormonism Unveiled,* pp. 323 ff. All quotations are from that source.

Chapter Thirty-two

Page 235. "*Employing his most artful . . . manner . . .*" As in the preceding chapter, my account of the last hours of the massacre are drawn principally from Lee, *Mormonism Unveiled,* pp. 232 ff.

Page 241. "*Three members of the ambushed train . . .*" The escape of John Baker and two companions prior to the massacre, and their subsequent murder, were long spoken of in Mormon circles; their story came from no single source but was widely reported by almost every commentator, Mormon and Gentile.

Chapter Thirty-three

Page 244. "In later times . . . '*We went along the field . . .*'" Lee, *Mormonism Unveiled,* pp. 247 ff.

Page 244. "It was Lee's contention . . . *George Powers . . . who witnessed the conduct of the Saints . . .*" *Daily Alta California,* 27 October 1857.

Page 245. "Relieved for the moment . . . *into Brigham Young's private office . . .*" For this account see Lee, *Mormonism Unveiled,* pp. 252 ff.

Page 248. "Two months later . . . '*My last report . . .*'" Lee's letter to Young has been widely reproduced. Among others, see Brooks, *The Mountain Meadows Massacre,* p. 151, and Lee, *Mormonism Unveiled,* pp. 255–56.

Page 248. "At the end of the letter . . . '*I never gave the Indians one of the articles named in the letter . . .*'" Lee, *Mormonism Unveiled,* p. 257.

Page 248. "*There remained one further act . . .*" Stewart's voucher may be found in National Archives Record Group 217, Voucher 9, 4th Quarter, Records of the United States General Accounting Office.

Chapter Thirty-four

Page 250. "Between 1857 and 1860 . . . *without the aid of Thomas Leiper Kane . . .*" For information about Kane's activities, see Linn, pp.

501–3 and note on p. 515; also, *Disruption of the American Democracy*, by Roy Franklin Nichols, pp. 110–11; and 183–84.

Page 256. "*Now, at last, during the spring and summer . . .*" The four separate parties amassed a vast store of information about the massacre, must of it widely published afterward. My own sources have included Carleton's *Report*, Forney's *Report* and evidence unearthed by Judge Cradlebaugh, much of it described by Deputy William Rodgers in the *Valley Tan*, February 29, 1860. An informative and rather typical passage from Carleton's *Report*, p. 11, says: "The property was brought to Cedar City and sold at public auction. It was called in Cedar City, and is so called now by the facetious Mormons, 'property taken at the siege of Sebastopol . . .' The clothing stripped from the corpses, bloody and with bits of flesh in it . . . was placed in the cellar of the tithing house. . . . It is said the cellar smells of it even to this day." And in a most vital passage Carleton's *Report*, p. 9, says: "A Pah-Ute chief, of the Santa Clara band, named 'Jackson,' . . . *says that orders came down in a letter from Brigham Young that the emigrants were to be killed*; and a chief of the Pah-Utes named Touche, now living on the Virgin River, told me that a letter from Brigham Young to the same effect was brought down to the Virgin River band *by a man named Huntington*, who, I learn, is an Indian interpreter and lives at present at Salt Lake City." (My italics.)

Page 257. "Speaking particularly . . . *Judge Cradlebaugh told the jury . . .*" Thomas Stenhouse, p. 408.

Chapter Thirty-five

Page 261. "Yet all the while . . . *a popular local ballad . . .*" Brooks, *John Doyle Lee*, pp. 251–52.

Page 262. "*Despite his retirement . . .*" For this period in Lee's life, see Brooks, *John Doyle Lee*, p. 267.

Page 262. "Journeying back . . . '*I asked . . . how it was . . .*'" Brooks, *John Doyle Lee*, p. 295.

Page 264. "*Within a few weeks . . .*" For Lee's arrest, see Brooks, *John Doyle Lee*, pp. 334 ff.; also *The Mormon Menace* by John D. Lee, which includes Sheriff William Stokes's account of the way he tracked Lee down and arrested him at his home.

Page 265. "*The line chosen by the defense . . .*" For two summaries of the trial, see Dunn, pp. 280–81; and Brooks, *John Doyle Lee*, p. 291.

Page 267. "Yet at the very close . . . '*I have been . . . betrayed . . .*'" Lee, *Mormonism Unveiled*, p. 291.

Page 268. "Patiently now . . . '*I am ready to die . . .*'" Brooks, *John Doyle Lee*, p. 367.

Page 268. "With Lee's execution . . . '*to put the saddle on the right horse . . .*'" Brooks, *John Doyle Lee*, p. 357.

Page 269. "*As for the site of the massacre . . .*" Brooks, *The Mountain Meadows Massacre*, p. xviii.

Page 269. "'*In the end, there is no way . . .*'" Morris Cohen, *The Faith of a Liberal*, p. 453.

Bibliography

Official Publications

National Archives Record Group 75. *Utah Superintendency.*

National Archives Record Group 217 Voucher 9, 4th Quarter, 1857. Records of the United States General Accounting Office.

Senate Executive Document 2, 36th Congress, 1st Session. *Message from the President of the United States to the Two Houses of Congress.*

Senate Executive Document 42, 36th Congress, 1st Session. Includes Forney's *Report.*

House of Representatives Executive Document 605, 57th Congress, 1st Session. Carleton's *Report.*

Senate Executive Document 3, Special Session, March 1851. *Exploration and Survey of the Great Salt Lake of Utah, by Captain Howard Stansbury.*

House of Representatives Executive Document 71, 35th Congress, 1st Session. *Utah Expedition, 1851–1858.*

House of Representatives Executive Document 25, 32nd Congress, 1st Session. *Conditions in Utah.*

33rd Congress, 2nd Session, *Report* No. 39, 29 January 1855. *Utah Expenses in Surpressing Indian Hostilities.*

House of Representatives, 41st Congress, 2nd Session. *Report* No. 21, Part 2.

National Archives, Adjutant General's Office, Record Group 94.

National Archives, U.S. Army Continental Commands, Record Group 393.

40th Congress, 2nd Session, House Report No. 79. General Records of the Department of Justice, National Archives Record Group 60.

Records of the United States Court of Claims, Record Group 123.

Records of the Court of Claims Section, Department of Justice, Record Group 205.

Records of the Supreme Court of the United States, Record Group 267.

General Records of the Department of State, Record Group 59.

Court of Claims of the United States, Indian Depredation No. 9239, *Payton Y. Welch v. The United States and the Ute Indians.*

Laws of the State of Illinois, Passed by the Twelfth General Assembly: *An Act to Incorporate the City of Nauvoo, February 1841.*

An Act to Establish a Territorial Government for Utah, 9 September 1850.

Congressional Globe, 1858, 35th Congress, 1st Session.
Congressional Globe, 1859, 35th Contress, 2nd Session.
Utah (Territory) Report of the Grand Jury, 2nd District of Utah,
    September 1859.

Newspapers

Daily Alta California.
Deseret News
Millennial Star
New York Herald
New York Post
New York Times
New York Tribune
St. Louis Republican
Valley Tan

Books, Periodicals, Scrapbooks, Speeches

Beadle, J. H., *Life in Utah*, National Publishing Co., Philadelphia, 1870.
Bancroft, Hubert H., *The History of the Pacific States*, Vol. XXI, *Utah*,
    1540–1886, History Company Publishers, San Francisco, 1889.
Berrian (William) Collection, New York Public Library; tracts, pam-
    phlets, etc., including Plea of George A. Smith, Charge of Judge
    Zerubbabel Snow upon the Trial of Howard Egan; Speech of Hon.
    John Thompson of New York in the House of Representatives, 27
    January 1858; Hon. John Cradlebaugh, Address delivered in the
    House of Representatives, 7 February 1863; Speech of Hon. Aaron
    Craigin, House of Representatives, 18 May 1870.
Brodie, Fawn M., *No Man Knows My History*, Alfred A. Knopf, New
    York, 1945.
Brooks, Juanita, *John Doyle Lee*, Zealot-Pioneer-Builder-Scapegoat,
    Arthur H. Clark Co., Glendale, Cal. 1964.
——*The Mountain Meadows Massacre*, University of Oklahoma
    Press, Norman, Okla., 1970.
Buchanan, James, *The Works of*, J. P. Lippincott, Philadelphia, 1908.
Burton, Richard, *The City of the Saints*, Alfred A. Knopf, New York,
    1963.
Clark, William, "A Trip Across the Plains," *Iowa Journal of History and
    Politics*," April 1922.
Cleland, Robert, and Juanita Brooks, (eds.), *A Mormon Chronicle*,
    Huntington Library, San Marino, 1955.
Cohen, Morris R., *The Faith of a Liberal*, Henry Holt & Co., New York,
    1946.
Corle, Edwin, *Desert Country*, Duell, Sloan & Pearce, New York, 1941.

Cradlebaugh, Hon. John M., "Utah and the Mormons," Speech on the Admission of Utah as a State, delivered in the House of Representatives, Feb. 7, 1863.

DeVoto, Bernard, *1846, The Year of Decision*, Little, Brown & Co., Boston, 1943.

Dunn, Jacob P. Jr., *Massacres of the Mountains*, A History of the Indian Wars of the Far West, 1815–1875, Archer House, New York.

Fancher, William Hoyt, *The Fancher Family*, Cabinet Press, Milford, 1947.

Ferris, Benjamin, *Utah and the Mormons*, Harper & Bros., 1854.

Ferris, Mrs. Benjamin, *The Mormons at Home*, Dix & Edwards, New York, 1856.

Fillmore, Millard, Papers, The Buffalo Historical Society, Buffalo, N.Y., 1907.

Forney, John K. *The Forney Family of Lancaster County, Pennsylvania*, Privately printed at Abilene, Kan., 1926.

Gibbs, Josiah F., *The Mountain Meadows Massacre*, Salt Lake Tribune Publishing Co., 1910.

Ginn, John L., typescript, untitled manuscript.

Gunnison, Captain John W., *The Mormons or Latter-Day Saints in the Valley of the Great Salt Lake*, J.P. Lippincott, Philadelphia, 1852.

Haines, Francis, *The Buffalo*, Thomas Y. Crowell, New York, 1970.

Hickman William (Bill), *Brigham's Destroying Angel, Confession of Bill Hickman*, J.F. Beadle (ed.), Shepard Publishing Co., Salt Lake City, 1904.

Hirshon, Stanley P., *The Lion of the Lord*, Alfred A. Knopf, New York, 1969.

Huntington, Dimick B., *Vocabulary of the Utah and Sho-Shoe-Ne or Snake Dialects, with Indian Legends and Traditions*, 1870.

Hyde, John Jr., *Mormonism, Its Leader and Designs*, W.P. Fetridge & Co., New York, 1857.

Kane, Thomas L., *The Mormons*, A Discourse, Philadelphia, 1850.

——*The Mormons*, J.P. Lippincott, Philadelphia, 1852.

——"*The Situation in Utah*," an address to the New York Historical Society, 1859.

Kelly, Charles, and Birney Hoffman, *Holy Murder*, The Story of Porter Rockwell, Milton, Balch & Co., New York, 1934.

Lee, John Doyle, *Journals, 1846–7 and 1859*, Charles Kelly (ed.), Western Printing Co., 1938.

——*The Life and Confessions of John D. Lee, the Mormon*, Barclay & Co., Philadelphia, 1872.

——*The Mormon Menace*, Home Protection Publishing Co., New York, 1905.

——*Mormonism Unveiled*, Excelsior Publishing Co., St. Louis, 1891.

Linn, William A., *The Story of the Mormons*, MacMillan Co., New York, 1923.

Mulder, William and Mortensen, A. Russell (eds.), *Among the Mormons,* Alfred A. Knopf, New York, 1958.

Mumey, Dr. Nolie, "John Williams Gunnison, Centenary of his Survey and Tragic Death," an address delivered on December 23, 1953; reprinted in the *Colorado Magazine.*

Nichols, Roy Franklin, *The Disruption of American Democracy,* Free Press, New York, 1968.

Parkman, Francis, *The Oregon Trail,* Modern Library, New York, 1949.

Polk, James K., *Diaries,* Allan Nevins (ed.), Longmans, Green, 1929.

Slater, Nelson, *Fruits of Mormonism,* Harmon & Spring, Coloma, Cal., 1851.

Smith, Mary Ettie V., *Fifteen Years Among the Mormons,* H. Dayton, New York, 1860.

Stanley, Reva, *A Biography of Parley P. Pratt, The Archer of Paradise,* Caxton Publishers, Caldwell, Idaho, 1937.

Stegner, Wallace, *Mormon Country,* Bonanza Books, New York, 1942.

——*The Gathering of Zion,* McGraw-Hill, New York, 1964.

Stenhouse, Fanny, *"Tell It All,"* A.D. Worthington & Co., Hartford, Conn., 1890.

Stenhouse, Thomas, *The Rocky Mountain Saints,* D. Appleton, New York, 1873.

Swartzell, William, *Mormonism Exposed,* published by the author, Pekin, Ohio, 1840.

Utah, A Guide to the State, American Guide Series, Hastings House, 1945.

Waite, Catherine, *The Mormon Prophet,* Riverside Press, Cambridge, Mass., 1866.

Wallace, Irving, *The Twenty-Seventh Wife,* Simon & Schuster, New York, 1961.

Werner, M.R., *Brigham Young,* Harcourt Brace, New York, 1925.

Woodward, Charles C., 2 vols. of scrapbooks. *The 1st Half Century of Mormonism,* Berrian Collection, unpublished, New York Public Library.

INDEX